# THE TIMES TOP 100 GRADUATE EMPLOYERS

The definitive guide to the leading employers recruiting graduates during 2025-2026.

**HIGH FLIERS**

**HIGH FLIERS PUBLICATIONS LTD**
**IN ASSOCIATION WITH THE TIMES**

Published by High Fliers Publications Limited
The Gridiron Building, 1 Pancras Square, London, N1C 4AG
*Telephone:* 020 7428 9100   *Web:* www.Top100GraduateEmployers.com


*Editor*  Martin Birchall
*Publisher*  Gill Thomas
*Production Manager*  Ellie Goodman
*Marketing & Social Media*  Ellie Goodman
*Portrait Photography*  Phil Ripley cityspacecreative.co.uk


**Copyright © 2025 High Fliers Publications Limited**


All rights reserved. Without limiting the rights under the copyright reserved above, no part of this publication may be reproduced, stored in or introduced into a retrieval system, or transmitted, in any form or by any means (electronic, mechanical, photocopying, recording or otherwise), without the prior written permission of the publisher of this book.

*The Times Top 100 Graduate Employers* is based on research results from *The UK Graduate Careers Survey 2025*, produced by High Fliers Research Ltd.

The greatest care has been taken in compiling this book. However, no responsibility can be accepted by the publishers or compilers for the accuracy of the information presented.

Where opinion is expressed it is that of the author or advertiser and does not necessarily coincide with the editorial views of High Fliers Publications Limited or *The Times* newspaper.


Printed and bound in Italy by L.E.G.O. S.p.A.

A CIP catalogue record for this book
is available from the British Library.
ISBN  978-1-9160401-6-8

# Contents

*Page*

**Foreword** 4

**Researching The Times Top 100 Graduate Employers** 10

**Understanding the Graduate Job Market** 24

**Successful Graduate Job Hunting** 34

**Employer Entries**

| | Page | | Page | | Page |
|---|---|---|---|---|---|
| A&O Shearman | 50 | Diageo | 98 | Microsoft | 146 |
| AECOM | 52 | DLA Piper | 100 | Mott Macdonald | 148 |
| Aldi | 54 | EDF | 102 | Network Rail | 150 |
| Amazon | 56 | Enterprise Mobility | 104 | Newton | 152 |
| AON | 58 | Environment Agency | 106 | NHS | 154 |
| Army | 60 | EY | 108 | P&G | 156 |
| Arup | 62 | Forvis Mazars | 110 | Penguin | 158 |
| AstraZeneca | 64 | Freshfields | 112 | Pfizer | 160 |
| AtkinsRéalis | 66 | Google | 114 | Police Now | 162 |
| Babcock | 68 | Grant Thornton | 116 | PwC | 164 |
| BAE Systems | 70 | HMRC | 118 | RAF | 166 |
| Bank of America | 72 | Hogan Lovells | 120 | Revolut | 168 |
| Barclays | 74 | HSBC | 122 | Rolls-Royce | 170 |
| BBC | 76 | IBM | 124 | Royal Navy | 172 |
| BCG | 78 | ITV | 126 | Savills | 174 |
| BlackRock | 80 | JPMorganChase | 128 | Scottish Power | 176 |
| Bloomberg | 82 | KPMG | 130 | Shell | 178 |
| BNY | 84 | L'Oréal | 132 | Slaughter and May | 180 |
| British Airways | 86 | Latham & Watkins | 134 | Teach First | 182 |
| Capgemini | 88 | Lidl | 136 | Tesco | 184 |
| Civil Service | 90 | Linklaters | 138 | TfL | 186 |
| Clyde & Co | 92 | Lloyds Banking Group | 140 | Unilever | 188 |
| Deloitte | 94 | Lockheed Martin | 142 | White & Case | 190 |
| Deutsche Bank | 96 | M&S | 144 | | |

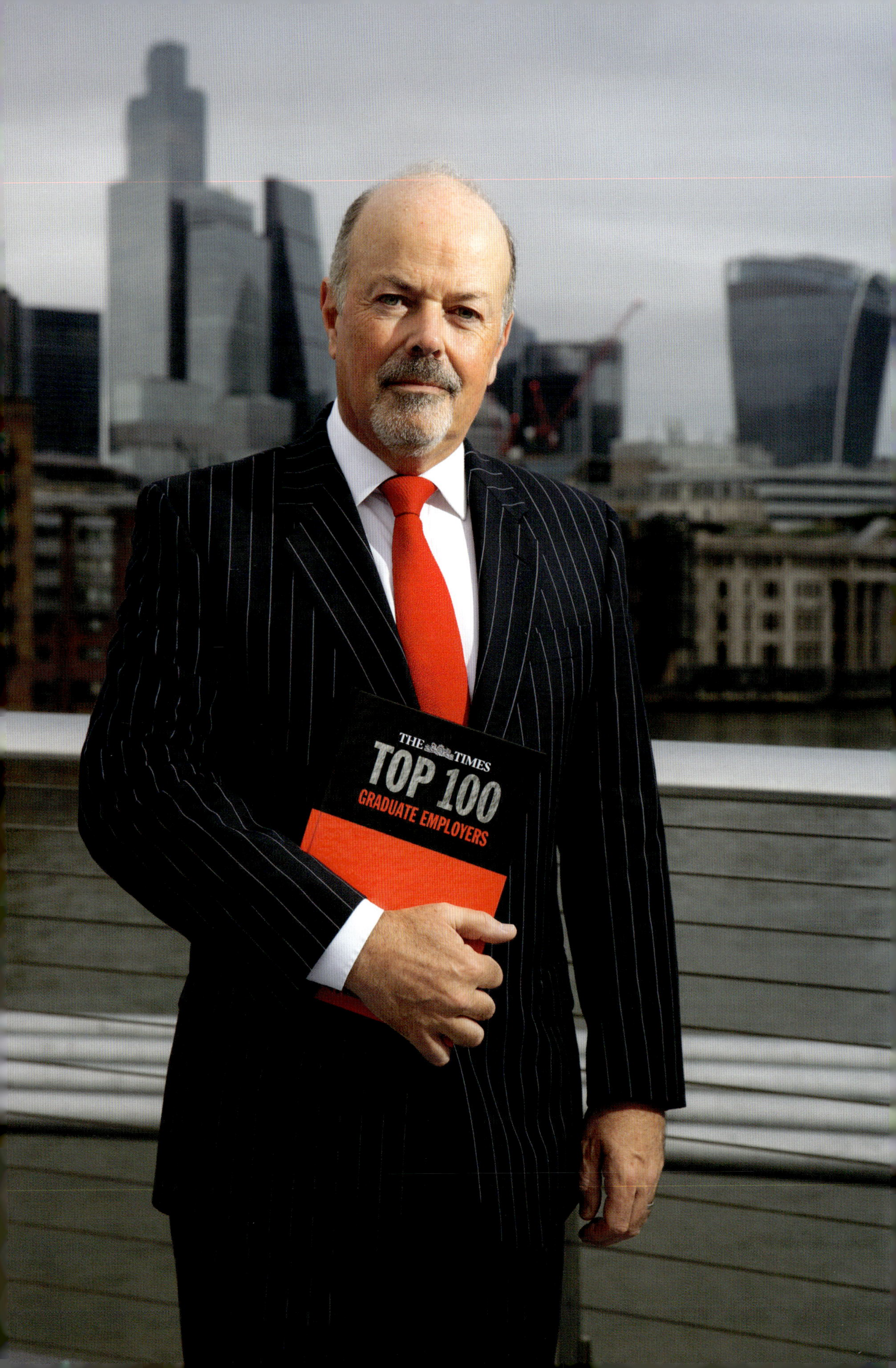
THE TIMES
TOP 100
GRADUATE EMPLOYERS

# Foreword

By **Martin Birchall**
Editor, *The Times Top 100 Graduate Employers*

Welcome to the twenty-seventh edition of *The Times Top 100 Graduate Employers*, your annual guide to the UK's most prestigious and sought-after graduate employers.

A year ago, Sir Kier Starmer's new Labour Government put growing the economy at the heart of its priorities. Yet its first Budget landed employers with substantial tax increases, business confidence dropped sharply, unemployment has risen to its highest level for four years, and the Bank of England now expects the UK economy to grow by just 1.25% in 2025.

This has had a profound impact on the graduate job market. The country's best-known employers hired 22 per cent fewer graduates than they originally planned to in 2024 – and reduced their graduate recruitment further in 2025.

In the past three years, the number of entry-level vacancies available for new graduates has been cut by more than a fifth – and it seems inevitable that there will be even fewer opportunities in the year ahead.

Over the past two and a half decades, *The Times Top 100 Graduate Employers* has tracked university students' success in the graduate job market. Our latest research with new graduates from the 'Class of 2025' reveals that they worked harder than any of the previous cohorts of university-leavers to secure their first graduate job, but have struggled with the worsening economic situation and the reduced number of graduate opportunities.

Almost half began researching their career options in their first year, almost as soon as they arrived at university – and more than two-fifths completed an internship or work placement with a graduate employer at the end of their second year.

By their final year, unprecedented numbers of students took part in university careers fairs, employers' on-campus recruitment presentations, skills workshops, and other careers promotions during their search for a graduate job.

> *In the past three years, the number of entry-level vacancies available for new graduates has been cut by more than a fifth.*

When it came to applying for jobs, those graduating in the summer of 2025 completed a record number of applications – averaging twenty-two applications per graduate, nearly twice the number made just two years ago.

But even with all of this preparation and engagement with employers, the number of graduates from the 'Class of 2025' who received a definite job offer before leaving university actually dropped by ten per cent, compared with 2024.

This means the proportion of new graduates who achieved a job offer was the second-lowest of the past decade – only the 2021 pandemic year led to a lower rate of graduate job offers.

This disappointing outcome is a reminder of just how much competition there is currently for

## Foreword

graduate-level opportunities. Employers featured in *The Times Top 100 Graduate Employers* typically receive between 50 and 100 applications per graduate vacancy – and some of the most sought-after graduate programmes can attract double this number.

The experience of the 'Class of 2025' shows that students who are most-likely to be successful in the post-university job market are those who start thinking about potential future careers early and spend their time at university developing the key skills and experience that graduate employers are looking for.

Very few, if any, of the country's top employers recruit graduates based on their academic record – or the content of their university degree. Many have removed school and university results from their applications altogether and are instead relying on their own battery of aptitude and psychometric tests and recorded, AI-assessed interviews to determine applicants' abilities and suitability for their graduate roles.

This move away from academic achievement to demonstrating the broad range of skills – from teamwork and leadership, to problem solving, critical thinking and resilience – that employers demand for their graduate programmes can be a difficult one to navigate.

The editorial features in this edition of *The Times Top 100 Graduate Employers* explain how your university careers service can help you research your career options, prepare your graduate job applications, and get ready for employers' selection processes. There are tips, advice and guidance on what employers are looking for, in-depth analysis of the current graduate job market, plus full details of graduate employers in more than fifteen different industries and business sectors.

Since the first edition was published in 1999, over 1.5 million copies of *The Times Top 100 Graduate Employers* have been produced, helping students and graduates at universities across the UK to research their career options and find their first graduate job. And during the past five years, more than 500,000 students and graduates have read the popular digital edition of the *Top 100* that accompanies the print edition.

More than a quarter of a century after its launch, *The Times Top 100 Graduate Employers* continues to provide the nation's university-leavers with an unrivalled, independent assessment of the UK's most highly-rated graduate employers.

### Finding out about the Top 100 Graduate Employers

**PRINT EDITION**

Each employer featured in this edition of the *Top 100* has their own **Employer Entry**, providing details of graduate vacancies for 2026, minimum academic requirements, starting salaries, for new graduates, plus this year's application deadlines.

**DIGITAL EDITION**

You'll find the **digital edition** of the *Top 100* on the official *Top 100* website, giving you access to the very latest information about the UK's most sought-after graduate employers..

Get ready for your graduate job search with full details of employers' forthcoming application deadlines.

And register on the website to receive regular updates about the country's top graduate employers.

**www.Top100GraduateEmployers.com**

**BY EMAIL**

Once you've registered with the *Top 100* website, you'll receive **weekly email bulletins** with news of the employers you're interested in, details of their latest graduate vacancies, and their application deadlines.

"Meeting people on the same journey as me, *making friends*, and getting excited about our future careers together has been truly special."

Read more about Amz's story here!

Scan here

Amz joined a community of over 300 graduates, where Capgemini's support and mentorship gave her the confidence to grow and shape a career that's truly her own.

Capgemini

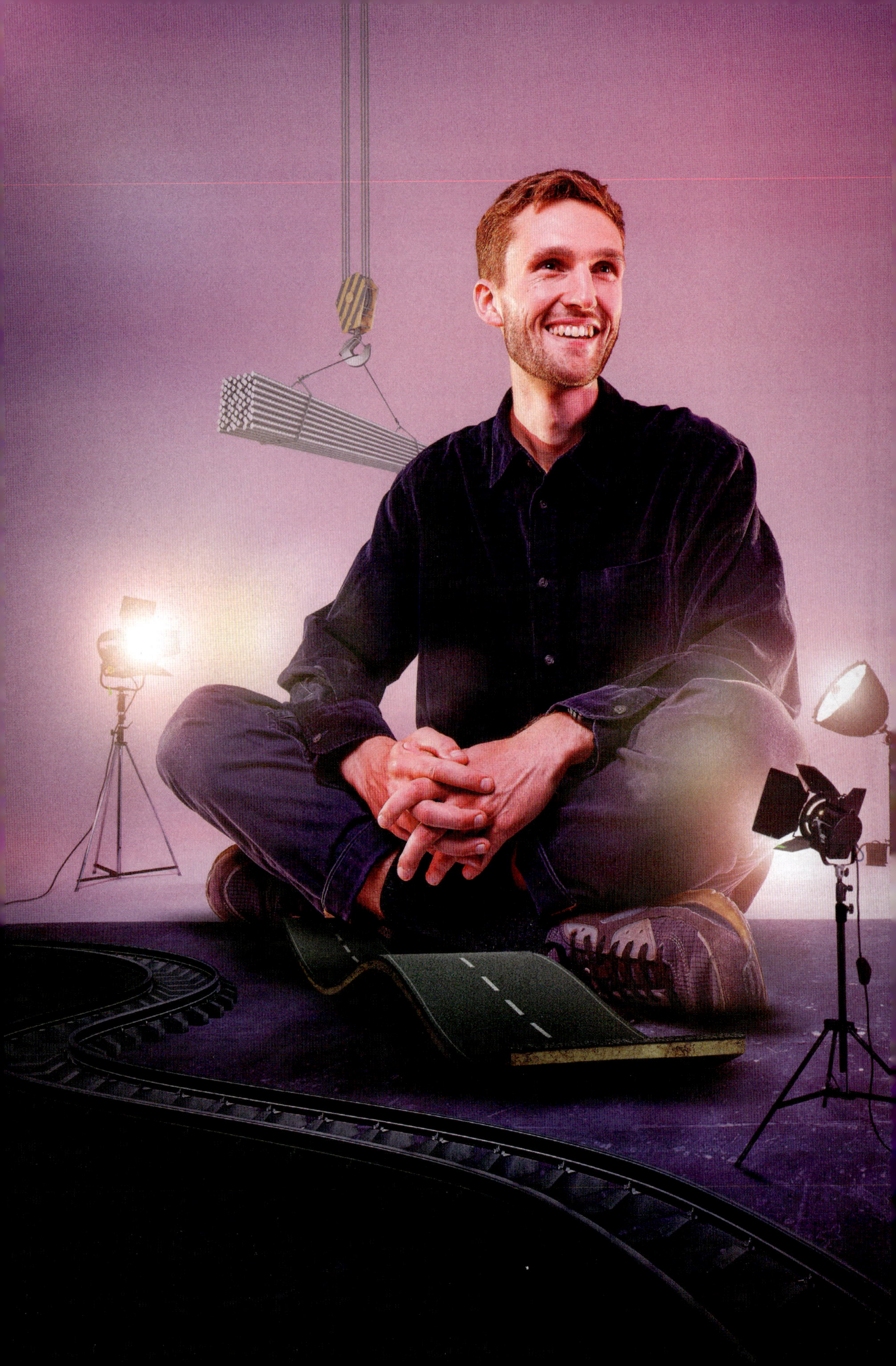

Civil Service
Fast Stream

Grow like nowhere else

# BOOST YOUR KNOWLEDGE

## SHAPE NATIONWIDE CHANGE

### Graduate Leadership and Management Development Programme
Nationwide Opportunities

Developing future leaders and managers UK-wide, we're building a Civil Service that represents – and is geographically closer to – the communities that we serve.

We offer 17 different schemes, with opportunities to build your career in England, Scotland and Wales. No matter where you join us, you can grow the knowledge, skills and networks you'll need to advance your career to a senior role in the Civil Service.

With high-quality training and on-the-job learning, you'll gain a breadth of experience in a range of postings. You'll progress your career path in a government profession, making meaningful change for millions of people.

**faststream.gov.uk**

# THE TIMES
# THE TIMES
# THE TIMES
# THE TIMES
# THE TIMES
# THE TIMES
# THE TIMES
# THE TIMES
# THE TIMES
# THE TIMES

TOP 100 GRADUATE EMPLOYERS 2016-2017
TOP 100 GRADUATE EMPLOYERS 2017-2018
TOP 100 GRADUATE EMPLOYERS 2018-2019
TOP 100 GRADUATE EMPLOYERS 2019-2020
TOP 100 GRADUATE EMPLOYERS 2020-2021
TOP 100 GRADUATE EMPLOYERS 2021-2022
TOP 100 GRADUATE EMPLOYERS 2022-2023
TOP 100 GRADUATE EMPLOYERS 2023-2024
TOP 100 GRADUATE EMPLOYERS 2024-2025
TOP 100 GRADUATE EMPLOYERS 2025-2026

# Researching The Times Top 100 Graduate Employers

By **Gill Thomas**
Publisher, High Fliers Publications

There were an estimated five thousand employers, large and small, recruiting graduates from UK universities when the first edition of *The Times Top 100 Graduate Employers* was published in 1999.

Over the two and a half decades since then, the number of employers recruiting graduates has risen steadily and for those due to leave university in 2026 and beyond, there are expected to be up to 200,000 graduate-level vacancies available annually.

But finding the 'right' graduate employer can often be a daunting prospect. What basis can you use to evaluate such a large number of different organisations and the employment opportunities they offer for new graduates after university?

*The Times Top 100 Graduate Employers* is compiled annually by the independent market research company, High Fliers Research, through interviews with final year students at the country's leading universities.

This latest edition is based on research with 15,105 students who were due to graduate from universities across the UK in the summer of 2025. The research examined students' experiences during their search for a first graduate job and asked them about their attitudes to employers.

Final year undergraduates from the 'Class of 2025' who took part in the study were selected at random to represent the full cross-section of finalists at their universities, not just those who had already confirmed their career plans and secured graduate employment.

The question used to produce the *Top 100* rankings was "Which employer do you think offers the best opportunities for graduates?". The question was deliberately open-ended and students were not shown a list of employers to choose from or prompted during the interview.

> *"Best-known for its prestigious Fast Stream programme, the Civil Service has returned to number one in this year's rankings."*

The wide selection of answers given during the research shows that final year students used very different criteria to decide which employer offered the best opportunities for graduates.

Some evaluated employers based on the quality of the recruitment promotions they'd seen whilst at university – either online or in-person – or their recent experiences during the application and graduate selection process.

Other final year students focused on the 'graduate employment proposition' as their main guide – the quality of training and development an employer offers, the starting salary and remuneration package available, and the practical aspects of a first graduate job, such as its location or the likely working hours.

Across the full survey sample, final year students

# Researching The Times Top 100 Graduate Employers

## The Times Top 100 Graduate Employers 2025

| 2025 | 2024 | Employer | 2025 | 2024 | Employer |
|---|---|---|---|---|---|
| 1 | 2 | CIVIL SERVICE | 51 | 46 | ITV |
| 2 | 1 | PWC | 52 | 29 | NATWEST GROUP |
| 3 | 3 | NHS | 53 | 54 | UBS |
| 4 | 4 | DELOITTE | 54 | 30 | BP |
| 5 | 5 | BBC | 55 | 47 | ACCENTURE |
| 6 | 7 | JPMORGANCHASE | 56 | 35 | IBM |
| 7 | 6 | EY | 57 | 42 | JLR |
| 8 | 8 | GOOGLE | 58 | 65 | BANK OF AMERICA |
| 9 | 19 | L'ORÉAL | 59 | 74 | AON |
| 10 | 13 | HSBC | 60 | 56 | HERBERT SMITH FREEHILLS KRAMER |
| 11 | 12 | LLOYDS BANKING GROUP | 61 | 52 | SHELL |
| 12 | 11 | KPMG | 62 | 62 | LATHAM & WATKINS |
| 13 | 15 | TEACH FIRST | 63 | 72 | DLA PIPER |
| 14 | 16 | CLIFFORD CHANCE | 64 | NEW | ENVIRONMENT AGENCY |
| 15 | 14 | GOLDMAN SACHS | 65 | 41 | ATKINSRÉALIS |
| 16 | 9 | BARCLAYS | 66 | 73 | SANTANDER |
| 17 | 18 | MCKINSEY & COMPANY | 67 | 84 | TRANSPORT FOR LONDON |
| 18 | 17 | ASTRAZENECA | 68 | 79 | BAIN & COMPANY |
| 19 | 20 | GSK | 69 | 95 | CAPGEMINI |
| 20 | 21 | AMAZON | 70 | 82 | HOGAN LOVELLS |
| 21 | 22 | ARUP | 71 | 58 | BLOOMBERG |
| 22 | 23 | UNILEVER | 72 | 64 | M&S |
| 23 | 27 | BAE SYSTEMS | 73 | 85 | VODAFONE |
| 24 | 31 | LINKLATERS | 74 | 92 | BAKER MCKENZIE |
| 25 | 49 | SLAUGHTER AND MAY | 75 | 69 | BDO |
| 26 | 25 | ROLLS-ROYCE | 76 | 81 | RAF |
| 27 | 10 | ALDI | 77 | 83 | MOTT MACDONALD |
| 28 | 36 | PENGUIN RANDOM HOUSE | 78 | 93 | FORVIS MAZARS |
| 29 | 32 | BCG | 79 | 96 | DEUTSCHE BANK |
| 30 | 34 | MORGAN STANLEY | 80 | 98 | GRANT THORNTON |
| 31 | 26 | P&G | 81 | NEW | NETWORK RAIL |
| 32 | 28 | NEWTON | 82 | 75 | CITI |
| 33 | 53 | BRITISH ARMY | 83 | NEW | HMRC |
| 34 | 33 | POLICE NOW | 84 | 63 | AECOM |
| 35 | 50 | JANE STREET | 85 | NEW | CMS |
| 36 | 24 | A&O SHEARMAN | 86 | NEW | SCOTTISH POWER |
| 37 | 37 | BLACKROCK | 87 | NEW | SONY |
| 38 | 57 | WHITE & CASE | 88 | 39 | ROYAL NAVY |
| 39 | 45 | FRESHFIELDS | 89 | 89 | BT |
| 40 | 40 | PFIZER | 90 | 97 | SAVILLS |
| 41 | 48 | LIDL | 91 | NEW | EDF |
| 42 | 60 | LOCAL GOVERNMENT | 92 | NEW | BNY |
| 43 | 43 | SKY | 93 | NEW | LOCKHEED MARTIN |
| 44 | 67 | AIRBUS | 94 | NEW | REVOLUT |
| 45 | 38 | APPLE | 95 | 61 | CLYDE & CO |
| 46 | 76 | SIEMENS | 96 | 70 | WSP |
| 47 | 59 | ENTERPRISE MOBILITY | 97 | 100 | DIAGEO |
| 48 | 44 | MICROSOFT | 98 | NEW | BABCOCK |
| 49 | 68 | TESCO | 99 | NEW | WELLCOME |
| 50 | 66 | BRITISH AIRWAYS | 100 | NEW | ALPHASIGHTS |

**Source** High Fliers Research  15,105 final year students leaving UK universities in the summer of 2025 were asked the open-ended question "Which employer do you think offers the best opportunities for graduates?" during interviews for *The UK Graduate Careers Survey 2025* named over 1,500 different organisations, from well-known national and international organisations to small and medium-sized regional and local employers. The responses were analysed and the one hundred organisations that were named most often make up *The Times Top 100 Graduate Employers* for 2025.

In a dramatic twist, the Civil Service has returned to number one in this year's rankings, after two years in second place. Best-known for its prestigious Fast Stream programme, this is the sixth time the Civil Service has been named as the UK's leading graduate employer and a total of 6.7 per cent of final year students from the 'Class of 2025' voted for the organisation.

The accounting & professional services firm PwC has moved down to second place, having been the country's top graduate employer in both 2023 and 2024. The firm holds the unsurpassed record of being voted number one seventeen times in the twenty-seven year history of the *Top 100*.

The NHS, the accounting & professional services firm Deloitte, and the BBC are each unchanged in third, fourth and fifth places respectively. JPMorganChase moves up for the third year running, this time to sixth place, the highest-ever position for an investment bank in the *Top 100*. EY slips back one place, just ahead of Google which remains in eighth place, its lowest position for a decade. The consumer goods company L'Oréal jumps an impressive ten places, to reach the top ten for the for first time. And banking giant HSBC climbs to tenth place, its highest ranking for eighteen years.

The Teach First programme has moved up two places to this year's 13th place, and both law firm Clifford Chance and consulting firm McKinsey & Company have achieved their best-ever rankings, with moves to 14th and 17th places respectively. But after two years in the top ten, banking group Barclays has dropped back to 16th place. Engineering & defence company BAE Systems has climbed to 23rd place, its highest ranking yet. And publishing company Penguin Random House has moved up the rankings for the third year running, to reach the top thirty for the first time.

Within the new *Top 100*, the year's highest climbers are led by industrial company Siemens, which has leapt thirty places to 46th place, its best position yet. Capgemini, the technology company, has had a similar rise, jumping twenty-six places to 69th place. Law firm Slaughter and May, aerospace manufacturer Airbus, and the British Army have also moved up more than twenty places in this year's rankings.

The Royal Navy has had the most significant fall of the year, dropping forty-nine places from 39th place in 2024 to 88th place. Law firm Clyde & Co is down thirty-four places from last year's 61st place, and engineering consultants WSP has dropped back twenty-six places. Other graduate employers ranked lower in 2025 include engineering company Atkins, oil & energy company BP, NatWest Group, AECOM and IBM, who have each fallen at least twenty places this year.

There are thirteen employers new or re-entries in this year's *Top 100*, the highest being for the Environment Agency, which returns in 64th place. Network Rail reappears in 81st place following a five-year absence, and HM Revenue & Customs makes its debut in 83rd place. There are new entries for international bank BNY, defence & aerospace company Lockheed Martin, fintech company Revolut, Babcock International and knowledge company AlphaSights. There are a further four re-entries, for law firm CMS, Scottish Power, Sony, EDF Energy and Wellcome, the global charitable foundation.

Among the graduate employers leaving the *Top 100* in 2025 is Unlocked – the inspiring charity that has recruited hundreds of graduates into the prison service over the past decade – which had its funding unexpectedly withdrawn by the Ministry of Justice last year. Other employers leaving the rankings this year include MI5 and MI6, Dyson, law firm Irwin Mitchell, the Bank of England, engineering consultants Jacobs, the BMW Group, Nestlé, consultants Oliver Wyman, semiconductor and design company ARM, and two employers that had been ranked in the *Top 100* in each of its previous twenty-six years – McDonald's and Mars.

Since the original edition of *The Times Top 100 Graduate Employers* was published over a quarter of a century ago, just three organisations have made it to number one in the rankings.

Andersen Consulting (now Accenture) held on to the top spot for the first four years, beginning in 1999, and its success heralded a huge surge in popularity for careers in consulting. At its peak in 2001, almost one in six graduates applied for jobs in the sector.

In the year before the firm changed its name from Andersen Consulting to Accenture, it astutely introduced a new graduate package that

# Deloitte.

## Taking the first step...

Right now, you're exploring options for what direction to take as you start your career. We have opportunities in a wide range of business areas from Audit and Assurance to Technology, Tax Consulting and much more.

Choosing your path isn't always easy. Our aim is to make things simpler for you – whether that means you end up joining us, or pursuing another great opportunity.

Here's a snapshot of our programmes, and a few free resources to help get started.

### Spring into Deloitte
On this two-day course, you'll meet inspirational people through business activities, skills sessions and networking opportunities to gain an insight into what working in professional services really looks like.

### Summer Vacation Scheme
If you're in your penultimate year or about to do a Master's, test what you've learnt to solve complex challenges for our clients on our 4-6 week placement.

### Industrial Placement
For 12 months, you'll train alongside our first-year graduates.

You'll be paid a competitive salary throughout and if we're a right fit for each other, you could be offered a place on our graduate scheme.

### Graduate Programme
You'll receive world-class training, gain professional qualifications and work on meaningful projects with the chance to innovate on a global scale, making an impact that matters every day.

Scan the QR code or visit Deloitte.co.uk/earlycareers to find out more and apply.

## Researching The Times Top 100 Graduate Employers

included a £28,500 starting salary (a sky-high figure for graduates in 2000) and a much-talked-about £10,000 bonus, helping to assure the firm's popularity, irrespective of its corporate branding.

In 2003, after two dismal years in graduate recruitment when vacancies for university-leavers dropped by more than a fifth following the 9/11 terrorist attacks in 2001, the Civil Service was named the UK's leading graduate employer.

Just twelve months later it was displaced by PricewaterhouseCoopers, the accounting and professional services firm formed from the merger of Price Waterhouse and Coopers & Lybrand in 1998. At the time, the firm was the largest private sector recruiter of graduates, with an intake in 2004 of more than a thousand trainees.

Now known simply as PwC, the firm remained at number one for an impressive fifteen years, increasing its share of the student vote from 5 per cent in 2004 to more than 10 per cent in 2007, and fighting off the stiffest of competition from rivals Deloitte in 2008, when just seven votes separated the two employers.

PwC's reign as the UK's leading graduate employer represented a real renaissance for the entire accounting & professional services sector. Twenty years ago, a career in accountancy was often regarded as a safe, traditional employment choice, whereas today's profession is viewed in a very different light. The training required to become a chartered accountant is now seen as a prized business qualification, and the sector's leading firms are regularly described as 'dynamic' and 'international' by undergraduates looking for their first job after university – and continue to dominate the annual graduate employer rankings.

Sixteen years after first reaching number one, the Civil Service regained the top spot in the *Top 100* rankings in 2019 and remained there for four years until PwC returned to number one in 2023.

A total of 243 different organisations have now appeared within *The Times Top 100 Graduate Employers* since its inception, and thirty-four of these graduate employers hold the inspiring record of being ranked within the *Top 100* in all twenty-seven editions since 1999.

### THE TIMES TOP 100 GRADUATE EMPLOYERS — Number Ones, Movers & Shakers in the Top 100

| Year | NUMBER ONES | HIGHEST CLIMBING EMPLOYERS | HIGHEST NEW ENTRIES |
|---|---|---|---|
| 1999 | ANDERSEN CONSULTING | SCHLUMBERGER (UP 13 PLACES) | PFIZER (31st) |
| 2000 | ANDERSEN CONSULTING | CAPITAL ONE (UP 32 PLACES) | MORGAN STANLEY (34th) |
| 2001 | ACCENTURE | EUROPEAN COMMISSION (UP 36 PLACES) | MARCONI (36th) |
| 2002 | ACCENTURE | WPP (UP 36 PLACES) | GUINNESS UDV (44th) |
| 2003 | CIVIL SERVICE | ROLLS-ROYCE (UP 37 PLACES) | ASDA (40th) |
| 2004 | PRICEWATERHOUSECOOPERS | J.P. MORGAN (UP 29 PLACES) | BAKER & MCKENZIE (61st) |
| 2005 | PRICEWATERHOUSECOOPERS | TEACH FIRST (UP 22 PLACES) | PENGUIN (70th) |
| 2006 | PRICEWATERHOUSECOOPERS | GOOGLE (UP 32 PLACES) | FUJITSU (81st) |
| 2007 | PRICEWATERHOUSECOOPERS | PFIZER (UP 30 PLACES) | BDO STOY HAYWARD (74th) |
| 2008 | PRICEWATERHOUSECOOPERS | CO-OPERATIVE GROUP (UP 39 PLACES) | SKY (76th) |
| 2009 | PRICEWATERHOUSECOOPERS | CADBURY (UP 48 PLACES) | BDO STOY HAYWARD (68th) |
| 2010 | PRICEWATERHOUSECOOPERS | ASDA (UP 41 PLACES) | SAATCHI & SAATCHI (49th) |
| 2011 | PWC | CENTRICA (UP 41 PLACES) | APPLE (53rd) |
| 2012 | PWC | NESTLÉ (UP 44 PLACES) | EUROPEAN COMMISSION (56th) |
| 2013 | PWC | DFID (UP 40 PLACES) | SIEMENS (70th) |
| 2014 | PWC | TRANSPORT FOR LONDON (UP 36 PLACES) | FRONTLINE (76th) |
| 2015 | PWC | DIAGEO, NEWTON (UP 43 PLACES) | DANONE (66th) |
| 2016 | PWC | BANK OF ENGLAND (UP 34 PLACES) | SANTANDER (63rd) |
| 2017 | PWC | CANCER RESEARCH UK (UP 38 PLACES) | DYSON (52nd) |
| 2018 | PWC | MCDONALD'S (UP 30 PLACES) | ASOS (52nd) |
| 2019 | CIVIL SERVICE | POLICE NOW (UP 43 PLACES) | UNLOCKED (49th) |
| 2020 | CIVIL SERVICE | DLA PIPER/WHITE & CASE (UP 32 PLACES) | CHANNEL FOUR (77th) |
| 2021 | CIVIL SERVICE | CHARITYWORKS (UP 45 PLACES) | BDO (49th) |
| 2022 | CIVIL SERVICE | JAGUAR LAND ROVER (UP 30 PLACES) | BMW GROUP (66th) |
| 2023 | PWC | UNLOCKED (UP 45 PLACES) | DLA PIPER (51st) |
| 2024 | PWC | BLACKROCK (UP 42 PLACES) | ITV (46th) |
| 2025 | CIVIL SERVICE | SIEMENS (UP 30 PLACES) | ENVIRONMENT AGENCY (46th) |

*Source* High Fliers Research

## Researching The Times Top 100 Graduate Employers

The most consistent performers have been PwC, KPMG and the Civil Service, each of which have never been lower than 10th place in the league table. The NHS has also had a formidable record, appearing in every top ten since 2003, while the BBC and EY (formerly Ernst & Young) have both remained within the top twenty throughout the past twenty-five years. And consumer goods company Unilever and investment bank Goldman Sachs are two more employers that have appeared in the top quarter of the rankings every year from 1999 onwards.

Retailer Tesco is the highest-climbing employer within the *Top 100*, having risen eighty-eight places in its first thirteen years in the rankings, reaching 12th place in 2012. Google is another graduate employer that made very rapid progress during its early years in the *Top 100* rankings, jumping over eighty places in a decade, to reach the top three for the first time in 2015. But car manufacturer Jaguar Land Rover holds the record for being the fastest-moving employer in the *Top 100*, after leaping more than seventy places in just five years, between 2009 and 2014.

Other well-known graduate employers haven't been so successful. British Airways ranked in 6th place in 1999 but dropped out of the *Top 100* a decade later, and Ford, which was once rated as high as 14th, disappeared out of the list in 2006 after cancelling its graduate recruitment programme two years previously. Sainsbury's appeared in the top twenty in both 2003 and 2004 but left the *Top 100* nine years ago and hasn't been ranked since.

More recent high-ranking casualties include the John Lewis Partnership which – having been 9th in 2003 – tumbled out of the *Top 100* in 2020, and Boots, the pharmacy and health retailer that had appeared in 10th place in the inaugural edition of The Times Top 100 Graduate Employers,

### THE TIMES TOP 100 GRADUATE EMPLOYERS — Winners & Losers in the Top 100

| EMPLOYERS CLIMBING HIGHEST | NEW ENTRY RANKING | HIGHEST RANKING |
|---|---|---|
| TESCO | 100th (1999) | 12th (2012) |
| GOOGLE | 85th (2005) | 3rd (2015) |
| LIDL | 89th (2009) | 13th (2017) |
| NEWTON | 94th (2013) | 19th (2019) |
| AMAZON | 81st (2015) | 10th (2022) |
| JAGUAR LAND ROVER | 87th (2009) | 16th (2014) |
| ALDI | 65th (2002) | 2nd (2015-2016) |
| MI5 – THE SECURITY SERVICE | 96th (2007) | 33rd (2010) |
| POLICE NOW | 90th (2018) | 28th (2021) |
| TEACH FIRST | 63rd (2003) | 2nd (2014) |
| APPLE | 87th (2009) | 27th (2012) |
| DEUTSCHE BANK | 81st (1999) | 23rd (2005) |
| ATKINS | 94th (2004) | 37th (2009) |
| SLAUGHTER AND MAY | 90th (2001) | 36th (2022) |
| FRONTLINE | 76th (2014) | 26th (2018) |

| EMPLOYERS FALLING FURTHEST | HIGHEST RANKING | LOWEST RANKING |
|---|---|---|
| BRITISH AIRWAYS | 6th (1999) | Not ranked (2010, 2011, 2017, 2019-2022) |
| MARKS & SPENCER | 7th (1999) | Not ranked (2021-2022) |
| MARS | 9th (2000) | Not ranked (2025) |
| JOHN LEWIS PARTNERSHIP | 9th (2013) | Not ranked (FROM 2020) |
| BOOTS | 10th (1999) | Not ranked (FROM 2021) |
| FORD | 11th (1999) | Not ranked (FROM 2006) |
| UBS | 17th (2002) | Not ranked (2018) |
| SAINSBURY'S | 18th (2003) | Not ranked (FROM 2016) |
| EXXONMOBIL | 19th (1999) | Not ranked (FROM 2021) |
| SHELL | 11th (2006) | 90th (2021) |
| THOMSON REUTERS | 22nd (2001) | Not ranked (2009-2012, FROM 2014) |
| FRONTLINE | 26th (2018) | Not ranked (2024) |
| BANK OF AMERICA | 27th (2000) | Not ranked (FROM 2017-2020) |
| ASDA | 27th (2004) | Not ranked (FROM 2018) |
| McDONALD'S | 29th (2003) | Not ranked (2025) |

*Source* High Fliers Research

# Benefits that benefit you

#lidlgrads

At Lidl, we give our grads all the perks they deserve! With a **£40,000 salary**, plus amazing benefits that help you thrive both at work and at home, there's never been a better time to join.

**Find your place at lidlearlycareers.co.uk**

# Researching The Times Top 100 Graduate Employers

disappeared completely from the rankings in 2021. ExxonMobil, the oil & energy company that was a top twenty employer in the original *Top 100*, has also been unranked since 2021. And retailer Marks & Spencer, which was in 7th place in the *Top 100* in 1999, dropped out of the rankings altogether in 2022.

More than thirty graduate employers – including Nokia, Maersk, the Home Office, Cable & Wireless, United Biscuits, Nationwide, Samsung, Mercedes, the Met Office and TikTok – have the dubious record of having only been ranked in the *Top 100* once during the last twenty-six years. And former engineering & telecommunications company Marconi had the unusual distinction of being one of the highest-ever new entries, in 36th place in 2001, only to vanish from the list entirely the following year.

One of the most spectacular ascendancies in the *Top 100* has been the rise of discount retailer Aldi, which joined the list in 65th place in 2002, rose to 3rd place in 2009 and was ranked in 2nd place in both 2015 and 2016. Teach First, the first of five inspirational schemes launched to bring top graduates into different aspects of public service, did similarly well. It appeared as a new entry in 63rd place in 2003, before climbing the rankings every year for a decade and reaching 2nd place in the *Top 100* in 2014. Consulting firm Newton is another impressive climber, having jumped more than seventy places from 94th place in 2013 to reach the top twenty for the first time in 2019.

The Covid pandemic had a very significant impact on the annual rankings, and a fifth of the employers that appeared in *The Times Top 100 Graduate Employers* in 2020 – the final rankings

## THE TIMES TOP 100 GRADUATE EMPLOYERS – Employers Ranked from 1999-2025 in the Top 100

| MOST CONSISTENT EMPLOYERS | HIGHEST RANKING | LOWEST RANKING |
|---|---|---|
| PWC | 1st (2004-2018, 2023-2024) | 3rd (1999-2001, 2003, 2022) |
| CIVIL SERVICE | 1st (2003, 2019-2022, 2025) | 8th (2011) |
| KPMG | 3rd (2006-2008, 2011-2012) | 11th (2024) |
| BBC | 5th (2005-2007, 2024-2025) | 14th (1999) |
| GSK | 10th (2017-2018) | 22nd (2002-2003) |
| EY (FORMERLY ERNST & YOUNG) | 6th (2021-2024) | 20th (2001) |
| GOLDMAN SACHS | 5th (2001) | 25th (1999) |
| HSBC | 6th (2003) | 29th (1999) |
| NHS | 2nd (2022) | 27th (1999, 2002) |
| BARCLAYS | 9th (2024) | 35th (2006) |
| UNILEVER | 7th (2002) | 23rd (2008, 2024) |
| BAE SYSTEMS | 23rd (1999, 2025) | 49th (2015) |
| DELOITTE | 2nd (2013) | 30th (2001) |
| BP | 14th (2003-2004) | 54th (2021) |
| CLIFFORD CHANCE | 14th (2025) | 45th (2007, 2012) |
| McKINSEY & COMPANY | 17th (2025) | 48th (2008) |
| IBM | 13th (2000) | 46th (2022) |
| A&O SHEARMAN (FORMERLY ALLEN & OVERY) | 24th (2010, 2024) | 57th (2005) |
| PROCTER & GAMBLE | 4th (1999-2001) | 39th (2022) |
| MICROSOFT | 21st (2004-2005) | 58th (1999) |
| JPMORGANCHASE | 6th (2025) | 45th (2003) |
| ARUP | 21st (2025) | 60th (2001) |
| LINKLATERS | 19th (2021) | 59th (2000) |
| LLOYDS BANKING GROUP | 11th (2025) | 56th (2001) |
| BRITISH ARMY | 4th (2003) | 53rd (2024) |
| ACCENTURE | 1st (1999-2002) | 55th (2025) |
| ROLLS-ROYCE | 15th (2019) | 68th (2002) |
| ROYAL NAVY | 35th (2010) | 88th (2013, 2025) |
| CITI | 30th (2008) | 89th (2023) |
| DEUTSCHE BANK | 23rd (2005) | 96th (2018) |
| BT | 14th (2000) | 89th (2024-2025) |
| L'ORÉAL | 19th (2022-2023) | 85th (2018) |
| SHELL | 11th (2006) | 90th (2021) |
| TESCO | 12th (2012) | 100th (1999) |

*Source* High Fliers Research

# We hire people. Not just degrees

Don't want to be judged by your degree? Great, because we feel the same. We use skills-based hiring to find a career that suits you, not just what you studied.
**Apply now at hsbc.com/careers**

HSBC | Opening up a world of opportunity

### Researching The Times Top 100 Graduate Employers

before the onset of the pandemic – were no longer ranked two years later.

Together, the twenty-seven annual editions of *The Times Top 100 Graduates Employers* have produced a definitive record of the graduate employers that different generations of students and recent graduates have aspired to join after leaving university – and these latest results provide a unique insight into how the 'Class of 2025' rated the country's leading graduate employers.

## The UK's Number 1 Graduate Employer 2025

"We are so proud that the Civil Service has returned to the top spot in *The Times Top 100 Graduate Employers*. It's really important that we get the best talent coming into the Civil Service and we work very hard each year to make that happen.

The Fast Stream is the Civil Service's long-standing graduate programme that currently recruits around 700 graduates each year. It was reformed in 2024 so that each of the seventeen schemes within the programme aligns closely with different professions within the civil service. It now includes specialist areas such as cyber security and risk management, alongside more familiar roles like policy, economics, project delivery and science & engineering.

There are opportunities right across the UK, in many civil service departments like the Foreign Commonwealth & Development Office, Department for Work and Pensions, Ministry of Defence, and HM Revenue & Customs, as well as in government agencies like the Environment Agency. Our ambition is for 50% of Fast Stream roles to be based outside of London by 2030.

The Fast Stream is designed to give graduates all the knowledge, skills and experiences they need to become a brilliant civil servant. Each programme lasts three or four years and is based around 12-month placements in different roles. We place a heavy emphasis on graduates developing their networks too, so that as they develop in their future careers within the civil service they can utilise the networks and relationships they've built on the programme.

At many of our on-campus recruitment events, you'll have the opportunity to talk to our current 'Fast Streamers' – graduates already on the Fast Stream programme – who can share their experiences and give you the inside knowledge about what it's really like.

And new for 2026, we're offering a summer internship programme for students from

*Beaulah Chadwick, Head of Civil Service Fast Stream*

lower-income backgrounds, to enable them to experience working in the civil service first-hand. On successful completion of the programme, these interns will receive a fast-pass directly into the assessment centre stage for the Fast Stream.

There is no such thing as a typical Fast Streamer – our graduates come from many different walks of life and a very wide range universities.

Competition for places on the Fast Stream can be considerable. But we've done a lot of work to streamline our assessments and selection process, and make our advice and guidance to prospective candidates as simple and easy to understand as possible.

We're not expecting polished applicants who know the answers to everything – we're looking for people who can show a real commitment to public service, who have a diverse range of skills and talents, and have the potential to become Civil Service leaders and managers in the future."

# CLYDE&CO

## Redefine *success* with us.

**50+**
Training contracts

**70+**
Global offices

**5.5k+**
Global employees

Clyde & Co's programmes offer the perfect opportunity for those seeking experience with a business at the heart of global trade and commerce. Participants benefit from the chance to learn with the best and broaden their outlook in a global firm with big ambitions.

If you're looking to develop your career and are committed to delivering exceptional outcomes, explore our opportunities today.

Go further. Search Early Careers at Clyde & Co.

- careers.clydeco.com
- clydecoearlycareers

## Success & Beyond

# It's not who you are.
# It's what you will become.

The NHS Graduate Management Training Scheme (GMTS) offers you a fast track to becoming a non-clinical senior leader in an organisation that can positively impact 57 million people - beginning a life changing journey for you.

**THE TIMES GRADUATE RECRUITMENT AWARDS 2025** — Graduate Employer of Choice **GENERAL MANAGEMENT**

**THE TIMES GRADUATE RECRUITMENT AWARDS 2025** — Graduate Employer of Choice **HUMAN RESOURCES**

**gti | cibyl** UK Graduate Survey **No. 2** Public Sector 2025

# NHS
## Graduate Management Training Scheme

**Start your leadership journey with the NHS Graduate Management Training Scheme (GMTS) – and help shape the future of healthcare in your community.**

With placements across England, funded postgraduate education, and a starting salary of £30,277, GMTS offers a unique opportunity to make a real difference.

The GMTS is more than a graduate scheme – it's a launchpad for future leaders in the NHS, the UK's largest and most trusted public service. Ranked 3rd in The Times Top 100 Graduate Employers, GMTS offers a structured, 2–2.5 year programme combining real-world NHS placements, postgraduate education, and expert mentoring.

As a GMTS trainee, you'll be at the forefront of the NHS's transformation, helping to deliver the three major shifts outlined in the 10 Year Health Plan: moving care closer to home, harnessing digital innovation, and prioritising prevention over treatment. Whether you're improving access to services in underserved communities, shaping data-driven policy, or leading inclusive workforce initiatives, your work will directly impact the health and wellbeing of people where you live.

**Applications open 24th September. Register your interest now at graduates.nhs.uk and take the first step toward a career that matters.**

nhsgraduatescheme

NHS Graduate Management Training Scheme (GMTS)

## Start your journey here

www.graduates.nhs.uk

**Employment**

**Graduate job openings at lowest level since 2018**

# Graduates account for 1 in 8 of those claiming universal credit

# Gen Z mired in debt and unhappiness

# England 'has too many overqualified graduates'

**BUSINESS**

**Graduate salaries dive in 'brain waste' crisis**

# Is AI killing graduate jobs

# When AI steals our jobs we create new ones
Throughout history technology has upended the labour market; this time, whizz-kids but also carers will be winners

# Graduate scheme jobs slump by a third following Reeves's tax raid

# UK economy takes a hit after Labour tax increases
Pound, stocks and retail sales all suffer falls

# Unemployment hits four-year high as wage growth declines

# Trump unleashes tariffs

# Tight job market raises stakes for graduates

**Recruitment**

# Civil service internships will be reserved for working class

# Evidence of cooling UK labour market mounts

# Understanding the Graduate Job Market

By **Martin Birchall**
Managing Director, High Fliers Research

During the past quarter of a century since the first edition of *The Times Top 100 Graduate Employers* was published in 1999, graduate recruitment at the UK's leading employers has increased substantially.

The number of graduate vacancies on offer to university-leavers has increased in sixteen of the past twenty-six years and reached a new record level in 2022, with almost twice as many opportunities available, compared to graduate recruitment at the beginning of the new the millenium.

But this sustained period of growth in graduate jobs has been punctuated by five significant downturns in recruitment – and vacancies for new graduates in 2026 are expected to be at their lowest level for fourteen years.

In the two years following the 9/11 terrorist attacks in the US, the worsening economic outlook prompted employers in the UK to reduce their entry-level vacancies for new graduates by over 15 per cent.

Graduate recruitment recovered in 2004 and vacancies for university-leavers grew at between 10 and 12 per cent annually over the next three years, before the global financial crisis of 2008 and 2009 heralded the worst recession in the UK since the Second World War.

Graduate vacancies at the country's top employers plunged by an unprecedented 23 per cent in less than 18 months – and almost 10,000 jobs were cut or left unfilled from a planned intake of more than 40,000 new graduates during this period. A record fifty-nine of the employers featured in *The Times Top 100 Graduate Employers* reduced their graduate hiring in 2009 alone.

Although the graduate job market bounced back successfully in 2010, with an annual increase in vacancies of more than 12 per cent, it took a further five years for graduate recruitment to return to the pre-recession peak recorded in 2007.

The uncertainty that followed Britain's referendum vote to leave the European Union in 2016 saw graduate vacancies dip again in 2017. But growth returned a year later and by 2019 entry-level recruitment was up by 43 per cent compared to the number of vacancies available in 2009 – the low point in graduate recruitment during the economic crisis – and had been expected to rise even higher in 2020.

But the start of the Covid pandemic in March 2020 forced the UK's top employers to pause or re-evaluate their graduate recruitment and many were unable to continue with that year's planned annual intake of university-leavers. Graduate recruitment was cut in thirteen out of fifteen industries and business sectors, most noticeably at major engineering & industrial companies and

> **" *Opportunities for new graduates at the country's leading employers have now slumped by almost a quarter since 2023.* "**

**Nat & Amal's scribble inspired a team volunteering day.**

KPMG

Come and make a real-world difference, like Nat and Amal, on a KPMG graduate programme.

Apply to 2026 graduate roles at
**kpmgcareers.co.uk/graduate**

accounting & professional services firms, where over 700 planned vacancies were left unfilled. The final number of graduates recruited by employers featured in *The Times Top 100 Graduate Employers* in 2020 was 12.3 per cent lower than in 2019.

Recruitment began to bounce back in 2021 with a substantial 9.4 per cent rise in entry-level vacancies – the 'V-shaped' pandemic recovery in the graduate job market largely mirroring the recovery in the wider economy.

This strong growth gathered pace the following year when graduate vacancies increased in all fifteen industries and business sectors represented in *The Times Top 100 Graduate Employers*. In all, the number of graduate jobs available jumped by 14.5 per cent in 2022, the largest-ever year-on-year rise in recruitment at the UK's leading employers.

The 2023 graduate recruitment season began optimistically, with many of the country's top employers expecting to match their bumper intake from the previous year. But as the year progressed, fears of a possible recession in the UK grew and graduate recruitment was cut back by 6.4 per cent, compared with 2022.

With a General Election looming, the economic uncertainty increased substantially in 2024 and employers downgraded their recruitment targets dramatically as the year progressed. The number of graduates recruited dropped by 14.6 per cent year-on-year – the largest annual fall since 2009 – and an even bigger reduction than during the Covid pandemic. In all, the UK's leading employers took on 6,000 fewer graduates than they had originally expected to in 2024.

Post-election, employer confidence continued to worsen, with graduate recruitment decreasing by a further 1.3 per cent in 2025. At the beginning of the 2025-2026 recruitment season, employers in *The Times Top 100 Graduate Employers* are predicting that they will have a total of 22,880 graduate vacancies for autumn 2026 start dates.

This equates to another cut in graduate recruitment, this time by 3.5 per cent, the fourth consecutive annual reduction in entry level vacancies. This discouraging news means that opportunities for new graduates at the country's leading employers have now slumped by almost a quarter since 2023, taking graduate recruitment back to a level last recorded in 2012.

Accounting & professional services firms featured in the *Top 100* are among the hardest-hit in this downturn in recruitment – having recruited

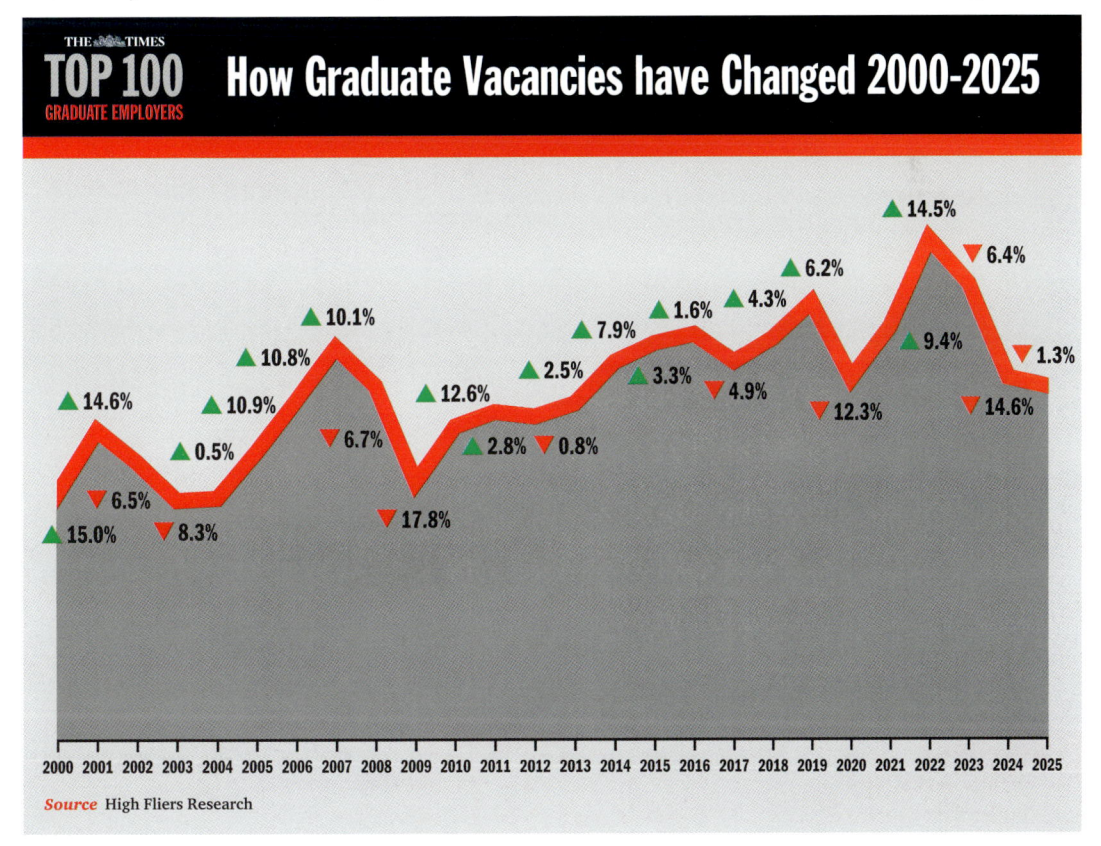

**THE TIMES TOP 100 GRADUATE EMPLOYERS — How Graduate Vacancies have Changed 2000-2025**

|  |  |
|---|---|
| 2000 | ▲ 15.0% |
| 2001 | ▼ 6.5% |
| 2002 | ▲ 14.6% |
| 2003 | ▼ 8.3% |
| 2004 | ▲ 0.5% |
| 2005 | ▲ 10.9% |
| 2006 | ▲ 10.8% |
| 2007 | ▲ 10.1% |
| 2008 | ▼ 6.7% |
| 2009 | ▼ 17.8% |
| 2010 | ▲ 12.6% |
| 2011 | ▲ 2.8% |
| 2012 | ▼ 0.8% |
| 2013 | ▲ 2.5% |
| 2014 | ▲ 7.9% |
| 2015 | ▲ 3.3% |
| 2016 | ▲ 1.6% |
| 2017 | ▼ 4.9% |
| 2018 | ▲ 4.3% |
| 2019 | ▲ 6.2% |
| 2020 | ▼ 12.3% |
| 2021 | ▲ 9.4% |
| 2022 | ▲ 14.5% |
| 2023 | ▼ 6.4% |
| 2024 | ▼ 14.6% |
| 2025 | ▼ 1.3% |

Source: High Fliers Research

## Understanding the Graduate Job Market

almost 6,500 graduate trainees in 2023, there are expected to be fewer than 4,500 graduate vacancies in the sector in 2026.

Graduate recruitment is predicted to fall in twelve out of fifteen key industries and business sectors in the next 12 months, with the biggest drops expected at oil & energy companies, consulting firms, media organisations and employers in the banking & finance sector.

The two employers from *The Times Top 100 Graduate Employers* with the largest graduate recruitment targets for 2026 are Teach First, the popular programme that recruits graduates to teach in schools in low-income communities around the UK, which has 1,300 places available – and car & van rental company Enterprise Mobility which is offering 1,100 graduate vacancies

Other very substantial individual graduate recruiters in 2026 include the accounting & professional services firms PwC, Deloitte and EY, which are each aiming to recruit 1,000 new trainees in the year ahead, and online retailer and technology company Amazon which also has 1,000 graduate positions available

More than half of *Top 100* employers have vacancies for graduates in technology and finance, two fifths have opportunities in engineering, and a third are recruiting for human resources roles

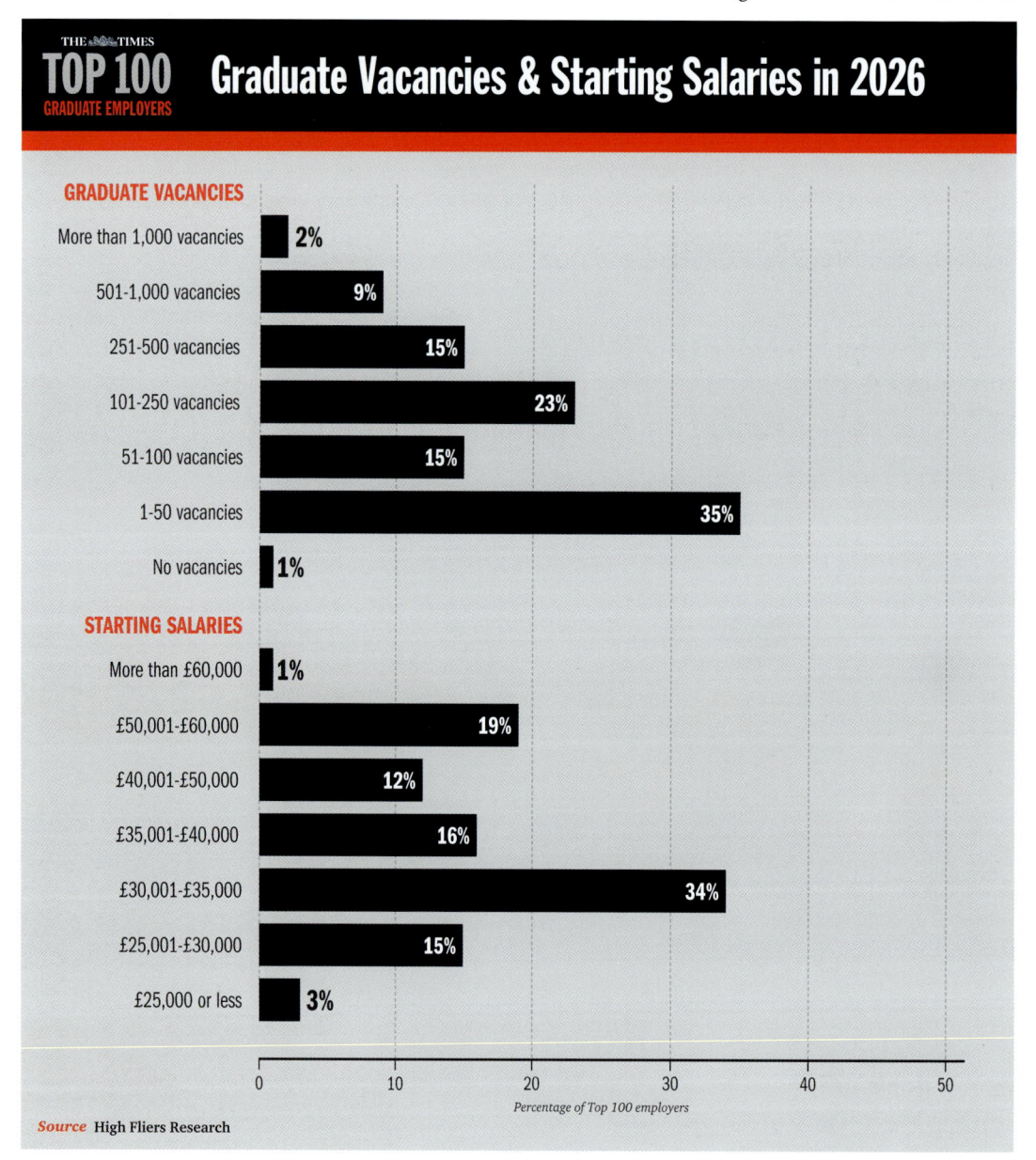

### THE TIMES TOP 100 GRADUATE EMPLOYERS — Graduate Vacancies & Starting Salaries in 2026

**GRADUATE VACANCIES**

| Category | Percentage |
|---|---|
| More than 1,000 vacancies | 2% |
| 501-1,000 vacancies | 9% |
| 251-500 vacancies | 15% |
| 101-250 vacancies | 23% |
| 51-100 vacancies | 15% |
| 1-50 vacancies | 35% |
| No vacancies | 1% |

**STARTING SALARIES**

| Category | Percentage |
|---|---|
| More than £60,000 | 1% |
| £50,001-£60,000 | 19% |
| £40,001-£50,000 | 12% |
| £35,001-£40,000 | 16% |
| £30,001-£35,000 | 34% |
| £25,001-£30,000 | 15% |
| £25,000 or less | 3% |

*Percentage of Top 100 employers*

*Source* High Fliers Research

# Enterprise Mobility™

# JOIN WITH GREAT IDEAS.

## STAY BECAUSE THEY'RE HEARD.

Ready to make an impact on mobility and the communities we serve? Then the Management Trainee role is for you.

**Learn more**

MAKE YOUR MOVE.
**Become a Management Trainee at**
**enterprisemobility.co.uk/careers**

## Understanding the Graduate Job Market

or general management positions. A quarter of the country's top graduate employers are looking for new recruits to work in marketing, sales or consulting, and a fifth have entry-level roles in research & development. There are fewer graduate jobs available in retailing or in more specialist areas, such as purchasing, logistics & supply chain, property and the media.

Over four-fifths of *Top 100* employers have graduate vacancies in London in 2025, and three-fifths have posts available elsewhere in the south east of England. More than half also have roles in the north west of England, the south west, the Midlands, Yorkshire and the north east. Half are recruiting for graduate roles in Scotland, but Northern Ireland, Wales and East Anglia have the fewest employers with vacancies this year.

Graduate starting salaries at *The Times Top 100 Graduate Employers* changed little between 2012 and 2021, increasing by just £1,000 in this nine-year period to a median of £30,000. But this went up to £32,000 in 2022, the first annual boost in starting salaries for seven years. And it has continued rising since – to £33,500 in 2023, £34,000 in 2024, and £35,000 in 2025.

These rates could increase further in 2026, with the most generous starting salaries available at the leading investment banks & fund managers (a median of £60,000), law firms (£56,000) and consulting firms (£50,000). It is noticeable that employers in each of these popular destinations for new graduates have opted to step-up their starting salaries in the past two years, with substantial increases at several of the top City and international law firms.

A fifth of the employers featured in *The Times Top 100 Graduate Employers* now offer starting salaries in excess of £50,000 for their new recruits. The most alluring salaries publicised within this edition are at law firms White & Case and Latham & Watkins, which are offering their new trainees starting salaries of £62,000 and £60,000 respectively in 2026. Away from the legal sector, retailer Aldi continues to pay a sector-leading graduate salary of £50,750, and consulting firm Newton is offering a starting salary of £48,000.

One in three of the UK's leading employers recruit graduates year-round, or in different phases during the year, and will accept applications throughout the 2025-2026 recruitment season until all their vacancies are filled. For employers with an annual application deadline, most are in November or December, although a limited number have October or post-Christmas deadlines for their graduate programmes.

This means that there is every incentive to apply early for the graduate vacancies that are available at *The Times Top 100 Graduate Employers* in 2026.

### THE TIMES TOP 100 GRADUATE EMPLOYERS — Graduate Vacancies at Top 100 Employers in 2026

| 2026 | 2025 | | GRADUATE VACANCIES IN 2026 | % CHANGE IN 2026 | % CHANGE IN 2025 | MEDIAN STARTING SALARY IN 2026 |
|---|---|---|---|---|---|---|
| 1. | 1 | ACCOUNTANCY & PROFESSIONAL SERVICES FIRMS | 4,450 | ▼ 0.4% | ▲ 0.9% | £37,000 |
| 2. | 2 | PUBLIC SECTOR EMPLOYERS | 3,385 | ▼ 6.0% | ▼ 6.4% | £31,200 |
| 3. | 3 | ENGINEERING & INDUSTRIAL COMPANIES | 3,240 | ▼ 6.1% | ▼ 4.3% | £31,000 |
| 4. | 5 | INVESTMENT BANKS & FUND MANAGERS | 2,055 | ▼ 1.7% | NO CHANGE | £60,000 |
| 5. | 6 | BANKING & FINANCIAL SERVICES | 1,875 | ▼ 7.9% | ▼ 3.1% | £45,000 |
| 6. | 7 | ARMED FORCES | 1,550 | ▲ 6.2% | ▼ 0.7% | £34,700 |
| 7. | 4 | TECHNOLOGY COMPANIES | 1,405 | ▼ 1.4% | ▲ 14.4% | £33,500 |
| 8. | 10 | RETAILERS | 1,145 | ▼ 17.0% | ▲ 14.2% | £34,000 |
| 9. | 8 | MEDIA ORGANISATIONS | 825 | ▼ 9.3% | ▼ 13% | £28,700 |
| 10. | 9 | LAW FIRMS | 817 | ▲ 0.6% | ▼ 3.4% | £56,000 |
| 11. | 13 | OIL & ENERGY COMPANIES | 290 | ▼ 15.7% | ▼ 39.1% | £35,000 |
| 12. | 12 | CONSULTING FIRMS | 255 | ▼ 13.6% | ▲ 41.7% | £50,000 |
| 13. | 11 | CONSUMER GOODS MANUFACTURERS | 220 | ▼ 7.9% | ▲ 13.7% | £38,000 |
| 14. | 15 | PROPERTY COMPANIES | 120 | NO CHANGE | NO CHANGE | £28,500 |
| 15. | 14 | CHEMICAL & PHARMACEUTICALS COMPANIES | 53 | ▼ 3.6% | ▼ 8.3% | £34,100 |

*Source* High Fliers Research

# How would you shape your world?

campus.bankofamerica.com

@BofA_Careers

All of our internships, placements and programs offer training, development and support. We'll help you learn, grow and belong while you begin a career with global impact.

Here at Bank of America, you'll be supported to succeed through mentorship programs and development opportunities. We foster a diverse, inclusive culture, where you'll build networks and find friendships. You'll be given real responsibilities, develop skills for the future, and discover which areas of our business most appeal to you.

**BANK OF AMERICA**

© 2023 Bank of America Corporation. All rights reserved.

# Turn your passion into your profession

**If you're interested in training to teach, Get Into Teaching will tell you everything you need to know.**

Teaching is a varied and rewarding career that shapes you, as much as it does others. Where **no two days are the same**, and where you can turn your passion into your profession and have lots of opportunities to grow.

You can bring creativity to the classroom every day, and in turn have a **lasting impact**; inspiring the next generation. You will be challenged and rewarded, and you'll make a difference.

In teaching, as you grow, so does your career. **Opportunities for progression are varied**, whether that be through a position as head of year or head of subject, or through taking on a pastoral role. With added responsibilities you can expect additional pay rewards.

Whether you're just thinking about a career in teaching or are ready to apply, Get Into Teaching offers **free advice and support** to help you decide if teaching in a primary or secondary school in England is right for you.

Search: **Get Into Teaching**

Department for Education

# Teaching ✓
## Every Lesson Shapes a Life

- You'll receive **one-to-one support** from an adviser with years of classroom experience. They'll guide you through the steps and answer any questions you may have.

- With **generous bursaries and scholarships** available across certain subjects, including STEM, you'll get advice on how to fund your training year.

- You'll find out how to get a taste of life in the classroom, from school experience days to paid internships.

- You'll learn about the career progression teaching offers, with a **minimum starting salary of £32.9k** (or more in London) and the opportunity to earn **over £45k within five years.**

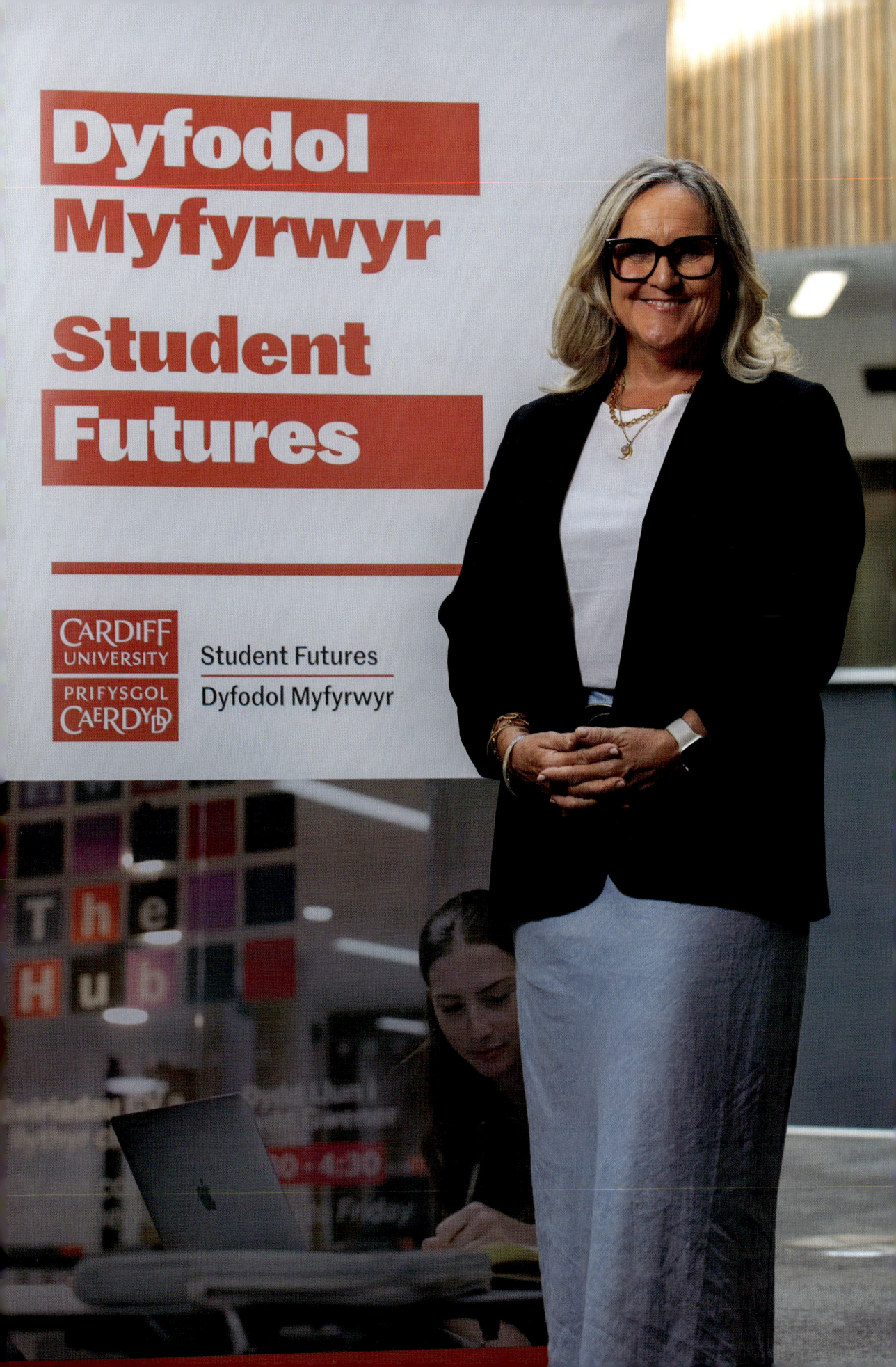

# Dyfodol Myfyrwyr
# Student Futures

**CARDIFF UNIVERSITY**
**PRIFYSGOL CAERDYDD**

Student Futures
Dyfodol Myfyrwyr

# Successful Graduate Job Hunting

By **Megan Jenkins**
Head of Student Futures, Cardiff University

The journey to finding a graduate job and your career beyond begins with self-awareness. The sooner you start thinking about what you're good at, what makes you tick, what gives you a buzz, and what you're passionate about – the easier it will be to work out what kind of graduate job could be right for you when you leave university.

You're going to be working for a very, very long time – maybe committing as much as fifty years to the workplace – so it's incredibly important to find something you're going to love and will excite you in the years ahead.

But what you do immediately after leaving university may not be the same as what you're doing in five or ten years' time. You don't need to worry if you can't find your 'ideal' job straightaway. You should see your first job as just that – a first step towards doing something that you have a real passion for.

The curriculum of your degree will encourage you to think about the skills you're developing and the values that are important to you. But your whole university experience is going to round you into the person you'll be at the end of your degree. Joining university societies, volunteering, taking part in social enterprises, doing part-time jobs alongside your studies, and getting work experience in the university holidays will all increase your skillset – and will help you to work out what you're aiming for in the future.

One of the first things you need to do is find out where your university careers service is and how to access the resources they offer. Every university in the UK has its own dedicated careers service, with professional careers advisers, a wealth of information and guidance, and extensive programmes of events, skills workshops and training courses. It's worth visiting your careers service in-person to see the facilities they offer, bookmark their website, find and follow them on socials – and check whether you need to set up an account with them.

Once you're in touch with your careers service, you can begin exploring your options and finding out about what's on offer

If you're in your first year, you'll be able to take part in the insight days and taster experiences that many graduate employers run during the year. With fewer academic pressures, you'll have more time to try different things out and reflect on what interests you, as well as building your confidence.

And if you're hoping to do work experience with one of the larger employers at the end of your second year, then these introductory sessions can be very useful preparation, as the deadline for applying for internship programmes can be as

> **"**AI can be very helpful to nuance your applications, but using it unintelligently is a disaster and very easy for an employer to spot.**"**

**ICAEW**

"The ACA gave me the confidence to do a job I never thought I could."

Evie Dolega-Ossowski,
Internal Auditor,
Marks & Spencer

# THIS IS ACCOUNTANCY

"When you tell someone you're an accountant or an auditor, they think you must be really good at maths.

But that's not necessarily true. It's more about critical thinking and being able to analyse, interpret data, talk to people, build relationships, and challenge conventional wisdom.

I studied the ACA under an apprenticeship programme, so I got to work and build up skills around things like communication and teamworking, while also studying he technical side of accounting. Even after you've completed your exams, there's always somebody to talk to if you need help."

**START YOUR CAREER:**

early as September or October in your second year.

Now could also be the time to find out about careers mentors – graduates from your university, maybe even from your degree course, who can share their experiences with you and guide you as you look for work experience or your first job.

Your careers service will help you find out about the very wide range of events that take place each year at your university. Employers large and small take part in on-campus careers fairs and they can be a great place to see what's out there and talk to different organisations, to find out what excites you – and what doesn't. And there'll be a whole programme of employer presentations, skills training events, student challenges, and introductory evenings on individual careers areas.

All of these events are designed to introduce you to what's available in the employment market and help you find your passion, and you can learn a great deal very quickly by taking part in them. Absorb as much information as you can, talk to people and ask questions, and build up your knowledge by doing more research on the employers you meet.

It's important to remember that the 'name over the door' of an organisation doesn't always convey the graduate jobs that lie beyond. For example, you might not be interested in working in retail, but by going along to a major retailer's presentation, you'll find out that they're also offering graduate roles in finance, technology, purchasing, logistics and even human resources.

And because 70 per cent of graduate jobs in the UK are open to graduates from any degree discipline, there's unlikely to be a direct link between what you're studying and the job you do after university. Just because you're doing an archaeology degree doesn't mean you're going to be on historical digs when you start work – it's just as likely that you could become a chartered accountant or have a career in marketing.

Talking to your university careers service can be very helpful at this point, particularly if you're not sure what you're interested in or how to approach your job search. This could be an informal chat with a student peer advisor, or a quick query about a particular employer or your CV, or it could be a longer one-to-one guidance appointment with an experienced careers adviser, either in-person or online.

These half-hour or one-hour sessions are especially popular and can be booked-up well in advance, but they're a fantastic opportunity for you to talk about who you are and what you've learned about yourself. Careers advisers are very skilled at picking out the information that will help with your decision-making – and will guide you on how to plan your next steps.

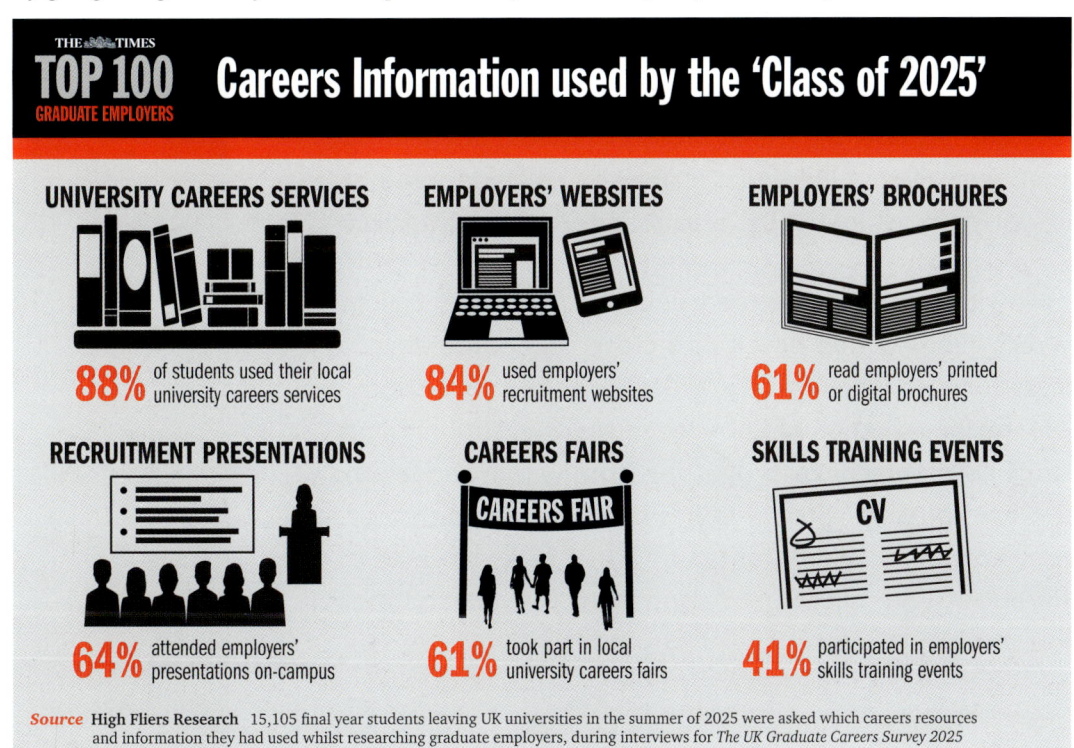

## THE TIMES TOP 100 GRADUATE EMPLOYERS — Careers Information used by the 'Class of 2025'

**UNIVERSITY CAREERS SERVICES**
**88%** of students used their local university careers services

**EMPLOYERS' WEBSITES**
**84%** used employers' recruitment websites

**EMPLOYERS' BROCHURES**
**61%** read employers' printed or digital brochures

**RECRUITMENT PRESENTATIONS**
**64%** attended employers' presentations on-campus

**CAREERS FAIRS**
**61%** took part in local university careers fairs

**SKILLS TRAINING EVENTS**
**41%** participated in employers' skills training events

*Source* **High Fliers Research** 15,105 final year students leaving UK universities in the summer of 2025 were asked which careers resources and information they had used whilst researching graduate employers, during interviews for *The UK Graduate Careers Survey 2025*

# SLAUGHTER AND MAY/

# A WORLD OF DIFFERENCE

Laws, international markets, global institutions... all changing every day. So how do we, as an international law firm, create the agility of mind that enables us to guide some of the world's most influential organisations into the future?

By allowing bright people the freedom to grow. By training lawyers in a way that develops a closer understanding of clients through working on a wider range of transactions. By fostering an ethos of knowledge sharing, support and mutual development by promoting from within and leaving the clocks outside when it comes to billing. To learn more about how our key differences not only make a world of difference to our clients, but also to our lawyers and their careers, visit:

## slaughterandmay.com/careers

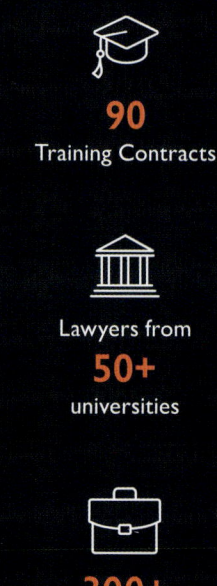

**90**
Training Contracts

Lawyers from
**50+**
universities

**300+**
places on
open days and schemes

## Successful Graduate Job Hunting

If you are hoping to get some formal work experience, like a six or eight-week internship or placement, then you'll usually need to apply for this during your second year. You should bear in mind that at the larger employers, internships are often linked directly to their graduate recruitment, so some – or sometimes all – of their graduate vacancies are filled by students who've completed a successful work experience placement with them. This means that getting a place on the internship is likely to be just as demanding and competitive as applying for a graduate position, with a formal application and multi-stage selection process.

Whether you're applying for work experience – or you've reached your final year and are preparing to make applications for graduate jobs – then putting together your CV is a critical first step. You won't necessarily use the CV itself when you make your applications, but preparing one is a very important part of getting your head in the game. Use it as self-reflection tool to note down the skills you've developed, the things you're interested in, and to collect together all your important educational and academic details.

When you come to fill in employers' individual applications, having all your dates and achievements in one place will be a big help. You'll find plenty of guidance on how to write your CV on your careers service website, along with workshops and training sessions, and online feedback to help you improve how you present yourself.

Your professional online presence is extremely important as you begin to enter the world of work, and the time you spend creating a focussed *LinkedIn* page is time well-spent. *LinkedIn* is the social media network for professionals and your page on it will be a 'digital CV' that showcases your education, experience and skills. It has the huge advantage of making you searchable by employers who are looking to recruit students like you. Your careers service will have lots of good examples available to help you build up your page and some universities often offer *LinkedIn* photo booths at careers fairs to provide you with a professional profile picture.

When you're drafting your CV, compiling your *LinkedIn* profile or preparing your answers on employers' application forms, you may be keen to turn to AI for assistance. AI can be very helpful to nuance your applications and improve the way you phrase things or structure your answers. In particular, if you're completely stuck as to how to start something, it can be brilliant. But using it unintelligently is a disaster and is very easy for an

---

### THE TIMES TOP 100 GRADUATE EMPLOYERS
### How the 'Class of 2025' Applied for Graduate Jobs

**WORK EXPERIENCE** 
More than a **third** of students who did internships or work placements at university received a **graduate job offer** from the employer they worked for

**JOB APPLICATIONS IN FINAL YEAR** 
Graduates made an average of **22 job applications** each, during their final year at university.

**SELECTION & ASSESSMENT** 
**4** out of **5** graduate job hunters found employers' online tests and recorded video interviews **difficult**

**GRADUATE JOB OFFERS** 
Only a **quarter** of graduates from the 'Class of 2025' received a **graduate job offer** before leaving university

*Source* **High Fliers Research** 15,105 final year students leaving UK universities in the summer of 2025 were asked about the job applications they had made to graduate employers and their progress with job offers, during interviews for *The UK Graduate Careers Survey 2025*

## Successful Graduate Job Hunting

employer to spot, so it's essential to understand how to use it effectively.

For example, if you upload your CV along with the description of the job you're applying for, and ask AI to answer the questions on the application form for you, then the answers it will generate are likely to be very generic and use a near-identical vocabulary to everyone else, who are also using AI to help them with their application.

In this instance, what AI gives you is a great starting point for your answers and can organise your content effectively. But you need to go through and do a very careful edit of the text it produces, to check that it's telling the right story and reflects who you are – and that your own 'voice' comes through clearly in your application. That's what employers are really after, they want a picture of you and want to be able to imagine you in their workforce when they're looking at your application and speaking to you during the selection process.

There is no 'right' number of applications to make – you will end up making as many as it takes to get the job you want. But firing off a hundred similar applications will be a waste of time. It's worth putting in as much effort as you can preparing for the application process, gathering information and honing your answers to different

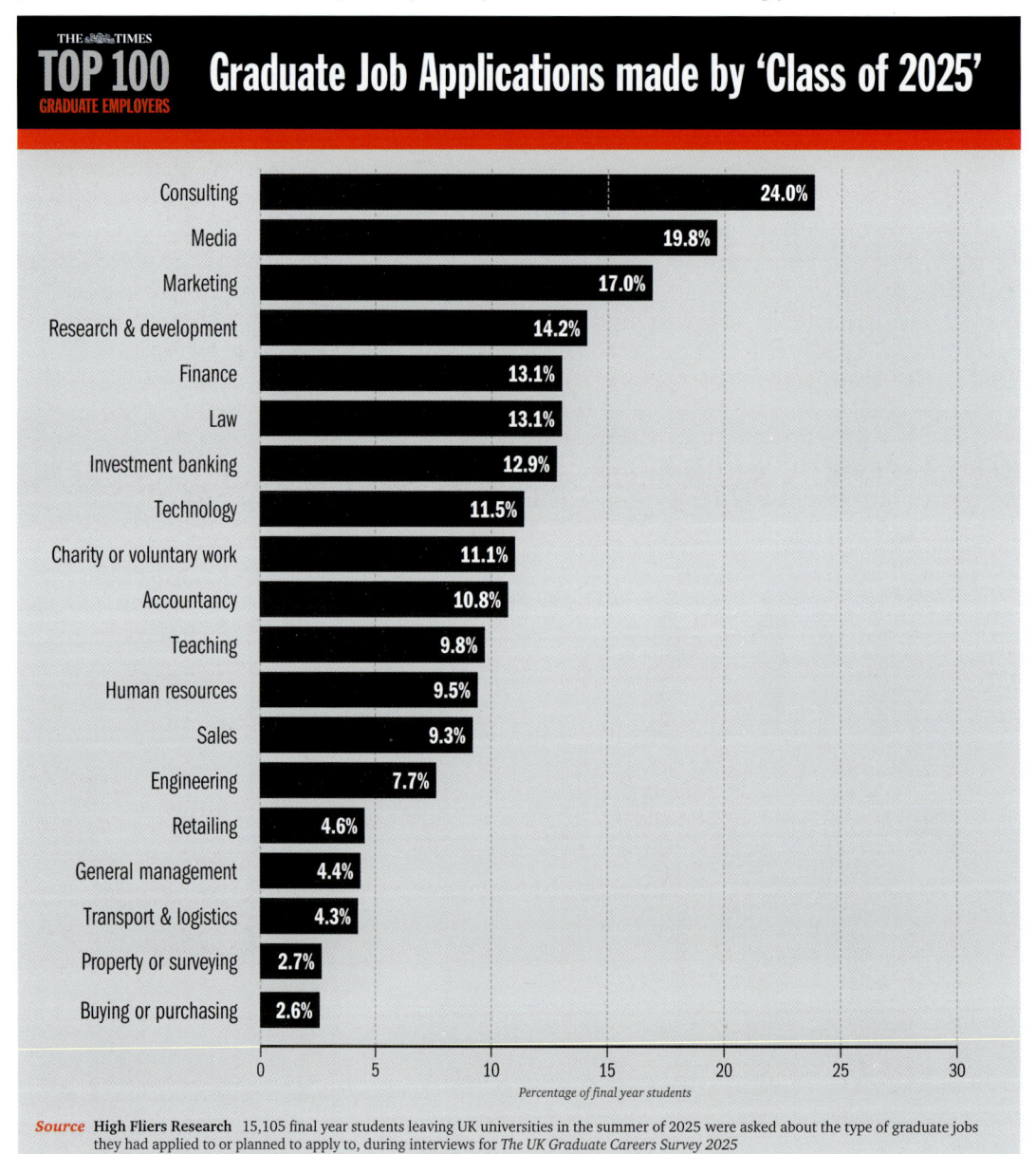

### THE TIMES TOP 100 GRADUATE EMPLOYERS
### Graduate Job Applications made by 'Class of 2025'

| Sector | Percentage |
|---|---|
| Consulting | 24.0% |
| Media | 19.8% |
| Marketing | 17.0% |
| Research & development | 14.2% |
| Finance | 13.1% |
| Law | 13.1% |
| Investment banking | 12.9% |
| Technology | 11.5% |
| Charity or voluntary work | 11.1% |
| Accountancy | 10.8% |
| Teaching | 9.8% |
| Human resources | 9.5% |
| Sales | 9.3% |
| Engineering | 7.7% |
| Retailing | 4.6% |
| General management | 4.4% |
| Transport & logistics | 4.3% |
| Property or surveying | 2.7% |
| Buying or purchasing | 2.6% |

*Percentage of final year students*

**Source** High Fliers Research  15,105 final year students leaving UK universities in the summer of 2025 were asked about the type of graduate jobs they had applied to or planned to apply to, during interviews for *The UK Graduate Careers Survey 2025*

# With ICAS, opportunity doesn't knock.
## It kicks down the door.

Learn more about how a Chartered Accountancy qualification with ICAS can fast-track your ambitions.

With ICAS, a career in Chartered Accountancy means open access to a whole world of possibilities – so there's no end to where your career could take you.

icas.com/opportunitykicks

ic as

# Successful Graduate Job Hunting

questions. So your first two or three applications will take you much longer to complete than the subsequent ones will.

Employers have many different application deadlines, from early in the academic year for the most competitive programmes, up until the following summer for some of the smaller employers or year-round recruiters. You should be prepared to make batches of applications throughout your final year, so it's important to find out when these deadlines are and prioritise those that close first. But remember, you'll be juggling your applications alongside getting a good degree. You'll have to balance job hunting with your academic commitments, your final year project and your part-time job too – so some careful planning is needed.

Once you've submitted your application, the next stage of selection is often online tests. For many of the larger employers, they automatically test everyone who applies, using a series of aptitude, ability and psychometric tests. If you've not done them before, they can seem extremely daunting. But your university careers service can help you practice different tests beforehand, so you don't go into them blind and will become more familiar with their format.

And as well as the tests, you're likely to be asked to do an online recorded video interview too, where you'll answer questions that pop-up on your laptop or phone screen. This can also be an intimidating experience, the first time you do one. So again, you should practice beforehand – find out the kind of questions you're likely to face, think through the sort of answers you might give, and ask for feedback from a careers adviser.

It's well worth committing time to these preparations, because so many well-known employers use tests and recorded interviews to decide who goes through to the last stages of their selection process.

When you reach a final-round assessment centre then you've done a cracking good job – and your odds of getting a job offer have improved dramatically. The employer is acknowledging that you have the ability to do this job, but they want to find out how much you want it, and how you compare with the other people who've also reached this stage.

To succeed, you'll need to really understand the company and find out what its values are – and then look at yourself and your own values, to make sure they align. If you can do your research and demonstrate you're a good 'fit' for the employer and have the same ethos, it will really stand out.

There is plenty of assistance available to prepare you for assessment centres – your university careers service will have lots of resources that explain the type of assessments that employers include, such as group exercises, presentations and one-to-one interviews. You can do mock assessment centres and interview practice, and get help preparing a presentation or selection task too. The more thorough your preparations are, the more likely you are to be successful.

If it all goes well and you get the job offer, then you're in a brilliant position. Even if the employer wasn't necessarily your first choice, then it will still give you invaluable experience, it'll build up your CV, help develop your skills, and make you much more employable in the future.

But if you reach the end of your final year and haven't achieved the job offer you were hoping for, then there will continue to be lots of help available and plenty of different options for you. The majority of university careers services offer on-going support, advice and guidance for two or three years post-graduation – and there are some universities that offer that for life. You can also access alumni networks too, which can be very helpful from an employability perspective.

Coming up with a 'Plan B' isn't easy. For example, doing a masters simply because it gives you an extra year's thinking time is definitely the wrong thing to do. But doing a masters where you develop new skills and knowledge, and is a stepping-stone on the way to a career path you're really interested in, is a much more positive decision.

Going travelling can teach you all sorts of things and will open you up to a whole panoply of experiences. But if you're not able to put those experiences to good use afterwards, it just becomes time spent abroad. Whatever you do next, think about who you are, how you're developing and how the things you do will make you more employable.

If you use your university careers service and take advantage of everything it's able to prepare you with, then you'll be given every tool necessary to navigate the world of work beyond university

So whether you're job hunting during your degree – or in the months or years afterwards – take these tools, learn from them, and keep them with you, as you make your way through the working world that lies ahead.

# AI is Changing the Job Market – Are You Ready?

Whether you're stepping into your first job or planning your next career move, this book gives you the tools to outpace the machines — and thrive.

**This game-changing guide reveals:**

- The 5 "killer career apps" every graduate needs
- How to stay relevant when roles are vanishing
- The soft skills AI can't replace – and how to master them

With practical advice, real-world examples and actionable strategies, don't just plan for the future – create it!

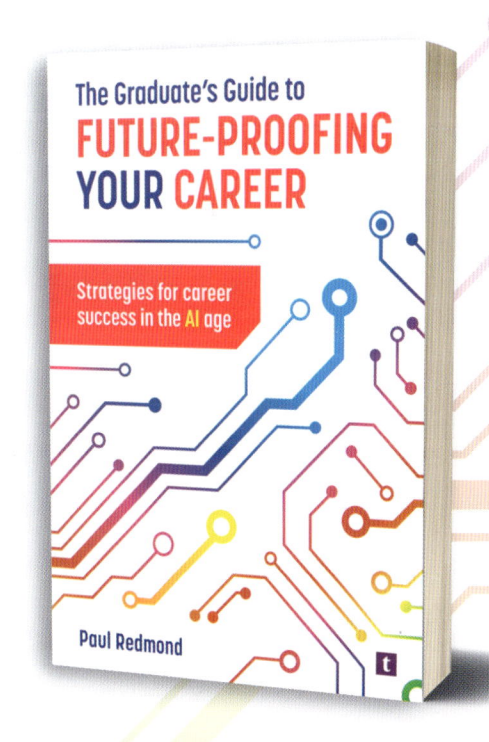

The Graduate's Guide to **FUTURE-PROOFING YOUR CAREER**

Strategies for career success in the AI age

Paul Redmond

**Buy now from Amazon**

Estd. 1969 trotman | t

# SOLVE PROBLEMS.
# SAVE LIVES.

Software Developer: **£60k**

Business Analyst: **£60k**

Technical Engineer: **£60k**

Service Analyst: **£45k**

Account Manager: **£60k**

Implementation Specialist: **£45k**

**NO EXPERIENCE REQUIRED**

www.tpp-careers.com

TPP Careers
@tpp_careers
@TPPCareers
TPP

tpp

# FIND CLARITY AMID THE CLAMOUR

**SUBSCRIBE WITH OUR STUDENT OFFER**

## £9.99 A YEAR FOR 3 YEARS*

Scan the QR code or search
**thetimes.com/student**

**LOUISE CALLAGHAN**
International Correspondent

**THE TIMES**
**THE SUNDAY TIMES**

*T&Cs apply. Offer is for verified students only. Billed as £9.99 a year for your first 3 years. Visit **thetimes.com/subscribe/student** for full Terms & Conditions.

# THE TIMES TOP 100 GRADUATE EMPLOYERS

| | Page | | Page | | Page |
|---|---|---|---|---|---|
| A&O Shearman | 50 | Diageo | 98 | Microsoft | 146 |
| AECOM | 52 | DLA Piper | 100 | Mott Macdonald | 148 |
| Aldi | 54 | EDF | 102 | Network Rail | 150 |
| Amazon | 56 | Enterprise Mobility | 104 | Newton | 152 |
| AON | 58 | Environment Agency | 106 | NHS | 154 |
| Army | 60 | EY | 108 | P&G | 156 |
| Arup | 62 | Forvis Mazars | 110 | Penguin | 158 |
| AstraZeneca | 64 | Freshfields | 112 | Pfizer | 160 |
| AtkinsRéalis | 66 | Google | 114 | Police Now | 162 |
| Babcock | 68 | Grant Thornton | 116 | PwC | 164 |
| BAE Systems | 70 | HMRC | 118 | RAF | 166 |
| Bank of America | 72 | Hogan Lovells | 120 | Revolut | 168 |
| Barclays | 74 | HSBC | 122 | Rolls-Royce | 170 |
| BBC | 76 | IBM | 124 | Royal Navy | 172 |
| BCG | 78 | ITV | 126 | Savills | 174 |
| BlackRock | 80 | JPMorganChase | 128 | Scottish Power | 176 |
| Bloomberg | 82 | KPMG | 130 | Shell | 178 |
| BNY | 84 | L'Oréal | 132 | Slaughter and May | 180 |
| British Airways | 86 | Latham & Watkins | 134 | Teach First | 182 |
| Capgemini | 88 | Lidl | 136 | Tesco | 184 |
| Civil Service | 90 | Linklaters | 138 | TfL | 186 |
| Clyde & Co | 92 | Lloyds Banking Group | 140 | Unilever | 188 |
| Deloitte | 94 | Lockheed Martin | 142 | White & Case | 190 |
| Deutsche Bank | 96 | M&S | 144 | | |

# Index

| EMPLOYER | RANK | ACCOUNTANCY | CONSULTING | ENGINEERING | FINANCE | GENERAL MANAGEMENT | HUMAN RESOURCES | INVESTMENT BANKING | LAW | LOGISTICS | MARKETING | MEDIA | PROPERTY | PURCHASING | RESEARCH & DEVELOPMENT | RETAIL | SALES | TECHNOLOGY | OTHER | VACANCIES | INSIGHT COURSES | DEGREE PLACEMENTS | SUMMER INTERNSHIPS | PAGE |
|---|---|---|---|---|---|---|---|---|---|---|---|---|---|---|---|---|---|---|---|---|---|---|---|---|
| A&O SHEARMAN | 36 | | | | | | | | ● | | | | | | | | | | | 80 | | | | 50 |
| AECOM | 84 | | ● | ● | | ● | | | | | ● | | | | | | ● | | | 250 | | ● | ● | 52 |
| ALDI | 27 | | | | | | | | | | | | | ● | | | | | | 15 | | ● | | 54 |
| AMAZON | 20 | | | ● | ● | ● | | | ● | ● | | | | | ● | ● | ● | | | 1,000+ | | | ● | 56 |
| AON | 59 | | ● | | ● | ● | | | | | | | | | | | | | | 100+ | | | ● | 58 |
| ARMY | 33 | | | ● | | ● | ● | | ● | ● | | | | | | | | ● | | 650+ | | | | 60 |
| ARUP | 21 | | ● | ● | ● | | | | | | ● | ● | ● | | ● | | | ● | | 300+ | | ● | ● | 62 |
| ASTRAZENECA | 18 | | | | | | | | | | | | | | ● | | | | | 10-20 | | ● | ● | 64 |
| ATKINSRÉALIS | 65 | | ● | ● | | | | | | | | | | | | | | | | 450+ | | | | 66 |
| BABCOCK | 98 | | | ● | ● | | | | ● | | | | | | ● | | | ● | | 300+ | | | | 68 |
| BAE SYSTEMS | 23 | | ● | ● | ● | ● | ● | | | | | | | | ● | | | ● | | 700+ | ● | ● | ● | 70 |
| BANK OF AMERICA | 58 | ● | | ● | ● | | | ● | | | | | | | | | | ● | | No fixed quota | ● | ● | ● | 72 |
| BARCLAYS | 16 | | ● | | ● | ● | | ● | | | | | | | ● | ● | ● | | | 600 | ● | ● | ● | 74 |
| BBC | 5 | ● | | ● | ● | ● | ● | | | | ● | ● | | | | | | ● | | 250 | | ● | ● | 76 |
| BCG | 29 | | ● | | | | | | | | | | | | | | | | | No fixed quota | ● | | ● | 78 |
| BLACKROCK | 37 | | | | ● | | ● | | | | ● | | | | | ● | ● | | | 225+ | ● | ● | ● | 80 |
| BLOOMBERG | 71 | | | ● | ● | | | | | | | | | | | | ● | ● | | 200+ | ● | | ● | 82 |
| BNY | 92 | | | ● | ● | ● | | ● | | | | | | | | | | ● | | 120+ | ● | | ● | 84 |
| BRITISH AIRWAYS | 50 | | | ● | ● | ● | | | | ● | | | | | | | | ● | | 50+ | ● | ● | ● | 86 |
| CAPGEMINI | 69 | | ● | ● | ● | ● | | | | | ● | | | | | | ● | ● | | 300+ | ● | ● | ● | 88 |
| CIVIL SERVICE | 1 | ● | | | | | | | | | | ● | ● | ● | | | | | | 700 | | ● | | 90 |
| CLYDE & CO | 95 | | | | | | | | ● | | | | | | | | | | | 50+ | ● | | ● | 92 |
| DELOITTE | 4 | ● | ● | | | | | | | | | | | | | | | | | 1,000+ | ● | | ● | 94 |
| DEUTSCHE BANK | 79 | | | | ● | | | ● | | | | | | | | | | | | 100+ | ● | ● | ● | 96 |
| DIAGEO | 97 | | | ● | ● | | ● | | | ● | | | | | | ● | ● | | | 30-50 | | | | 98 |
| DLA PIPER | 63 | | | | | | | | ● | | | | | | | | | | | 50+ | ● | | ● | 100 |
| EDF | 91 | ● | | ● | ● | | ● | | | | | | | ● | | | ● | | | 50+ | | | | 102 |
| ENTERPRISE MOBILITY | 47 | | | ● | | | | | | | | | | ● | ● | | | | | 1,100 | | | ● | 104 |
| ENVIRONMENT AGENCY | 64 | | | ● | ● | ● | | | ● | | | | ● | | | | | | | 30-40 | | ● | ● | 106 |
| EY | 7 | ● | ● | ● | | | | | | | | | | | | | | ● | | 1,000+ | ● | | ● | 108 |
| FORVIS MAZARS | 78 | ● | ● | | ● | | | | | | | | | | | | | ● | | 250 | ● | ● | ● | 110 |
| FRESHFIELDS | 39 | | | | | | | | ● | | | | | | | | | | | No fixed quota | ● | | ● | 112 |
| GOOGLE | 8 | | ● | ● | | ● | | | ● | | | | | | | | | ● | | No fixed quota | | ● | ● | 114 |
| GRANT THORNTON | 80 | ● | | ● | | | | | | | | | | | | | | ● | | 200 | ● | ● | ● | 116 |
| HMRC | 83 | ● | | ● | | | | | ● | | | | | | | | | | | 500 | | ● | ● | 118 |
| HOGAN LOVELLS | 70 | | | | | | | | ● | | | | | | | | | | | 50 | ● | | ● | 120 |

48 TOP 100 GRADUATE EMPLOYERS

| EMPLOYER | RANK | GRADUATE VACANCIES IN 2025 (Accountancy, Consulting, Engineering, Finance, General Management, Human Resources, Investment Banking, Law, Logistics, Marketing, Media, Property, Purchasing, Research & Development, Retail, Sales, Technology, Other) | VACANCIES | WORK EXPERIENCE (Insight Courses, Degree Placements, Summer Internships) | PAGE |
|---|---|---|---|---|---|
| HSBC | 10 | Engineering, Finance, Human Resources, Investment Banking, Technology | 600+ | Insight, Degree, Summer | 122 |
| IBM | 56 | Sales, Technology | 30+ | Degree, Summer | 124 |
| ITV | 51 | Accountancy, Engineering, Finance, General Management, Human Resources, Law, Marketing, Media, Research & Development, Sales, Technology | No fixed quota | Insight, Degree, Summer | 126 |
| JPMORGANCHASE | 6 | Accountancy, Engineering, Finance, General Management, Human Resources, Investment Banking, Technology | 450 | | 128 |
| KPMG | 12 | Accountancy, Consulting, Technology | 1,000 | Insight, Degree, Summer | 130 |
| L'ORÉAL | 9 | Engineering, Finance, General Management, Marketing, Purchasing, Research & Development | 40+ | Insight, Summer | 132 |
| LATHAM & WATKINS | 62 | Law | 32 | Insight, Degree, Summer | 134 |
| LIDL | 41 | Finance, Logistics, Marketing, Property, Purchasing, Retail | 30-50 | | 136 |
| LINKLATERS | 24 | Law | 100 | Insight, Summer | 138 |
| LLOYDS BANKING GROUP | 11 | Accountancy, Engineering, Human Resources, Investment Banking, Marketing, Technology | 250+ | Insight, Degree, Summer | 140 |
| LOCKHEED MARTIN | 93 | Consulting, Engineering, Technology | 15+ | | 142 |
| M&S | 72 | Finance, Property, Retail | 40+ | | 144 |
| MICROSOFT | 48 | Consulting, Engineering, Marketing, Sales, Technology | No fixed quota | Summer | 146 |
| MOTT MACDONALD | 77 | Consulting, Engineering, Technology | 350 | Insight, Degree, Summer | 148 |
| NETWORK RAIL | 81 | Accountancy, Engineering, Finance, General Management, Property, Purchasing, Technology | 120+ | | 150 |
| NEWTON | 32 | Consulting | 130+ | Summer | 152 |
| NHS | 3 | Accountancy, Finance, General Management, Human Resources, Technology | 200 | | 154 |
| P&G | 31 | Accountancy, Engineering, Finance, General Management, Marketing, Media, Research & Development, Technology | 100 | Insight, Degree, Summer | 156 |
| PENGUIN | 28 | Accountancy, Engineering, General Management, Marketing, Media, Research & Development, Retail, Sales | 250 | Insight, Summer | 158 |
| PFIZER | 40 | Engineering, Finance, Marketing, Sales, Technology | 15-20 | Degree, Summer | 160 |
| POLICE NOW | 34 | Other | 400 | | 162 |
| PWC | 2 | Accountancy, Consulting, Engineering, Law, Technology | Around 1,000 | Insight, Degree, Summer | 164 |
| RAF | 76 | Engineering, General Management, Human Resources, Law, Logistics, Technology | No fixed quota | | 166 |
| REVOLUT | 94 | Consulting, Engineering, Finance, Sales, Technology | 150 | Summer | 168 |
| ROLLS-ROYCE | 26 | Engineering, Finance, Technology | No fixed quota | Degree, Summer | 170 |
| ROYAL NAVY | 88 | Engineering, Finance, General Management, Law, Logistics, Marketing, Retail, Technology | No fixed quota | Insight, Degree, Summer | 172 |
| SAVILLS | 90 | Engineering, Property | 120+ | Degree, Summer | 174 |
| SCOTTISH POWER | 86 | | 160 | | 176 |
| SHELL | 61 | Engineering, Finance, General Management, Marketing, Media, Research & Development, Retail, Sales, Technology | 30+ | Summer | 178 |
| SLAUGHTER AND MAY | 25 | Law | 90 | Insight, Summer | 180 |
| TEACH FIRST | 13 | Other | 1,300 | Insight | 182 |
| TESCO | 49 | Engineering, Finance, Marketing, Property, Technology, Other | 50+ | Degree, Summer | 184 |
| TRANSPORT FOR LONDON | 67 | Engineering, Finance, General Management, Property, Purchasing, Technology | 50+ | Insight, Summer | 186 |
| UNILEVER | 22 | Engineering, Finance, General Management, Marketing, Media, Research & Development, Technology | 40+ | Insight, Summer | 188 |
| WHITE & CASE | 38 | Law | 50 | Insight, Summer | 190 |

# A&O SHEARMAN

earlycareersuk.aoshearman.com
linkedin.com/company/aoshearman
earlycareersuk@aoshearman.com
@AOShearmanEarlyCareersUK
youtube.com/@AOShearmanEarlyCareersUK

A&O Shearman is a new type of legal industry leader. Formed via a merger of two leading UK and US firms in 2024, Allen & Overy and Shearman & Sterling, the firm is an unparalleled combination of truly global capabilities helping the world's leading businesses grow, innovate and thrive.

In a fast-moving world, A&O Shearman continue to lead from the front. The firm work with companies, organisations and governments on their most complex legal issues to build strong client relationships. With offices across the world, graduates are guaranteed to work on the most interesting, high profile legal work.

The most common entry into the firm is the paid summer and winter vacation schemes. Open to students and graduates from all disciplines, they immerse students in how to excel at the highest level of law. Students experience the excitement of tackling complex challenges and being part of a friendly and dynamic firm that supports their growth from day one.

The A&O Shearman training contract is built on the same principles. Defined by flexibility and choice, trainees receive a foundation to find their strengths and grow into exceptional lawyers. This is where talent excels. Training is based on four six-month rotations through leading practice areas. All trainees see as many parts of the firm as possible and experience hands-on learning and guidance from senior colleagues. Some trainees do international or client secondments and gain contentious experience by spending a seat in the firm's litigation department, or completing a litigation course and obtaining experience via legal advice clinics.

A&O Shearman has strong values and a commitment to sustainability, where individuals with different backgrounds belong and excel.

---

### GRADUATE VACANCIES IN 2026
LAW

**NUMBER OF VACANCIES**
**80 graduate jobs**
For training contracts starting in 2028.

**LOCATIONS OF VACANCIES**

**STARTING SALARY FOR 2026**
**£56,000**
Raising to £61,000 in year two and £150,000 for NQ.

**UNIVERSITY PROMOTIONS DURING 2025-2026**
BATH, BIRMINGHAM, BRISTOL, CAMBRIDGE, EDINBURGH, EXETER, KENT, KING'S COLLEGE LONDON, LANCASTER, LEEDS, LEICESTER, LIVERPOOL, LONDON SCHOOL OF ECONOMICS, MANCHESTER, NEWCASTLE, NOTTINGHAM, OXFORD, QUEEN MARY LONDON, UNIVERSITY COLLEGE LONDON, YORK
Please check with your university careers service for full details of A&O Shearman's local promotions and events.

**MINIMUM ENTRY REQUIREMENTS**
**2.1 Degree, 136 UCAS points**

**APPLICATION DEADLINE**
Please see website for full details.

**FURTHER INFORMATION**
www.Top100GraduateEmployers.com
Register now for the latest news, local promotions, work experience and graduate vacancies at A&O Shearman.

# A&O SHEARMAN

# ~~Enabled~~
# *Empowered to grow*

Following a merger of two leading global firms, this is a unique chance to become an exceptional lawyer in an increasingly global legal world. We help organisations with their most complex challenges. We provide every trainee with the chance to find your strengths. We help you be at your absolute best.

From day one, you'll work on complex matters, directly supported by senior colleagues and as part of a high performance firm culture. That combination is how we nurture talented trainees into lawyers capable of handling the most exciting cases in the industry. There's high expectations and constant guidance. This is where you can truly excel.

*Belong.Excel.*

**Learn more:**
https://earlycareersuk.aoshearman.com/

© A&O Shearman 2025

# A=COM

aecom.com/graduates-and-early-careers/uk-ireland/

AecomTechnologyCorporation  grad_recruit.europe@aecom.com
@AECOM  linkedin.com/company/aecom
@aecom  youtube.com/@AECOM/shorts

AECOM is the world's trusted infrastructure consulting firm, bringing bold ideas and practical action to challenges. From reconnecting communities with climate-resilient infrastructure to restoring river habitats. Low-carbon transport to clean energy. Greener cities to flood defences that protect homes.

AECOM has graduate opportunities in energy; water; environment; building engineering & sustainability; architecture & interior design; urban, planning & economics; geotechnical & tunnelling; surveying & project management; transportation; and landscape. With a diversity of opportunities, they are looking for students across various disciplines. They offer permanent roles from day 1 and have opportunities in 28 offices across the UK & Ireland, and globally.

Each year AECOM offer around 100 summer and industrial placement opportunities. Summer placements tend to be 6-12 weeks and industrial placements 12 months. This gives graduates the opportunity to develop technical and industry knowledge, experience the AECOM culture, and demonstrate their skills and attributes which may lead to a permanent graduate opportunity.

The Ignite programme is a two-year development journey that builds technical skills and grows confidence on projects that matter, backed by formal training in over 30 business, technical and digital skills. With three more years of structured support including mentorship, professional development and progression opportunities, graduates are set up to shape their own career that's truly their own.

AECOM provides talks with senior leaders, and opportunities to grow a network, from conferences and technical practice groups to random global coffee chats. They support their graduates every step of the way.

### GRADUATE VACANCIES IN 2026
CONSULTING
ENGINEERING
HUMAN RESOURCES
PROPERTY
TECHNOLOGY

### NUMBER OF VACANCIES
**250 graduate jobs**

### LOCATIONS OF VACANCIES

*Vacancies also available in Europe, the USA, Asia and elsewhere in the world.*

### STARTING SALARY FOR 2026
**£27,500-£32,500**

### WORK EXPERIENCE
DEGREE PLACEMENTS | SUMMER INTERNSHIPS

### UNIVERSITY PROMOTIONS DURING 2025-2026
BATH, CAMBRIDGE, CARDIFF, HERIOT-WATT, LEEDS, LOUGHBOROUGH, NEWCASTLE, NOTTINGHAM, OXFORD BROOKES, QUEEN'S BELFAST, READING, SHEFFIELD, SOUTHAMPTON, ULSTER
*Please check with your university careers service for full details of AECOM's local promotions and events.*

### MINIMUM ENTRY REQUIREMENTS
**2.1 Degree**

### APPLICATION DEADLINE
**Year-round recruitment**

### FURTHER INFORMATION
**www.Top100GraduateEmployers.com**
*Register now for the latest news, local promotions, work experience and graduate vacancies at AECOM.*

# Care about the planet? People? Doing work that matters? So do we.

Yes, we're a global consultancy. But at our core, we're a team of people who care about solving complex challenges and building a better future — socially, environmentally, and everything in between.

| | |
|---|---|
| Architecture and Interior Design | Landscape Architecture |
| Building Engineering and Sustainability | Surveying and Project Management |
| Design, Planning and Economics | Transportation Engineering and Planning |
| Energy | Water Engineering and Consulting |
| Environmental Consulting | |
| Geotechnical and Tunnelling Engineering | |

aecom.com/uk/impact

AECOM

Delivering a better world

**aldirecruitment.co.uk**

AldiCareersUK [Facebook]   @aldicareersuk [Instagram]
linkedin.com/company/aldi-uk [LinkedIn]
@AldiCareersUK [X]   @aldicareersuk [TikTok]

Arriving in the UK back in 1990, Aldi is now the UK's fourth largest supermarket, with over 1,050 stores and 45,000 colleagues – and don't forget about their global presence. It's a business with integrity – everything Aldi does is for the benefit of customers, colleagues and the community.

Third year students or recent graduates can apply for Aldi's Area Manager Programme, renowned for the £50,750 starting salary rising to £95,655, fully expensed electric BMW for personal and work use, and incredible level of responsibility. Through the support of a dedicated training programme and network of experienced colleagues, graduates will become responsible for a portfolio of stores after they complete their extensive training. They will shadow an experienced Area Manager mentor and take charge of their own area for a short period, leading their teams to provide an outstanding customer experience and deliver exceptional performance.

Area Managers will spend time with other departments also, equipping them with a 360-degree view of the business. As personnel leader to their store teams, Area Managers coach and lead their teams to success. Supporting large volumes of colleagues within their area, the ability to motivate and drive their teams is essential. Once they are ready, graduates will take on their own designated group of stores and hit the ground running for a rewarding career.

For penultimate year university students, Aldi offer 12-month long placements across the UK. The Retail Management Placement offers a pathway to the Area Manager Programme. Students will spend six months in store, shadowing the Store Manager and Area Manager, learning what it takes to run a successful store. Students will then take on a national project – solving real-life business problems.

**GRADUATE VACANCIES IN 2026**
RETAIL

**NUMBER OF VACANCIES**
15 graduate jobs

**LOCATIONS OF VACANCIES**

**STARTING SALARY FOR 2026**
£50,750
*Plus a fully expensed company car.*

**WORK EXPERIENCE**
DEGREE PLACEMENTS

**UNIVERSITY PROMOTIONS DURING 2025-2026**
*Please check with your university careers service for full details of Aldi's local promotions and events.*

**MINIMUM ENTRY REQUIREMENTS**
2.1 Degree, 96 UCAS points

**APPLICATION DEADLINE**
Year-round recruitment

**FURTHER INFORMATION**
www.Top100GraduateEmployers.com
*Register now for the latest news, local promotions, work experience and graduate vacancies at Aldi.*

# GRADUATES OF TODAY.
# LEADERS OF TOMORROW.

## GRADUATE AREA MANAGER PROGRAMME

**Starting salary of £50k, rising to £95k, plus a fully expensed BMW**

Why join our Graduate Area Manager programme? The opportunity to kick start your career with one of the world's leading retailers, the exposure and training... and yes, the salary and the car! But our Graduate Area Manager programme is about more than that. It's about delivering an experience that's **Everyday Amazing**. You'll progress at pace (just like our tills) and help to shape the future of retail! And as you lead and inspire your teams to run a group of £multi-million stores, you'll unlock your true potential too. Ready for more?

aldirecruitment.co.uk/graduates

Scan the QR code to find out more...

## ALDI MEANS MORE

**ALDI — Everyday Amazing.**

**MORE REWARDS**
Earn a market leading salary of £50,750 rising to £95,655

**MORE BENEFITS**
Electric **BMW** for personal and work use, five weeks' holiday and **more**

**MORE DEVELOPMENT**
Learn through our **12 month training plan** and dedicated mentors

**MORE RESPONSIBILITY**
Manage, coach and **lead** multiple store teams

UK 300

**The Grocer Gold Awards 2025**
WINNER
Employer of the Year (Retailer)

RATEMYPLACEMENT 2024-2025
Best 100 Student Employers

# amazon

**amazon.jobs/content/en/career-programs**

linkedin.com/company/amazon-careers
youtube.com/@insideamazonvideos

Amazon is guided by four principles: customer obsession rather than competitor focus, passion for invention, commitment to operational excellence, and long-term thinking. Amazon strives to be Earth's most customer-centric company, Earth's best employer, and Earth's safest place to work.

Customer reviews, 1-Click shopping, personalised recommendations, Prime, Fulfilment by Amazon, AWS, Kindle Direct Publishing, Kindle, Career Choice, Fire tablets, Fire TV, Amazon Echo, Alexa, Just Walk Out technology, Amazon MGM Studios, and The Climate Pledge are some things pioneered by Amazon.

There are thousands of opportunities across Amazon's offices, with robotics, fulfilment and data centres across EMEA for students who have graduated within the last 2 years. The career path a graduate can take is endless, ranging from leadership development programmes to technical, machine learning, engineering, finance, operations, business, account management roles and more! They'll be part of a team that is constantly innovating, disrupting and delivering efficiencies - making what seems impossible, possible.

Amazon is a global company of unique individuals with different experiences and backgrounds, yet they unite around a pursuit to delight customers and make their lives easier. At Amazon, every day is filled with exciting challenges. Discover incredible mentors, transformative experiences, and an inclusive culture that inspires employees to shape a better future. Amazon knows that experiences will help make everyday better – for customers, employees, and communities around the world. Graduates are empowered to take ownership over their career. They challenge each other, constructively question ideas, and then commit to delivering the best results. Amazon guides graduates on how to make fast decisions, take calculated risks and fearlessly chase excellence.

## GRADUATE VACANCIES IN 2026
- ENGINEERING
- FINANCE
- GENERAL MANAGEMENT
- HUMAN RESOURCES
- LOGISTICS
- MARKETING
- RETAIL
- SALES
- TECHNOLOGY

### NUMBER OF VACANCIES
**1,000+ graduate jobs**

### LOCATIONS OF VACANCIES

*Vacancies also available in Europe, the USA, Asia and elsewhere in the world.*

### STARTING SALARY FOR 2026
**£Competitive**
*Plus RSUs and other benefits offered on top of base salary.*

### WORK EXPERIENCE
SUMMER INTERNSHIPS

### UNIVERSITY PROMOTIONS DURING 2025-2026
*Please check with your university careers service for full details of Amazon's local promotions and events.*

### MINIMUM ENTRY REQUIREMENTS
*Relevant degree required for some roles.*

### APPLICATION DEADLINE
**Year-round recruitment**

### FURTHER INFORMATION
**www.Top100GraduateEmployers.com**
*Register now for the latest news, local promotions, work experience and graduate vacancies at **Amazon**.*

# amazon

# Define Tomorrow

**How often can you say that your work truly changes the world?**

You'll say it often enough with us. At Amazon, what we do touches the world every day, and you will have the opportunity to leave your imprint on our work. Here, you'll be encouraged and rewarded to disrupt the status quo, think big and redefine normal as you team with other curious and open-minded innovators. Our people will help you grow into the visionary, high-impact person you know you're ready to be.

**Graduate & Internship Opportunities:**
**Join Our Corporate, Operations & Data Center Teams**

**For Graduates**
bit.ly/AmazonGrads2026

**For Internships**
bit.ly/AmazonInterns2026

# AON

aon.com/careers/uk

Aonplc **f**  graduates@aon.co.uk
@aon_plc **X**  linkedin.com/company/aon

**GRADUATE VACANCIES IN 2026**
CONSULTING
FINANCE

**NUMBER OF VACANCIES**
100+ graduate jobs

**LOCATIONS OF VACANCIES**

**STARTING SALARY FOR 2026**
£Competitive

**WORK EXPERIENCE**
DEGREE PLACEMENTS | SUMMER INTERNSHIPS

**UNIVERSITY PROMOTIONS DURING 2025-2026**
BATH, BIRMINGHAM, BRISTOL, CITY, HERIOT-WATT, IMPERIAL COLLEGE LONDON, LEEDS, LONDON SCHOOL OF ECONOMICS, MANCHESTER, QUEEN MARY LONDON, UNIVERSITY COLLEGE LONDON, WARWICK
*Please check with your university careers service for full details of Aon's local promotions and events.*

**MINIMUM ENTRY REQUIREMENTS**
2.1 Degree

**APPLICATION DEADLINE**
*Please see website for full details.*

**FURTHER INFORMATION**
www.Top100GraduateEmployers.com
*Register now for the latest news, local promotions, work experience and graduate vacancies at Aon.*

---

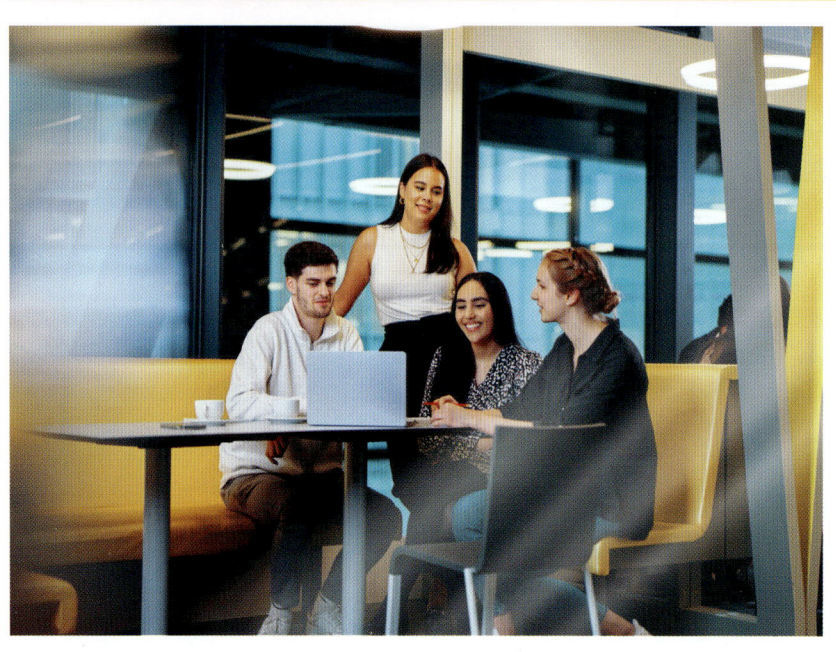

**Aon exists to shape decisions for the better and to protect and enrich the lives of people around the world. Through their global expertise across two key areas of need – Risk Capital and Human Capital – Aon's clients are better advised within, and across, their risk and people strategies.**

Aon believes that businesses thrive when the communities they serve and the people they employ flourish. Their values are the foundation of all they do. Living their values helps Aon to shape decisions for the better – for their colleagues, clients and communities.

Aon believes inclusive teams create better insights and solutions, deliver the best outcomes for clients and are vital to ensuring long-term success. Colleague wellbeing is a cornerstone and strong value, and Aon are dedicated to ensuring their workforce is representative of the communities in which they operate.

Aon's Early Careers Programme onboards and develops graduates, industrial placements, summer interns and apprentices through meaningful work experience, professional skills training, qualifications and technical expertise, and opportunities to grow their career. Cohorts join across a range of consulting and broking roles within areas including actuarial analysis, investment consulting, insurance, reinsurance, and catastrophe modelling, and receive ongoing support from leaders, colleagues and the talent development team.

Aon's market-leading study packages include fully funded professional qualifications, such as the Chartered Insurance Institute and Chartered Financial Analyst, tutorial support, study materials and study leave, combined with on-the-job experience to put the theory into practice immediately. Each qualification is supported by an external professional training company to ensure a rounded mixture of skills, knowledge and behaviours.

# AON

# Grow your career from day one

Whether you are interested in a graduate role, summer internship, placement or apprenticeship, Aon has the right early careers programme for you.

Visit our website to learn more:

aon.com/careers/uk

#AonEarlyCareers

- @Aonplc
- @aonplc
- @Aon
- @Aon_plc

Tania - Aon Graduate

# ARMY
## BE THE BEST

**jobs.army.mod.uk**

jobs.army.mod.uk
Armyjobs — facebook
linkedin.com/company/BritishArmy
@armyjobs_ — instagram
youtube.com/armyjobs

The British Army protects the UK and supports global security. It combines cutting-edge technology with strong leadership, values diversity, and fosters an inclusive culture. The British Army's people are trained to lead, respond to crises, and make a real difference at home and abroad.

Make a real difference. Live a life full of purpose and adventure. Officers in the British Army lead teams, help protect others, and work to make the world a safer place. It's a big responsibility, but also a chance to do something truly meaningful.

The journey begins at the Royal Military Academy Sandhurst. Here, Officer Cadets learn the skills they need to lead – from using equipment to surviving outdoors. They also build confidence and learn how to take care of their team.

After training, new Officers take charge of a platoon of around 30 soldiers. They then start specialist training in their chosen area – like engineering, intelligence, or flying an Apache helicopter. Army Officers live an exciting life. They might parachute in the UK or dive overseas. They train around the world, earn a good salary, and enjoy great benefits – including housing, sports, and gaining qualifications. There's financial support available too. The Army offers different types of bursaries to help future leaders while at university – especially if studying a technical subject.

The Army looks for people with leadership potential, a strong sense of purpose, and the drive to succeed. With training in areas like project management and strategic thinking – and even the option to earn a degree while working – there's something for everyone, helping each Officer grow and succeed in their role. With world-class training and support, they rise through the ranks and become leaders who make a real difference.

---

**GRADUATE VACANCIES IN 2026**
- ENGINEERING
- GENERAL MANAGEMENT
- HUMAN RESOURCES
- LAW
- LOGISTICS
- TECHNOLOGY

**NUMBER OF VACANCIES**
650+ graduate jobs

**LOCATIONS OF VACANCIES**

**STARTING SALARY FOR 2026**
£41,456
After training.

**WORK EXPERIENCE**
SUMMER INTERNSHIPS

**UNIVERSITY PROMOTIONS DURING 2025-2026**
BATH, BIRMINGHAM, BRISTOL, CARDIFF, DERBY, EDINBURGH, EXETER, GLASGOW, MANCHESTER
Please check with your university careers service for full details of the Army's local promotions and events.

**MINIMUM ENTRY REQUIREMENTS**
72 UCAS points

**APPLICATION DEADLINE**
Year-round recruitment

**FURTHER INFORMATION**
www.Top100GraduateEmployers.com
Register now for the latest news, local promotions, work experience and graduate vacancies at **the Army**.

---

60 TOP 100 GRADUATE EMPLOYERS

THERE'S A LEADERSHIP ROLE WAITING FOR YOU.

SEARCH ARMY OFFICER

ARMY
BE THE BEST

YOU BELONG HERE

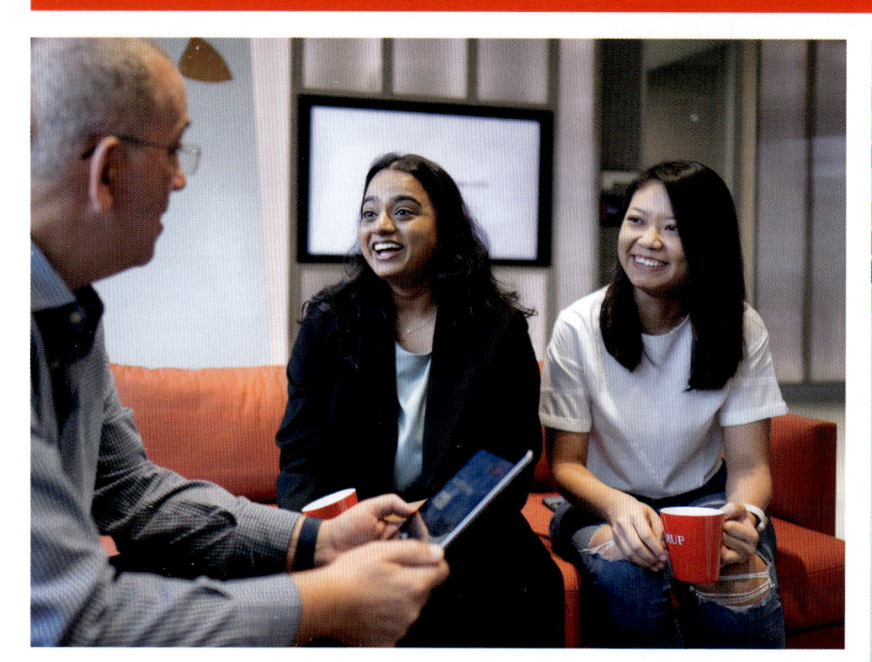

# ARUP

careers.arup.com/earlycareers

UKEarlyCareersRecruitment@arup.com
ArupGroup
linkedin.com/company/arup
@arupgroup
youtube.com/arupgroup

Arup advise on, plan and design the future of the built environment. As a global consultancy with technical and advisory expertise across more than 150 disciplines, they bring a total design approach to their work with their clients. This is how they shape a better world.

Arup need people who see the world through a unique lens. They embrace those who see things differently – it's essential for creating a sustainable future. With their people's ideas and thinking, they can solve the most complex challenges facing clients, climate and communities.

Arup are an employee-owned organisation – their members are their shareholders – empowering them to do purpose-driven work. They are dedicated to creating a sustainable future – it's at the heart of all their work. They believe their members' ideas and fresh thinking can help solve the future climate resilience, biodiversity, and social challenges faced in a rapidly changing world.

Arup recruits around 500 graduates, interns and apprentices in the UK every year and has vacancies across Climate & Sustainability Services, Energy, Water & Resources, Advisory, Building Services & Building Performance, Structural & Civil Engineering, Transport & Ground Engineering, Planning and Digital Services to name a few.

Graduates are encouraged to pursue a professional qualification of their choice with the support of a designated mentor. Arup partners with many professional institutes such as ICE, IStructE, IMechE, IET, CIBSE, RICS, so graduates can choose a path that suits them.

Arup have the vision and ability to influence a future with purpose, and they make it happen together - with each other, and their clients.

## GRADUATE VACANCIES IN 2026
- CONSULTING
- ENGINEERING
- FINANCE
- LOGISTICS
- MARKETING
- PROPERTY
- RESEARCH & DEVELOPMENT
- TECHNOLOGY

**NUMBER OF VACANCIES**
300 graduate jobs

**LOCATIONS OF VACANCIES**

**STARTING SALARY FOR 2026**
£30,200
*Plus a £2,500 bonus.*

**WORK EXPERIENCE**
DEGREE PLACEMENTS | SUMMER INTERNSHIPS

**UNIVERSITY PROMOTIONS DURING 2025-2026**
*Please check with your university careers service for full details of Arup's local promotions and events.*

**MINIMUM ENTRY REQUIREMENTS**
2.1 Degree
*Relevant degree required for some roles.*

**APPLICATION DEADLINE**
*Please see website for full details.*

**FURTHER INFORMATION**
www.Top100GraduateEmployers.com
*Register now for the latest news, local promotions, work experience and graduate vacancies at Arup.*

# ARUP

**Early Careers**

# see it differently

**Graduate | Apprenticeship | Internship**

Your ideas and perspective can shape a better world. Join us and help solve some of the biggest challenges facing our clients, climate and communities.

**Why join us?**
- Purpose-driven work
- Create remarkable outcomes
- Inclusive and supportive culture
- Career growth and development
- Work-life balance

"Working at Arup has expanded my perspective – embracing curiosity, collaboration, and diversity has turned challenges into incredible opportunities for growth."

**Santina Ajdari Bunting**
Assistant Technician

Early career opportunities

# AstraZeneca

careers.astrazeneca.com/early-talent

@astrazenecajobs  AstraZeneca
linkedin.com/company/astrazeneca  youtube.com/astrazeneca

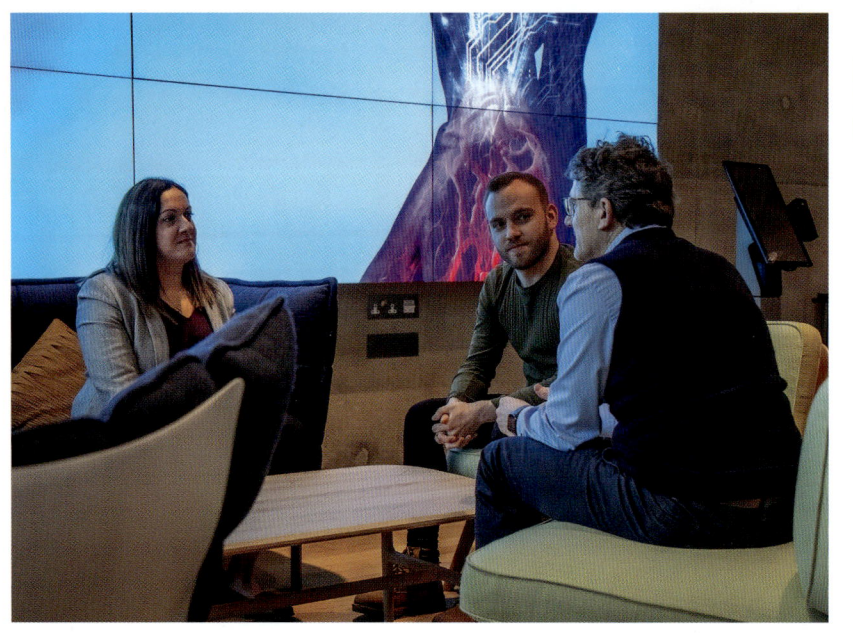

AstraZeneca is a global, science-led, patient-focused pharmaceutical company. AstraZeneca are dedicated to accelerating the delivery of life-changing medicines that create enduring value for patients, society, the planet and their shareholders.

AstraZeneca's graduate programmes are open to bachelor's and master's level applicants and cover a broad range of functions and specialities. They open doors and kick-start careers – helping graduates to create connections that will last a lifetime. They truly value their graduate talent, their experience, knowledge, ideas and who they are. Graduates will be empowered to jump in, take initiative and be part of meaningful project teams to make an impact and deliver real value for their patients and business.

AstraZeneca offers internships to gain an insight into a particular sector or role within their global organisation. Varying in length and aim, their internships are the perfect opportunity for a successful career. Undergraduate Industrial Placement Studentship (UIPS) introduces undergrads to the world of drug discovery, embedding students within highly dedicated teams driven to create impactful new medicines. Working on projects with real patient implications, graduates could have the opportunity to contribute to making a meaningful, life-changing impact for millions of people around the world.

The graduate programmes give a broad experience of the pharmaceutical industry by immersing graduates in real science, and responsibility on real projects from the outset with ongoing mentoring. Graduates can choose from a range of placements and tailor their development to their passion. As well as building scientific knowledge, AstraZeneca will help them to develop professional skills which will support their career progression.

## GRADUATE VACANCIES IN 2026
ENGINEERING
RESEARCH & DEVELOPMENT
TECHNOLOGY

### NUMBER OF VACANCIES
**10-20 graduate jobs**

### LOCATIONS OF VACANCIES

*Vacancies also available in Europe and the USA.*

### STARTING SALARY FOR 2026
**£35,000-£40,000**
*Plus flexible benefit funding, bonus and relocation allowance (where applicable).*

### WORK EXPERIENCE
DEGREE PLACEMENTS | SUMMER INTERNSHIPS

### UNIVERSITY PROMOTIONS DURING 2025-2026
CAMBRIDGE, LEICESTER, LIVERPOOL, OXFORD, QUEEN MARY LONDON, SOUTHAMPTON, UNIVERSITY COLLEGE LONDON
*Please check with your university careers service for full details of AstraZeneca's local promotions and events.*

### MINIMUM ENTRY REQUIREMENTS
**2.1 Degree**

### APPLICATION DEADLINE
**January 2026**

### FURTHER INFORMATION
www.Top100GraduateEmployers.com
*Register now for the latest news, local promotions, work experience and graduate vacancies at AstraZeneca.*

# AstraZeneca

# Build a broad skill base and accelerate your career

## Put your knowledge and skills to the test then take them further

Applying your knowledge and pushing it further. It's not always easy, but it's always rewarding. A place full of challenges and opportunity where you can be curious and courageous to push boundaries, change the game, innovate and make an impact.

Starting salary for 2026 programmes:

£35,000 - £40,000 plus benefits and relocation (where applicable)

*Find out more and apply at https://careers.astrazeneca.com/early-talent*

# AtkinsRéalis

**careers.atkinsrealis.com/uk-early-careers**

InsideAtkins

linkedin.com/company/atkinsrealis

@inside_atkinsrealis

youtube.com/@atkinsrealisglobal

AtkinsRéalis is a world-class engineering services and nuclear organisation. They work with clients on local, national and international projects across sectors including transportation, infrastructure, environment, water, energy, defence, technology, and aerospace.

AtkinsRéalis offers a wide range of graduate development programmes nationally across engineering, technical and non-technical disciplines. Roles typically include: environmental, project management, civil and structural engineering, ground engineering and tunnelling, mechanical engineering, electrical engineering, human factors, transport planning, digital and technology, nuclear fusion, software, management consulting, rail consulting, data intelligence, chemical and process engineering, along with opportunities in airport planning and surveying.

The graduate development programme features a series of training events and modules, professional development, mentoring and on-the-job experience, to help graduates gain the skills and knowledge they need to develop their career and work towards professional qualifications. Graduates join AtkinsRéalis from a wide range of disciplines including engineering, digital and technology, the sciences, mathematics, geography/GIS, project management, business studies, law, humanities, chemistry, data/computer science, and many more.

AtkinsRéalis offer two types of placements: 8-week summer schemes and 12-month industrial placements. Both are full-time paid work posts, designed to support and complement the academic learning of undergraduate and postgraduate students who are studying a relevant degree. On joining, graduates enjoy an induction and settling-in buddy scheme to familiarise themselves with the organisation. They also join a vibrant, sociable early careers community.

### GRADUATE VACANCIES IN 2026
CONSULTING
ENGINEERING

### NUMBER OF VACANCIES
**450+ graduate jobs**

### LOCATIONS OF VACANCIES

### STARTING SALARY FOR 2026
**£Competitive**
*Plus a £2,500 settling in payment.*

### WORK EXPERIENCE
DEGREE PLACEMENTS | SUMMER INTERNSHIPS

### UNIVERSITY PROMOTIONS DURING 2025-2026
READING, SURREY, IMPERIAL COLLEGE LONDON, SHEFFIELD, LOUGHBOROUGH, STRATHCLYDE, UNIVERSITY OF THE BUILT ENVIRONMENT, NOTTINGHAM, NOTTINGHAM TRENT, BIRMINGHAM, SWANSEA, BATH, BRISTOL, NEWCASTLE, UNIVERSITY COLLEGE LONDON, BRUNEL UNIVERSITY, QUEEN'S BELFAST, LIVERPOOL JOHN MOORES, LIVERPOOL, LEEDS, MANCHESTER, WEST OF ENGLAND
*Please check with your university careers service for full details of AtkinsRéalis' local promotions and events.*

### MINIMUM ENTRY REQUIREMENTS
**2.2 Degree**

### APPLICATION DEADLINE
**October 2025 - April 2026**
*Varies by scheme.*

### FURTHER INFORMATION
**www.Top100GraduateEmployers.com**
*Register now for the latest news, local promotions, work experience and graduate vacancies at AtkinsRéalis.*

# AtkinsRéalis

## In the company of...
# INNOVATORS

## Graduate Development Programmes – nationwide opportunities

Here you can have a real impact on some of the most significant global, national and local projects; engineering a better future for our planet and its people. Our work covers a variety of sectors, including transportation, infrastructure, environment, water, energy, defence, technology and aerospace.

You'll learn from some of the best minds, get involved with exciting projects, and work with some of the most prestigious companies. We'll support you to grow in the career direction that interests you, so you'll enjoy plenty of events, world-class training, professional development, and mentoring. And of course we offer numerous benefits; from a settling in payment, through to flexible leave, retail discounts, fitness funding and much, much more.

**Different is brilliant.** Here, everyone is valued, heard and supported and you'll love being part of our vibrant early careers community.

## At AtkinsRéalis, you'll be in great company

To learn more about our engineering, technical and non-technical careers, scan the QR code or visit

careers.atkinsrealis.com/uk-early-careers

# Babcock

earlycareers.babcockinternational.com/graduates

@babcockplc
recruitment.earlycareers@babcockinternational.com
BabcockFutureTalent
linkedin.com/company/babcock-international-group
@babcockinternationalgroup
youtube.com/BabcockInternational

Babcock is a FTSE 100 defence company delivering engineering and through-life technical support across naval, land, air and nuclear sectors. Its 26,000 employees work to solve critical global challenges and help create a safer, more secure world, together.

Babcock offers a range of graduate opportunities in engineering, science, business management and project management. While some roles require specific qualifications, many are open to graduates from a variety of degree backgrounds. Opportunities are available across the UK, with most roles based in Plymouth, Bristol, Leicester and Warrington in England, as well as Rosyth and HM Naval Base Clyde in Scotland.

Graduates at Babcock work on some of the UK's most impactful engineering projects, from supporting the UK's submarine fleet to delivering secure communications in space. Along the way, they'll sharpen their skills, develop leadership qualities, and play a vital role in creating a safer, more secure world.

Babcock offers undergraduates studying STEM subjects work experience through their placement years and 10–12-week summer internships. These programmes are designed to develop practical skills, build confidence and open pathways to future opportunities, including Babcock's graduate programmes.

Graduates receive structured support, mentorship and tailored training to help them excel during their programme and beyond. The Babcock Graduate Development Programme offers masterclasses in personal branding, resilience, wellbeing and more. Graduates are supported in achieving professional qualifications, including chartered or incorporated status, with fees covered. After the programme, clear career paths are mapped through the Babcock role framework, so employees always know their next step and how to get there.

## GRADUATE VACANCIES IN 2026
- ENGINEERING
- FINANCE
- GENERAL MANAGEMENT
- LOGISTICS
- PURCHASING
- TECHNOLOGY

### NUMBER OF VACANCIES
**300+ graduate jobs**

### LOCATIONS OF VACANCIES
*Vacancies also available elsewhere in the world.*

### STARTING SALARY FOR 2026
**£34,000+**

### WORK EXPERIENCE
DEGREE PLACEMENTS

### UNIVERSITY PROMOTIONS DURING 2025-2026
ASTON, BATH, BRISTOL, CAMBRIDGE, CARDIFF, EXETER, LANCASTER, LEICESTER, MANCHESTER, NEWCASTLE, NOTTINGHAM, PLYMOUTH, SHEFFIELD, SOUTHAMPTON, STRATHCLYDE, WEST OF ENGLAND, DE MONTFORT
*Please check with your university careers service for full details of Babcock's local promotions and events.*

### MINIMUM ENTRY REQUIREMENTS
*Relevant degree required for some roles.*

### APPLICATION DEADLINE
**October 2025 - December 2025**

### FURTHER INFORMATION
www.Top100GraduateEmployers.com
*Register now for the latest news, local promotions, work experience and graduate vacancies at Babcock.*

# Your future starts here

At Babcock, what you do matters. From submarines beneath the waves to communications in space, our graduates gain the skills to help solve global challenges and create a safer, more secure world.

And you won't do it alone. Here, you'll be part of a connected, ambitious team – united by the belief that when we grow together, we go further.

Join a company where careers have purpose, collaboration drives progress, and together, we make a lasting impact.

**Babcock**

Apply now and see how far we can go together.

# BAE SYSTEMS

**careers.baesystems.com**

@LifeatBAESystems
gart@baesystems.com
linkedin.com/company/bae-systems
lifeatbaesystems
youtube.com/@BAESystemsplc

**BAE Systems are proud to be pioneers in their industry, pushing the boundaries of innovation and excellence. Play a crucial role in creating a secure future for all by working on projects across air, land, sea, cyber and space as part of an international defence, aerospace and security company.**

BAE Systems graduate programmes develop skills of the future in engineering, technology or business and are non-rotational with varying durations and structures. Upon joining, graduates can expect to be supported and empowered to achieve their potential, with exposure to live projects and real responsibility from day one. With a starting salary of £34,000 and a £2,000 welcome bonus, graduates will be provided with all the training and support they need to achieve their ambitions. With opportunities available nationwide, BAE Systems graduates can build a career they can be proud of.

They offer 12 month industrial placements, 12 week summer internships and insight experiences, for undergraduates to get a head-start and gain valuable skills to take back to their studies, and secure their future.

With over 40 sites across the UK, BAE Systems give students a platform to build and launch their career – all whilst earning a competitive salary. They work on real projects, with real responsibilities, collaborating with the brightest minds developing valuable professional and personal networks, exploring what life is really like at the company.

BAE Systems graduates and undergraduates gain opportunities and support to shape their future. At every stage of their career, first-class training, coaching and development programmes, role models and mentors will help them embrace their potential. It's an inclusive and collaborative culture where everyone has the chance to build a varied career and is empowered to achieve their goals.

---

**GRADUATE VACANCIES IN 2026**
- CONSULTING
- ENGINEERING
- FINANCE
- GENERAL MANAGEMENT
- HUMAN RESOURCES
- RESEARCH & DEVELOPMENT
- TECHNOLOGY

**NUMBER OF VACANCIES**
**700+ graduate jobs**

**LOCATIONS OF VACANCIES**

**STARTING SALARY FOR 2026**
**£34,000**
*Plus a £2,000 welcome payment & an optional 20% salary advance.*

**WORK EXPERIENCE**
| INSIGHT COURSES | DEGREE PLACEMENTS | SUMMER INTERNSHIPS |

**UNIVERSITY PROMOTIONS DURING 2025-2026**
ASTON, BATH, BIRMINGHAM, BOURNEMOUTH, BRISTOL, BRUNEL, CAMBRIDGE, CARDIFF, COVENTRY, DURHAM, EDINBURGH, ESSEX, EXETER, GLASGOW, IMPERIAL COLLEGE LONDON, KENT, KING'S COLLEGE LONDON, LANCASTER, LEEDS, LEICESTER, LIVERPOOL, LIVERPOOL JOHN MOORES, LOUGHBOROUGH, MANCHESTER, NEWCASTLE, NORTHUMBRIA, NOTTINGHAM, OXFORD, PORTSMOUTH, QUEEN MARY LONDON, ROYAL HOLLOWAY LONDON, SALFORD, SHEFFIELD, SOUTHAMPTON, STRATHCLYDE, SURREY, UNIVERSITY COLLEGE LONDON, WARWICK, YORK
*Please check with your university careers service for full details of BAE Systems' local promotions and events.*

**MINIMUM ENTRY REQUIREMENTS**
**2.2 Degree**

**APPLICATION DEADLINE**
**Year-round recruitment**
*Early application is advised.*

**FURTHER INFORMATION**
**www.Top100GraduateEmployers.com**
*Register now for the latest news, local promotions, work experience and graduate vacancies at BAE Systems.*

# Pioneer + Protect

## Own your future.
## Shape a safer tomorrow.

**From the depths of the ocean to the far reaches of space, there's no limit to where a career at BAE Systems could take you.**

Designed for the future, our graduate programmes will enable you to develop the skills you need for today and tomorrow, in our international defence, aerospace and security company.

With opportunities in engineering, technology and business; you'll receive world-class training and mentoring, learn through structured learning pathways gaining industry-recognised qualifications.

You'll be empowered to be your best; encouraged to push boundaries and bring new ideas to groundbreaking projects – all whilst being supported within a growing global network.

Our inclusive, supportive team are committed to nurturing your potential in an environment where your unique skills and perspective will be valued and your contribution recognised.

**Join us and make a real difference – to customers, colleagues, communities and the world.**

| | |
|---|---|
| **£34,000** starting salary | **£2,000** starting bonus |
| **£1billion** total invested in education and skills by 2025 | **43%** of our power came from sustainable sources in 2024 |
| **40,959** | working hours volunteered with charities and not-for-profit organisations in 2024 |

Pioneer your future.
Apply now.

baesystems.com/graduates

Follow **Life at BAE Systems**

Copyright© 2025 BAE Systems. All rights reserved. BAE SYSTEMS is a registered trademark.

**BAE SYSTEMS**

# BANK OF AMERICA

campus.bankofamerica.com

@BankofAmerica  juniortalentemea@bofa.com

linkedin.com/company/bank-of-america-business

@BankofAmerica  youtube.com/bankofamerica

---

Bank of America is one of the world's leading financial institutions, serving individuals, small and middle-market businesses, large corporations, and governments with a full range of banking, investment management and other financial and risk management products and services.

Bank of America welcomes graduates from all universities, degrees and backgrounds into its diverse and inclusive workplace. They firmly believe all employees should be treated with respect and be able to bring their whole selves to work. This is core to who they are as a company and how they drive responsible growth. Bank of America offers a range of early careers programmes, including apprenticeships, insight courses, internships, industrial placements and full time Analyst and Associate graduate programmes.

Graduates can join Bank of America in areas including Audit, Research, Risk, Sales & Trading, Technology and more. Each line of business offers unique opportunities, and there's plenty of collaboration across the bank designed to shape a smarter, greener, safer and more inclusive world. This includes everything from helping clients achieve sustainable growth, and working with external partners to increase the number of women working in tech.

All programmes offer formal, ongoing training and development opportunities, structured performance evaluations, mentoring support and networking opportunities. As well as getting involved in exciting client projects, graduates are encouraged to make the most of the various internal groups and events such as sport and social club activities, employee network events and volunteering programmes. All of these opportunities give teammates the chance to shape a meaningful career, build connections both within and outside the bank and spend time on what matters to them.

---

### GRADUATE VACANCIES IN 2026
- ACCOUNTANCY
- FINANCE
- INVESTMENT BANKING
- TECHNOLOGY

### NUMBER OF VACANCIES
**No fixed quota**

### LOCATIONS OF VACANCIES

*Vacancies also available in Europe.*

### STARTING SALARY FOR 2026
**£Competitive**

### WORK EXPERIENCE
INSIGHT COURSES | DEGREE PLACEMENTS | SUMMER INTERNSHIPS

### UNIVERSITY PROMOTIONS DURING 2025-2026
BANGOR, BATH, BIRMINGHAM, BRISTOL, CAMBRIDGE, DURHAM, EDINBURGH, IMPERIAL COLLEGE LONDON, KING'S COLLEGE LONDON, LANCASTER, LEEDS, LIVERPOOL, LONDON SCHOOL OF ECONOMICS, MANCHESTER, NOTTINGHAM, OXFORD, QUEEN MARY LONDON, SOUTHAMPTON, SURREY, UNIVERSITY COLLEGE LONDON, WARWICK, YORK

*Please check with your university careers service for full details of Bank of America's local promotions and events.*

### MINIMUM ENTRY REQUIREMENTS
**2.1 Degree**

### APPLICATION DEADLINE
**25th October 2025**
*Recruiting on a rolling basis so early application is advised.*

### FURTHER INFORMATION
**www.Top100GraduateEmployers.com**
*Register now for the latest news, local promotions, work experience and graduate vacancies at Bank of America.*

## How would you shape your world?

campus.bankofamerica.com

@BofA_Careers

All of our internships, placements and programs offer training, development and support. We'll help you learn, grow and belong while you begin a career with global impact.

Here at Bank of America, you'll be supported to succeed through mentorship programs and development opportunities. We foster a diverse, inclusive culture, where you'll build networks and find friendships. You'll be given real responsibilities, develop skills for the future, and discover which areas of our business most appeal to you.

**BANK OF AMERICA**

© 2023 Bank of America Corporation. All rights reserved.

# BARCLAYS

search.jobs.barclays/grads-interns

ukandemeaprogrammaticrecruitment@barclays.com

@lifeatbarclays (TikTok)   @lifeatbarclays (Instagram)

Barclays is one of the world's biggest financial organisations, operating in 40 countries and employing around 90,000 people. For over 330 years, they've created financial solutions and technology. They work together for a better financial future for their customers, clients and communities.

Barclays' Graduate programmes are immersive experiences. Join them and they'll provide a wealth of experience and support during challenging, complex real-world projects that matter. They have opportunities in their UK offices working in areas such as Banking, Technology, Quantitative Finance, Operations, Wealth Management and their Function business areas.

Their internships are a great first experience of the finance world. Barclays immerse their interns in their culture, involve them in real projects and give them a thorough overview of the business. Interns take on responsibility from day one with a people leader to guide and challenge them, and a role model and mentor to support them as they build their knowledge and skills. Barclays connect interns with colleagues across teams and encourage them to explore new opportunities. Their performance during the internship will be assessed, and Barclays consider extending them an offer to join their graduate programme the following year.

They have opportunities across the UK in areas such as Banking, Technology, Quantitative Finance, Operations, Wealth Management and their Function business areas. Applicants need to be be in their penultimate year to be eligible.

Graduates receive focused training sessions during their induction programme, designed to give them the core knowledge and skills to get off to the very best start. Barclays help graduates to achieve professional qualifications and their learning Labs provide bespoke continuous training.

## GRADUATE VACANCIES IN 2026
- ENGINEERING
- FINANCE
- HUMAN RESOURCES
- INVESTMENT BANKING
- RESEARCH & DEVELOPMENT
- RETAIL
- SALES
- TECHNOLOGY

**NUMBER OF VACANCIES**
600 graduate jobs

**LOCATIONS OF VACANCIES**

*Vacancies also available in Europe, the USA and Asia.*

**STARTING SALARY FOR 2026**
£Competitive
*Plus a scholarship and bursary payments.*

**WORK EXPERIENCE**
| INSIGHT COURSES | DEGREE PLACEMENTS | SUMMER INTERNSHIPS |

**UNIVERSITY PROMOTIONS DURING 2025-2026**
ABERDEEN, ASTON, BATH, BIRMINGHAM, BRISTOL, CAMBRIDGE, DUNDEE, DURHAM, EDINBURGH, EXETER, GLASGOW, GLASGOW CALEDONIAN, GREENWICH, HERIOT-WATT, IMPERIAL COLLEGE LONDON, KING'S COLLEGE LONDON, LANCASTER, LIVERPOOL JOHN MOORES, LONDON BUSINESS SCHOOL, LONDON SCHOOL OF ECONOMICS, LOUGHBOROUGH, MANCHESTER, MANCHESTER METROPOLITAN, NORTHAMPTON, NOTTINGHAM, OXFORD, ST ANDREWS, STRATHCLYDE, UNIVERSITY COLLEGE LONDON, WARWICK, WEST OF SCOTLAND
*Please check with your university careers service for full details of Barclays' local promotions and events.*

**MINIMUM ENTRY REQUIREMENTS**
*Relevant degree required for some roles.*

**FURTHER INFORMATION**
www.Top100GraduateEmployers.com
*Register now for the latest news, local promotions, work experience and graduate vacancies at **Barclays**.*

# THERE'S MORE TO BECOME

## DISCOVER LIFELONG LEARNING AT BARCLAYS.

At Barclays, we're a community of people who care — about your ambitions, your development, and our future together.

From shaping smarter digital banking to financing sustainable innovation, graduates and interns get hands-on experience with work that matters. With managers that champion your learning, structured training and the freedom to explore, early careers here are built on driving you towards your full potential. As part of the team, you'll achieve things you never thought were possible, without ever compromising on who you are.

> *To find out more, search jobs at Barclays*

# BBC

**bbc.co.uk/earlycareers**

earlycareersrecruitment@bbc.co.uk

@lifeatthebbc — TikTok
linkedin.com/company/bbc
@BBCGetIn — X
@bbcgetin — Instagram
youtube.com/@LifeAtTheBBC

### GRADUATE VACANCIES IN 2026
- ACCOUNTANCY
- ENGINEERING
- FINANCE
- GENERAL MANAGEMENT
- HUMAN RESOURCES
- LAW
- MARKETING
- MEDIA
- RESEARCH & DEVELOPMENT
- TECHNOLOGY

**NUMBER OF VACANCIES**
250+ graduate jobs

**LOCATIONS OF VACANCIES**

**STARTING SALARY FOR 2026**
£22,950

**UNIVERSITY PROMOTIONS DURING 2025-2026**
Please check with your university careers service for full details of BBC's local promotions and events.

**MINIMUM ENTRY REQUIREMENTS**
Varies by scheme

**APPLICATION DEADLINE**
November 2025 - January 2026

**FURTHER INFORMATION**
www.Top100GraduateEmployers.com
Register now for the latest news, local promotions, work experience and graduate vacancies at **BBC**.

---

The BBC is the world's leading public service broadcaster, producing distinctive content that informs, educates, and entertains millions of people in the UK and around the world. More than 18,000 staff work across journalism, production, engineering, technology, and business.

BBC content is delivered through a range of television channels, national and local radio networks, the BBC World Service, and digital platforms. From BBC One and Radio 1 to BBC Sounds, iPlayer and BBC News Online, the BBC reaches audiences of all ages across the UK and globally. This commitment to accessibility and innovation ensures that BBC content continues to evolve in line with audience needs, technological advances, and changing media habits.

Alongside its role as a global broadcaster, the BBC is also a major provider of training and career development. With a strong focus on potential over academic qualifications, the BBC offers apprenticeship schemes for school leavers, graduates, and career changers alike, as well as at postgraduate-level. BBC apprenticeship opportunities are available across a diverse range of disciplines, including journalism, content production, engineering, artificial intelligence, software development, research and development, UX design, marketing, business, and law.

Apprenticeships at the BBC are designed to help people build skills and gain industry experience while earning a recognised qualification. Schemes vary in length and level, combining work placements with structured learning, delivered by training providers and universities. The BBC aims to open up pathways into careers in the creative and technology industries, ensuring that people from all backgrounds have the opportunity to contribute, develop, and thrive within one of the world's most respected media organisations or the wider creative sector.

# BBC GET IN!

## LAUNCH YOUR CAREER AT THE BBC

bbc.co.uk/earlycareers

Whether you're a school leaver, graduate, or seeking a career change, the BBC's early careers schemes can launch you into a job you'll love. Explore opportunities in Business, Digital, Engineering, Production, and Journalism.

# BCG

@BCGinUK  linkedin.com/company/boston-consulting-group

careers.bcg.com

When organisations face challenges they can't solve on their own, that's where BCG gets to work. As the pioneer in business strategy consulting, it has been helping to solve some of the world's toughest problems since it was founded nearly 60 years ago. Today, its work is more fascinating than ever.

Graduates will join a 33,000-strong global team of consultants and subject-matter experts to partner with clients on projects that make a difference. Whether in the UK or internationally, BCG works shoulder to shoulder with business leaders to shape their organisations for success – today and into the future.

At BCG, graduates benefit from exceptional opportunities for personal and professional growth. From day one, they're exposed to high-impact work and senior client stakeholders. The breadth of experience is vast – from advising on cutting-edge technologies like advanced robotics and agentic AI, to helping clients deliver on their net zero commitments. With exposure across a wide range of industries, consultants start learning immediately.

BCG's culture is performance-oriented and based on apprenticeship, diversity and an eagerness to forge new ways of working. Hands-on learning is fundamental to both BCG's business structure and career development. The firm continually invests in its employees with in-depth learning experiences.

BCG looks for bright students from any subject matter or discipline. It values people with high academic achievement, leadership skills, deep intellectual curiosity, and a problem-solving mindset. Diversity of thought, expertise, experience, and background are fundamental to BCG's success. For graduates looking to continue their learning journey and make a real difference in the world, BCG is the place to start.

**GRADUATE VACANCIES IN 2026**
CONSULTING

**NUMBER OF VACANCIES**
No fixed quota

**LOCATIONS OF VACANCIES**

**STARTING SALARY FOR 2026**
£Competitive
*Plus competitive compensation and benefits package including an annual discretionary performance related bonus.*

**WORK EXPERIENCE**
INSIGHT COURSES | SUMMER INTERNSHIPS

**UNIVERSITY PROMOTIONS DURING 2025-2026**
BATH, BIRMINGHAM, BRISTOL, CAMBRIDGE, CARDIFF, DURHAM, EDINBURGH, EXETER, GLASGOW, IMPERIAL COLLEGE LONDON, KING'S COLLEGE LONDON, LEEDS, LIVERPOOL, LONDON SCHOOL OF ECONOMICS, MANCHESTER, NEWCASTLE, NOTTINGHAM, OXFORD, SCHOOL OF AFRICAN STUDIES, SHEFFIELD, SOUTHAMPTON, ST ANDREWS, UNIVERSITY COLLEGE LONDON, WARWICK, YORK
*Please check with your university careers service for full details of BCG's local promotions and events.*

**MINIMUM ENTRY REQUIREMENTS**
2.1 Degree

**APPLICATION DEADLINE**
23rd October 2025

**FURTHER INFORMATION**
www.Top100GraduateEmployers.com
*Register now for the latest news, local promotions, work experience and graduate vacancies at BCG.*

*Felix, Nick and Ashna,* London

# Beyond growth.

We're dedicated to your success with deep career development and networking opportunities. Based on our own employees' ratings, Comparably ranked us as the #1 company for career growth in 2022 and 2023.

Scan Here

careers.bcg.com

Beyond is where we begin. | BCG

# BlackRock

careers.blackrock.com/students-and-graduates

@blackrock | EMEACampusRecruitment@blackrock.com
BlackRock | linkedin.com/company/blackrock
@blackrock | @blackrock | youtube.com/@LifeatBlackRock

BlackRock is a global investment management company that helps individuals and institutions achieve their financial goals. BlackRock offers a range of products and services, such as mutual funds, ETFs, portfolio management, risk analysis, and advisory solutions.

BlackRock offers a range of graduate programmes for students eager to begin their careers in fintech. These programmes cater to various interests and skill sets, including asset management, technology, analytics and business operations. Open to graduates from all academic backgrounds, BlackRock provides opportunities in several areas, including client & product, corporate & strategic, investments, technology, and operations. Specific tasks and responsibilities vary based on the role and team they join, but students can anticipate engaging in meaningful work, collaborating with colleagues and clients, and contributing to BlackRock's mission to forge a better financial future for all.

BlackRock is set to offer a variety of internships and work experience programmes in 2026, including an 8-week summer internship, spring insight event and 3-12 month placements.

BlackRock is dedicated to offering graduates unparalleled training and development opportunities to foster their growth and success in their careers. Graduates at BlackRock can expect a comprehensive training programme that encompasses both technical and soft skills, along with industry knowledge and insights. Graduates will benefit from on-the-job coaching, feedback, and support from their managers and team, as well as access to a wealth of online learning resources and courses. They will join a community that encourages collaboration, while embarking on a clear and transparent career path that facilitates their progression within the firm.

### GRADUATE VACANCIES IN 2026
- FINANCE
- HUMAN RESOURCES
- MARKETING
- SALES
- TECHNOLOGY

### NUMBER OF VACANCIES
**225+ graduate jobs**

### LOCATIONS OF VACANCIES

*Vacancies also available in Europe.*

### STARTING SALARY FOR 2026
**£Competitive**
*Plus a sign on bonus.*

### WORK EXPERIENCE
| INSIGHT COURSES | DEGREE PLACEMENTS | SUMMER INTERNSHIPS |

### UNIVERSITY PROMOTIONS DURING 2025-2026
BATH, BIRMINGHAM, BRIGHTON, BRISTOL, CAMBRIDGE, DURHAM, EDINBURGH, EXETER, GLASGOW, IMPERIAL COLLEGE LONDON, KING'S COLLEGE LONDON, LEEDS, LOUGHBOROUGH, LONDON SCHOOL OF ECONOMICS, MANCHESTER, NEWCASTLE, NOTTINGHAM, OXFORD, QUEEN MARY LONDON, SHEFFIELD, SOUTHAMPTON, ST ANDREWS, UNIVERSITY COLLEGE LONDON, WARWICK, YORK

*Please check with your university careers service for full details of BlackRock's local promotions and events.*

### MINIMUM ENTRY REQUIREMENTS
*Please check website for full details.*

### APPLICATION DEADLINE
**26th September - 24th October 2025**

### FURTHER INFORMATION
www.Top100GraduateEmployers.com
*Register now for the latest news, local promotions, work experience and graduate vacancies at BlackRock.*

# BlackRock

# Let's invest in each other

BlackRock manages more assets than any other firm in the world. But what we do is far bigger than that. We're responsible for the financial well-being of governments, foundations and people — including those saving for retirement, their children's education or a better life.

Accomplishing this mission would not be possible without our smartest investment – the one we make in our incoming students and graduates. That's why we're committed to creating an environment where you feel welcomed, valued and supported with learning opportunities, benefits and employee networks to help you thrive.

No matter what you're studying – whether it's liberal arts, computer science or anything in between – you can apply your skills at BlackRock.

**Explore opportunities at careers.blackrock.com.**

**Stay connected @BlackRock**

BlackRock is proud to be an Equal Opportunity Employer. We evaluate qualified applicants without regard to race, color, national origin, religion, sex, sexual orientation, gender identity, disability, protected veteran status, and other statuses protected by law. BlackRock will consider for employment qualified applicants with criminal histories in a manner consistent with the requirements of the law, including any applicable fair chance law.

# Bloomberg

bloomberg.com/company/early-careers/full-time
linkedin.com/company/bloomberg
youtube.com/InsideBloomberg

As a global information and technology company, Bloomberg uses its dynamic network of data, ideas and analysis to solve difficult problems every day. Its customers around the world rely on them to deliver accurate, real-time business and market information that helps them make important financial decisions.

Bloomberg offers insight weeks, internship and full-time entry-level roles at their London office across a range of business areas including analytics & sales, data, engineering and more. Candidates who join Bloomberg can build and define their own unique career, rather than a pre-defined path.

Bloomberg offers 10 week internships throughout the summer to provide an unparalleled combination of learning, networking, and project responsibilities. The internship programme aims to provide first-hand exposure to its business and unique culture, and is filled with training, seminars, senior leader speaker series, philanthropic events, and much more.

Bloomberg provides robust training and development opportunities for new joiners through a variety of structured programs. New employees receive comprehensive onboarding that includes both technical and soft skill development via Bloomberg University courses, mentorship, and access to employee-run communities.

Bloomberg's groundbreaking success reaches far beyond the finance and technology industries: they invest nearly all of their profits to help solve humanitarian issues globally and in Bloomberg's own communities. Their founder, Mike Bloomberg, is one of the world's top philanthropists, and through Bloomberg Philanthropies, they are committed to support worthy causes where the greatest good can be achieved. By harnessing the power of data, news and analytics, they help organize, understand and bring clarity to a complex world.

## GRADUATE VACANCIES IN 2026
- ENGINEERING
- FINANCE
- SALES
- TECHNOLOGY

### NUMBER OF VACANCIES
**200+ graduate jobs**

### LOCATIONS OF VACANCIES

*Vacancies also available in Europe, the USA, Asia and elsewhere in the world.*

### STARTING SALARY FOR 2026
**£45,000+**
Plus a £3,000+ salary bonus.

### WORK EXPERIENCE
INSIGHT COURSES | DEGREE PLACEMENTS | SUMMER INTERNSHIPS

### UNIVERSITY PROMOTIONS DURING 2025-2026
CITY, EDINBURGH, GLASGOW, GLASGOW CALEDONIAN, HERIOT-WATT, IMPERIAL COLLEGE LONDON, KING'S COLLEGE LONDON, LONDON SCHOOL OF ECONOMICS, MANCHESTER, QUEEN MARY LONDON, ST ANDREWS, UNIVERSITY COLLEGE LONDON, WARWICK

*Please check with your university careers service for full details of Bloomberg's local promotions and events.*

### APPLICATION DEADLINE
**Year-round recruitment**

### FURTHER INFORMATION
**www.Top100GraduateEmployers.com**
*Register now for the latest news, local promotions, work experience and graduate vacancies at Bloomberg.*

# Make it yours. ▸▸▸

**Ready to do real work from day one?**

At Bloomberg, you'll develop your career your way — backed by an inclusive, global team invested in your growth.

**Let's make it happen.**

BLOOMBERG.COM/EARLYCAREERS

Make it happen here.

© Bloomberg L.P. 2025 984279 0725

**Bloomberg**

# ➤BNY

bny.com/corporate/global/en/careers.html

linkedin.com/company/bnyglobal

Founded by Alexander Hamilton in 1784, BNY proudly holds the title of America's oldest bank and the longest continuously operating financial services company in New York City. They have a proven track record of evolving through challenging times and supporting the market through cycles.

BNY's graduate programme is open to final year students across all degree disciplines. This 24-month full-time programme is designed to develop future leaders through impactful projects and cross-functional exposure in financial services. Students can expect to rotate across their line of business to maximize exposure to their area of work and the bank as a whole. Graduates will be working in either the Manchester, London or Dublin offices.

BNY's summer internship is open to penultimate year students across all degree disciplines. This 10 week internship offers real-world experience across core areas of financial services and allows for insight into what it's like to work for a leading global financial services company touching nearly 20% of the worlds investible assets.

Students will lead meaningful projects that tackle real business challenges, access senior leaders and global peer networking and may be considered for conversion to the graduate programme at the end of the internship.

Graduates at BNY will have access to a 2 week induction and in depth introduction to BNY; an exclusive senior speaker series with a spotlight on professional development and hot topics; a peer mentor who can provide additional support and guidance through the transition from education to the workplace. They'll also receive a blended learning approach mixing classroom, peer and self guided learning, as well as the opportunity to apply for additional learning such as a masters degree or professional qualification

### GRADUATE VACANCIES IN 2026
ENGINEERING
FINANCE
HUMAN RESOURCES
INVESTMENT BANKING

### NUMBER OF VACANCIES
**120+ graduate jobs**

### LOCATIONS OF VACANCIES

*Vacancies also available in Europe, the USA and Asia.*

### STARTING SALARY FOR 2026
**£Competitive**

### WORK EXPERIENCE
SUMMER INTERNSHIPS

### UNIVERSITY PROMOTIONS DURING 2025-2026
BIRMINGHAM, LANCASTER, LEEDS, MANCHESTER, MANCHESTER METROPOLITAN, NOTTINGHAM, SALFORD, WARWICK

*Please check with your university careers service for full details of BNY's local promotions and events.*

### MINIMUM ENTRY REQUIREMENTS
**2.1 Degree**

### APPLICATION DEADLINE
**Year-round recruitment**

### FURTHER INFORMATION
**www.Top100GraduateEmployers.com**
*Register now for the latest news, local promotions, work experience and graduate vacancies at BNY.*

# COME TO LEARN.

# STAY TO LEAD.

**96%**
would accept a full time return offer

**50,000**
employees worldwide across 35 countries

**95%**
said BNY has a great culture

EXPLORE
**#LIFEATBNY**

BNY is a global financial services company overseeing over $50 trillion in assets for our clients — managing it, moving it and keeping it safe.

We offer early careers opportunities for both penultimate and final year students to experience what life is like working for a global leader at the centre of the world's financial ecosystem.

Our summer internship program is a 10 week program open to penultimate year students that offers real-world experience across core areas of financial services.

Our Analyst program is a 24-month full-time program available to final year students, designed to develop future leaders through impactful projects and cross-functional exposure in financial services.

Scan the QR code to learn more about our early careers programs.

➤ BNY

# BRITISH AIRWAYS

**careers.ba.com/graduates-bps-and-interns**

emerging.talent@ba.com

@british_airways (TikTok)  linkedin.com/company/british-airways
@british_airways (Instagram)  youtube.com/FlyBritishAirways

---

British Airways are looking to the future as an airline that loves embracing the best of modern Britain. The country's creativity, diversity and style are the same qualities that make British Airways who they are. Now, they are looking to build on this spirit and passion to make tomorrow even better.

The UK flag carriers are offering a variety of Graduate Schemes across Finance, Commercial, Management and Engineering. These programmes offer graduates the opportunity to complete rotational placements, working on projects that sit at the very heart of the business, with genuine decision-making responsibility.

British Airways graduates can get involved with the sustainability vision, support the community investment programmes, and take part in fundraising challenges for partnership charities - supporting causes close to the company's heart. Being a part of the British Airways graduate community, gives the opportunity to engage with graduates from all schemes across the business and learn from former graduates who are now in senior management positions. An exciting opportunity; not mentioning the access to heavily discounted flights to go globetrotting. British Airways also offer a 10 week Summer Internship and 11 month Business Placement – as well as some new exciting work experience opportunities coming soon!

Taking the first step into the world of work can be daunting, but this is a fantastic development opportunity for young people, creating new experiences and moments that allow them to expand their horizons and explore every possibility with one of the world's leading airlines.

Join a British Airways Graduate scheme to discover how great it feels to connect Britain with the world, and the world with Britain.

---

### GRADUATE VACANCIES IN 2026
- ENGINEERING
- FINANCE
- GENERAL MANAGEMENT
- LOGISTICS
- TECHNOLOGY

### NUMBER OF VACANCIES
**50+ graduate jobs**

### LOCATIONS OF VACANCIES

### STARTING SALARY FOR 2026
**£33,000-£35,200**

### WORK EXPERIENCE
| INSIGHT COURSES | DEGREE PLACEMENTS | SUMMER INTERNSHIPS |

### UNIVERSITY PROMOTIONS DURING 2025-2026
ASTON, BATH, BIRMINGHAM, BRUNEL, CARDIFF, COVENTRY, EDINBURGH, EXETER, IMPERIAL COLLEGE LONDON, KING'S COLLEGE LONDON, LIVERPOOL JOHN MOORES, LOUGHBOROUGH, LONDON SCHOOL OF ECONOMICS, QUEEN MARY LONDON, SHEFFIELD HALLAM, SOUTHAMPTON, UNIVERSITY COLLEGE LONDON, WARWICK

*Please check with your university careers service for full details of British Airways' local promotions and events.*

### MINIMUM ENTRY REQUIREMENTS
**2.2 Degree**

### APPLICATION DEADLINE
**November 2025**

### FURTHER INFORMATION
**www.Top100GraduateEmployers.com**
*Register now for the latest news, local promotions, work experience and graduate vacancies at **British Airways**.*

# THE SKY IS NEVER THE LIMIT

## YOUR JOURNEY WITH BRITISH AIRWAYS WILL TAKE YOU FURTHER THAN YOU EVER IMAGINED

Scan below to start your journey:

**BRITISH AIRWAYS**

# Capgemini

capgemini.com/gb-en/careers/career-paths

graduate.careers.uk@capgemini.com
linkedin.com/company/capgemini
@capgemini_uk
CapgeminiUK
youtube.com/capgeminimedia

For over 50 years, Capgemini has supported graduates in working collaboratively to solve real-world challenges for clients. Every day, Capgemini's 340,000+ strategy, business, and technology specialists deliver innovation and excellence, across a variety of projects.

With a strong industry focus, graduates can build careers in sectors such as healthcare, retail, utilities, manufacturing, the public sector, and more. Capgemini's two award-winning graduate programmes combine hands-on experience with structured development, helping graduates grow their consulting, technology, industry, and soft skills. Graduates thrive with tailored feedback and mentoring, alongside individualised development in areas such as business analysis, data, project management, software development, cybersecurity, and creative design.

The Empower Programme prepares graduates for dynamic roles that integrate both technology and business expertise. Built around six Power Skills, Empower combines client work, role-specific training, and collaborative projects. Learning Pods build cross-functional networks and follow personalised learning roadmaps.

The Accelerate Programme at Capgemini Invent fast-tracks graduates into specialist consulting roles. It begins with a four-month immersive experience at the Institute, where graduates learn core consulting skills in a safe learning environment, before progressing to 18 months of real client engagement.

Regular social and networking events foster strong connections and a collaborative culture. With access to over 250,000 learning resources, volunteering days, and industry-recognised certifications, graduates gain the confidence and skills to grow their careers in the direction that's right for them.

## GRADUATE VACANCIES IN 2026
CONSULTING
ENGINEERING
FINANCE
MARKETING
SALES
TECHNOLOGY

**NUMBER OF VACANCIES**
300+ graduate jobs

**LOCATIONS OF VACANCIES**

**STARTING SALARY FOR 2026**
£30,000+

**WORK EXPERIENCE**
INSIGHT COURSES | DEGREE PLACEMENTS | SUMMER INTERNSHIPS

**UNIVERSITY PROMOTIONS DURING 2025-2026**
ASTON, BATH, BIRMINGHAM, BRIGHTON, BRISTOL, CAMBRIDGE, COVENTRY, DURHAM, EDINBURGH, EXETER, GLASGOW, GLASGOW CALEDONIAN, IMPERIAL COLLEGE LONDON, KING'S COLLEGE LONDON, LANCASTER, LEEDS, LEICESTER, LOUGHBOROUGH, LONDON SCHOOL OF ECONOMICS, MANCHESTER, NOTTINGHAM, NOTTINGHAM TRENT, OXFORD, QUEEN MARY LONDON, SALFORD, SHEFFIELD, SHEFFIELD HALLAM, SOUTHAMPTON, ST ANDREWS, STRATHCLYDE, SUSSEX, UNIVERSITY COLLEGE LONDON, WARWICK

*Please check with your university careers service for full details of Capgemini's local promotions and events.*

**MINIMUM ENTRY REQUIREMENTS**
*Relevant degree required for some roles.*

**APPLICATION DEADLINE**
Year-round recruitment

**FURTHER INFORMATION**
www.Top100GraduateEmployers.com
*Register now for the latest news, local promotions, work experience and graduate vacancies at Capgemini.*

# Capgemini

# What impact could you have?

At Capgemini, we believe in the power of people. We know starting your career is more than just the job. It's about feeling supported, finding your people, and doing work that truly matters. From your first day, you'll join an inclusive and feedback-rich environment where your growth is a shared priority.

You'll work on projects that make a difference – from using AI to transform healthcare, to innovating systems and enhancing digital customer experiences. You'll work alongside experts who'll support your development every step of the way. Whether you're exploring new technologies, building client relationships, or shaping strategy, you'll be part of a team that values curiosity, collaboration, and creativity.

We'll help you build the skills and confidence to thrive through hands-on experience, tailored learning, and a culture that celebrates individuality. With access to mentoring, professional qualifications, and a global network, you'll have everything you need to shape a career that's uniquely yours.

| 340,000+ employees worldwide | 50+ countries | Work in 15+ industries | Technology, Consulting & Business roles | Starting salary dependent on programme |
| Access to 250,000+ courses | | Regular social & networking events | A buddy & a mentor | 300+ peers on programme |

For information on our graduate programmes

**Scan here**

**Rewrite your future.
Join us.**

# Civil Service Fast Stream

**faststream.gov.uk**

faststream | @civilservicefaststream
@faststreamuk | linkedin.com/company/civil-service-fast-stream

The Civil Service supports the government to implement its policies on behalf of every community across the UK. The award-winning Fast Stream is a leadership and management programme that equips talented graduates with the knowledge, skills and networks to operate effectively across the Civil Service.

With 17 different schemes, the Fast Stream is designed to help accelerate progression to senior roles in the Civil Service. There is no typical fast streamer. The programme welcomes individuals from all ages, cultures and backgrounds, ensuring the Civil Service reflects the diverse communities it serves. The Fast Stream is increasingly offering opportunities outside of London, with a new ambition for 50% of postings to be outside of London by 2030.

While the programme welcomes graduates across all degree subjects and backgrounds, the Civil Service is keen to attract more people with Science, Technology, Engineering and Maths (STEM) degrees. STEM graduates are crucial in realising the vision of building a skilled, innovative and ambitious Civil Service equipped for the future.

Offering career opportunities in England, Scotland and Wales, each scheme offers high-quality training and on-the-job learning where participants build practical skills and put their knowledge into practice across various government departments.

Alongside this, a range of Fast Stream networks offer a vibrant social life around work as well as enabling graduates to make lasting, professional connections.

Fast streamers are valued members of the wider Civil Service community. They make an impact every day, helping to deliver vital public services and government operations by shaping decisions that affect everyone's lives.

---

**GRADUATE VACANCIES IN 2026**
- ACCOUNTANCY
- ENGINEERING
- FINANCE
- HUMAN RESOURCES
- PROPERTY
- PURCHASING
- RESEARCH & DEVELOPMENT
- TECHNOLOGY

**NUMBER OF VACANCIES**
700 graduate jobs

**LOCATIONS OF VACANCIES**

**STARTING SALARY FOR 2026**
£31,186

**WORK EXPERIENCE**
SUMMER INTERNSHIPS

**UNIVERSITY PROMOTIONS DURING 2025-2026**
Please check with your university careers service for full details of the Civil Service's local promotions and events.

**MINIMUM ENTRY REQUIREMENTS**
2.2 Degree

**APPLICATION DEADLINE**
6th November 2025

**FURTHER INFORMATION**
www.Top100GraduateEmployers.com
Register now for the latest news, local promotions, work experience and graduate vacancies at *the Civil Service*.

# Civil Service Fast Stream

Grow like **nowhere else**

# REACH YOUR POTENTIAL
## BE A LEADER OF TOMORROW

**Graduate Leadership and Management Development Programme**
Nationwide Opportunities

Go further, sooner. Own your development on this career-accelerating programme. Gaining real-world skills and experience through high-quality training and postings across government, you'll put what you learn into practice, on work that impacts our nation. We're here to grow tomorrow's leaders and managers, building a productive and agile Civil Service for a fast-changing world. And you could help tackle some of our biggest challenges.

Get future-ready at faststream.gov.uk

# CLYDE&CO

careers.clydeco.com/en
EarlyCareers@clydeco.com
@clydecoearlycareers
linkedin.com/company/clydeco

Clyde & Co is a global law firm providing a complete service to clients in core sectors of insurance, transport, energy, infrastructure and trade & commodities. With over 5,500 people operating from nearly 70 offices, across six continents, Clyde & Co is committed to creating successful outcomes for clients.

Clyde & Co seek out early talents with ambition, independent thinking, curiosity and commitment, and will help trainees harness their skills to build a successful career. Their early talent programmes challenge, inspire, and prepare students and graduates for a future in a dynamic legal landscape.

Future lawyers at Clyde & Co are defined by their curiosity, teamwork, and willingness to think beyond the expected. Whether through structured programmes or hands-on experience, they equip their people with the tools to shape meaningful careers. Most of Clyde & Co's trainees are individuals who have impressed the firm through their vacation schemes or through internal recruitment from their paralegal population.

Clyde & Co's vacation schemes are the perfect opportunity for those seeking experience with a business at the heart of global trade and commerce. Their participants benefit from the chance to learn with the best and broaden their outlook in a global firm with big ambitions.

The firm's Bright Futures programme is a scheme designed to offer first year students exposure to the legal sector. It offers insight into life at an international law firm, including shadowing lawyers, networking, and development sessions.

With the Paralegal Academy, Clyde & Co also offers an alternative pathway into a legal career which targets graduates and candidates transitioning careers to match their ambition. By joining Clyde & Co, you can find and redefine success in every aspect of your career.

## GRADUATE VACANCIES IN 2026
LAW

**NUMBER OF VACANCIES**
50+ graduate jobs
*For training contracts starting in 2028.*

**LOCATIONS OF VACANCIES**

*Vacancies also available in Europe, the USA and Asia.*

**STARTING SALARY FOR 2026**
£24,500-£48,500

**WORK EXPERIENCE**
INSIGHT COURSES | SUMMER INTERNSHIPS

**UNIVERSITY PROMOTIONS DURING 2025-2026**
ASTON, BATH, BIRMINGHAM, BRISTOL, CARDIFF, CITY, DURHAM, EDINBURGH, GLASGOW, KENT, LANCASTER, LIVERPOOL, MANCHESTER, QUEEN MARY LONDON, QUEEN'S UNIVERSITY BELFAST, SALFORD, SHEFFIELD, SOAS, SOUTHAMPTON, SURREY, ULSTER, WARWICK
*Please check with your university careers service for full details of Clyde & Co's local promotions and events.*

**MINIMUM ENTRY REQUIREMENTS**
2.1 Degree

**APPLICATION DEADLINE**
5th January 2026

**FURTHER INFORMATION**
www.Top100GraduateEmployers.com
*Register now for the latest news, local promotions, work experience and graduate vacancies at Clyde & Co.*

# CLYDE&CO

# Reshape your *future* with us.

We offer brilliant opportunities to develop your skills and experience, working on exciting cases alongside some of the most respected and talented lawyers in their field.

You'll be encouraged and supported to realise your full potential, actively participating and collaborating with senior fee earners, partners and exposure to household clients.

If you're looking to develop your career and are committed to delivering exceptional outcomes, explore our opportunities today.

Go further. Search Early Careers at Clyde & Co.

🌐 careers.clydeco.com  ⓘ clydecoearlycareers

## Success & Beyond

# Deloitte.

deloitte.com/uk/en/careers/early-careers.html
@deloitte_uk
linkedin.com/company/deloitte
DeloitteUK
youtube.com/@DeloitteUK

**For more than 175 years, Deloitte has offered professional services to organisations – from the Global 500 to private businesses – to build better futures. Deloitte makes its impact through collaboration. All around the world, their colleagues spark positive progress for their clients, people and society.**

From audit and assurance to tax, legal, technology, and consulting, Deloitte's end-to-end programmes transform complex challenges into opportunities, building a more connected future. Their graduate programmes offer permanent positions, market-leading salaries, tailored benefits, and structured career paths leading to recognised professional qualifications and rapid progression. Graduates will gain invaluable experience with an unrivalled client list, working with local and global businesses across the 22 UK and offshore offices, developing both technical and personal skills.

Deloitte also offer work experience and placement schemes including Spring Into Deloitte, Summer Vacation Schemes, and Industrial Placements providing hands-on experience and to explore potential career paths.

Deloitte ensure a community who bring out the best in each other through sharing ideas, providing support and motivating one another to reach their potential. There's a genuine commitment to ongoing professional development that stretches far beyond initial qualifications. They help their graduates progress through technical, professional and leadership skills training, on-the-job learning, mentoring and much more.

From day one, graduates make significant contributions, working alongside incredible people who challenge and inspire one another to create work with real purpose. In an inclusive environment, graduates can dream bigger, think creatively, and deliver real impact, growing and progressing every day.

---

**GRADUATE VACANCIES IN 2026**
ACCOUNTANCY
CONSULTING

**NUMBER OF VACANCIES**
1,000+ graduate jobs

**LOCATIONS OF VACANCIES**

**STARTING SALARY FOR 2026**
£Competitive

**WORK EXPERIENCE**
INSIGHT COURSES | DEGREE PLACEMENTS | SUMMER INTERNSHIPS

**UNIVERSITY PROMOTIONS DURING 2025-2026**
ABERDEEN, BATH, BRISTOL, DURHAM, EDINBURGH, EXETER, GLASGOW, HERIOT-WATT, IMPERIAL COLLEGE LONDON, LANCASTER, LEEDS, LEICESTER, LIVERPOOL, LOUGHBOROUGH, MANCHESTER, NORTHUMBRIA, NOTTINGHAM, NOTTINGHAM TRENT, QUEEN MARY LONDON, QUEEN'S UNIVERSITY BELFAST, READING, ROYAL HOLLOWAY LONDON, SHEFFIELD, SOUTHAMPTON, SWANSEA, ULSTER, UNIVERSITY COLLEGE LONDON, YORK

*Please check with your university careers service for full details of Deloitte's local promotions and events.*

**MINIMUM ENTRY REQUIREMENTS**
2.1 Degree

**APPLICATION DEADLINE**
September - November 2025

**FURTHER INFORMATION**
www.Top100GraduateEmployers.com
*Register now for the latest news, local promotions, work experience and graduate vacancies at Deloitte.*

# Deloitte.

## What matters to you?

Innovating with cutting-edge tech.
Protecting our planet.
Working from home. Collaborating in the office.
Developing your skills.
Taking time off for yourself.
Feeling supported and included. Helping others feel the same.

**What matters** is different to everyone.
But you don't need to have it all figured out just yet.
**We're here to help you make the right choices, for you.**

**careers.db.com/students-graduates**

DeutscheBankCareers  uk.graduatequeries@db.com
@DeutscheBank  linkedin.com/company/deutsche-bank
@DeutscheBank  youtube.com/DeutscheBank

### GRADUATE VACANCIES IN 2026
**FINANCE**
**INVESTMENT BANKING**

### NUMBER OF VACANCIES
**100+ graduate jobs**

### LOCATIONS OF VACANCIES

### STARTING SALARY FOR 2026
**£Competitive**
Plus a sign on bonus.

### WORK EXPERIENCE
| INSIGHT COURSES | DEGREE PLACEMENTS | SUMMER INTERNSHIPS |

### UNIVERSITY PROMOTIONS DURING 2025-2026
BIRMINGHAM, BRISTOL, CAMBRIDGE, DURHAM, EDINBURGH, IMPERIAL COLLEGE LONDON, KING'S COLLEGE LONDON, LEEDS, LONDON SCHOOL OF ECONOMICS, MANCHESTER, NOTTINGHAM, OXFORD, QUEEN MARY LONDON, SHEFFIELD, ST ANDREWS, UNIVERSITY COLLEGE LONDON, WARWICK
*Please check with your university careers service for full details of Deutsche Bank's local promotions and events.*

### MINIMUM ENTRY REQUIREMENTS
**2.1 Degree**

### APPLICATION DEADLINE
**September 2025 - February 2026**

### FURTHER INFORMATION
**www.Top100GraduateEmployers.com**
*Register now for the latest news, local promotions, work experience and graduate vacancies at **Deutsche Bank**.*

---

**For over 150 years, Deutsche Bank has been dedicated to their client's lasting success at home and abroad. As the Global Hausbank, Deutsche Bank provides financial services to companies, governments, institutional investors, small and medium-sized businesses, and private individuals.**

The bank has four core businesses: the Corporate Bank, the Investment Bank, the Private Bank and the Asset Management business (DWS). All of which are well positioned to respond to trends that will shape the economy, and to deliver their combined expertise to clients. Deutsche Bank's Graduate Programme is a year-long comprehensive programme that provides graduates with ongoing professional and technical training, and a network of support to help them develop the skills they need to take initiative and pioneer real solutions. Whether embarking on a Graduate Programme in one of the business divisions, or in an infrastructure team like Technology, Data & Innovation, Chief Risk Office or Human Resources, graduates benefit from Deutsche Bank's collaborative culture.

Deutsche Bank's nine-week Summer Internship Programme and 3-6 month Seasonal Internship Programme is designed to enable early talent to develop skills that will help them succeed, through formal training and continuous support. These interns will learn first-hand how and what the bank deliver for clients worldwide and quickly gain the confidence it takes to impact real projects.

Deutsche Bank's Early Careers programmes are designed to support students and graduates develop the skills and knowledge they need to take charge of their career. Supported by a global network of talented colleagues, graduates are encouraged to work together while being given the autonomy to achieve their goals. As graduates grow, they will continue to benefit from a variety of in-person and on-demand training in an environment which encourages diverse careers.

Dedicated to you.
Building pathways
for your future.
careers.db.com
With deep dedication.
Deutsche Bank

# DIAGEO

diageo.com/en
@diageogb
linkedin.com/company/diageo

With over 200 brands sold in nearly 180 countries, Diageo are the world's leading premium drinks company. Every day, over 30,000 people come together to create the magic behind their much loved brands. From iconic names to innovative newcomers – the brands Diageo is building are rooted in culture and local communities.

Diageo's founders, such as Arthur Guinness, John Walker and Elizabeth Cumming, were visionary entrepreneurs whose brilliant minds helped shape the alcohol industry. Through Diageo's people, their legacy lives on. By joining Diageo, individuals will collaborate, explore, and innovate, challenging and being challenged. Together with passionate people from across the world, they will build brands consumers love.

Diageo's graduate programmes challenge, inspire, and provide the support needed to kick-start a rewarding career. As a graduate at Diageo, individuals will help build iconic brands consumers love, such as Guinness, Baileys, and Johnnie Walker. By aiming high, graduates will be supported to explore, learn, and grow while collaborating with passionate people from all corners of the world. Diageo's graduate schemes last for 1-3 years and are available across its regions: Great Britain, Ireland, Southern Europe, and Turkey. Diageo encourages graduates to come as they are, share their ideas, and learn from others. By bringing passion, curiosity, and a desire to learn and grow relentlessly, graduates will be celebrated for their contributions to progress and will enjoy an attractive benefits and rewards package.

Supported by a buddy, they will learn from experienced and knowledgeable colleagues. Graduates will develop leadership skills and knowledge through formal and informal training. From day one, graduates will make a real contribution to the business and industry.

## GRADUATE VACANCIES IN 2026
- ENGINEERING
- FINANCE
- HUMAN RESOURCES
- LOGISTICS
- MARKETING
- SALES
- TECHNOLOGY

## NUMBER OF VACANCIES
**30-50 graduate jobs**

## LOCATIONS OF VACANCIES

*Vacancies also available in Europe.*

## STARTING SALARY FOR 2026
**£38,000**
*Plus a 10% bonus scheme.*

## UNIVERSITY PROMOTIONS DURING 2025-2026
ASTON, GLASGOW, HERRIOT WATT, LONDON, LOUGHBOROUGH, MANCHESTER, SURREY, UNIVERSITY COLLEGE LONDON, WARWICK
*Please check with your university careers service for full details of Diageo's local promotions and events.*

## MINIMUM ENTRY REQUIREMENTS
*Relevant degree required for some roles.*

## APPLICATION DEADLINE
**6th October 2025 - 10th November 2025**

## FURTHER INFORMATION
**www.Top100GraduateEmployers.com**
*Register now for the latest news, local promotions, work experience and graduate vacancies at Diageo.*

# DIAGEO

# Kick-start *your* career with us

Join any of our graduate schemes and help build some of the world's most-loved brands, including Johnnie Walker, Guinness and Baileys. Just bring your passion and ideas, and we'll support you to build a career worth celebrating.

In a supportive environment, you'll be empowered to be you, with us.

**EXPLORE DIAGEO CAREERS**

JOHNNIE WALKER · GUINNESS · Tanqueray · BAILEYS · SMIRNOFF

# DLA PIPER

careers.dlapiper.com/early-careers

earlycareers@dlapiper.com
@dlapipercareers
linkedin.com/company/dla-piper

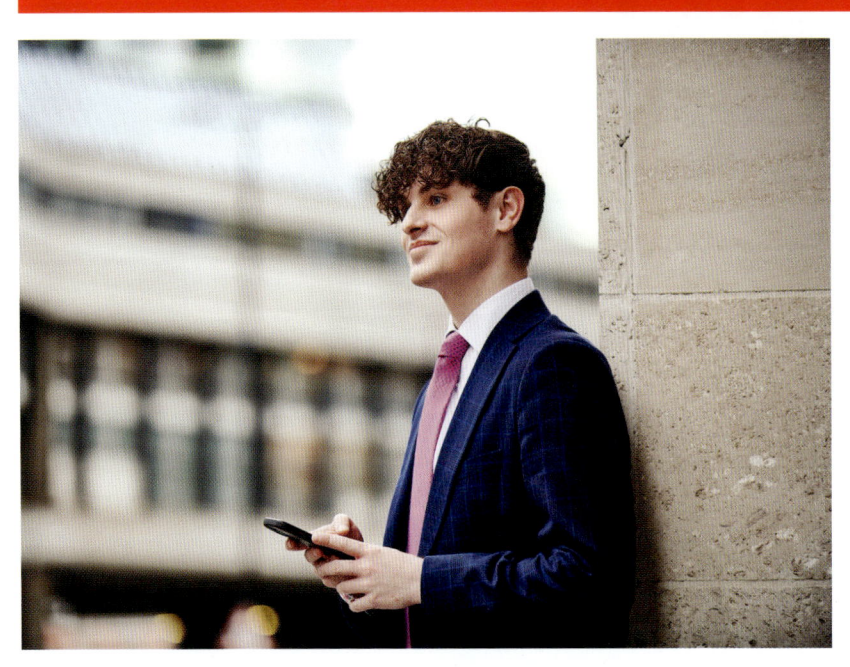

DLA Piper are the key to a global career. With over 90 offices in more than 40 countries, they offer global careers without limits. Trainees will experience the most interesting and challenging work, create exceptional results with high-profile clients globally, and enjoy the complexity of an interconnected world.

DLA Piper's three-and-a-half-week summer internship programme begins with a three-day induction in their London office, followed by three-weeks working in two practice groups. Law students must be a second-year student on a three-year course, or a third-year student on a four-year course; non-law applicants must be in their final year of study or already graduated. Successful completion of the award-winning summer internship could lead to the offer of a place on the international training programme. Find out more at DLA Piper Early Careers website.

They offer two programmes for students: an insight day and summer internship programme. Their "Law, *unlocked*" insight day is designed for first-year law students and second-year non-law students who want to explore what makes DLA Piper a different kind of law firm.

Trainees are sponsored to attend a Masters level preparatory course which includes the SQE1 and SQE2. For non-law degree joiners a law conversion course will be sponsored before the SQE. Trainees begin their two-year programme with an immersive international induction week in London, connecting with peers and leaders from across the globe. Across their programme, trainees rotate through four dynamic six-month placements within DLA Piper's market-leading practice groups, gaining depth of experience through their sector specific lens. Trainees benefit from international and client secondment opportunities, as well as continuous professional development.

---

**GRADUATE VACANCIES IN 2026**
LAW

**NUMBER OF VACANCIES**
**50+ graduate jobs**
For training contracts starting in 2028.

**LOCATIONS OF VACANCIES**

**STARTING SALARY FOR 2026**
**£35,500**

**WORK EXPERIENCE**
INSIGHT COURSES | SUMMER INTERNSHIPS

**UNIVERSITY PROMOTIONS DURING 2025-2026**
BIRMINGHAM, BRISTOL, CAMBRIDGE, DURHAM, EDINBURGH, EXETER, GLASGOW, KING'S COLLEGE LONDON, LEEDS, LIVERPOOL, MANCHESTER, NEWCASTLE, NOTTINGHAM, OXFORD, QUEEN MARY LONDON, SHEFFIELD, UNIVERSITY COLLEGE LONDON, WARWICK, YORK
*Please check with your university careers service for full details of DLA Piper's local promotions and events.*

**MINIMUM ENTRY REQUIREMENTS**
**2.1 Degree**
*Please see careers website for full details.*

**APPLICATION DEADLINE**
**November - December 2025**

**FURTHER INFORMATION**
www.Top100GraduateEmployers.com
*Register now for the latest news, local promotions, work experience and graduate vacancies at DLA Piper.*

# Build a different kind of legal career.

## Where law *unlocks* potential

## Ready to launch your legal career and give it the best platform?

At DLA Piper, we're not just shaping the future of law—we're redefining it.

As a trainee, you'll take on exciting, high-impact work with major international clients.

You'll be challenged, supported, and inspired to make a real difference—right from day one.

Scan the QR code to explore more about the firm and our opportunities

DLA Piper is a global law firm operating through various separate and distinct entities. Further details of these entities can be found at dlapiper.com. This may qualify as "Lawyer Advertising" requiring notice in some jurisdictions. Copyright © 2025 DLA Piper. All rights reserved. JUL25 | A29251-7

**DLA PIPER**

**careers.edfenergy.com/early-careers**

yourfuture@edfenergy.com
@edfenergy | linkedin.com/company/edf-energy
EDFEnergy | youtube.com/EDF

EDF UK is helping Britain achieve net zero by leading the transition to a cleaner, low emission, electric future and tackling climate change. As part of EDF Group, the world's largest electricity generator, EDF UK employs around 14,000 people across England, Scotland, Wales and Ireland.

At EDF UK, Success is Personal. Employees are supported to shape their own career paths, recognising that success looks different for everyone, and empowered to make their career everything it deserves to be. Graduates can start their career journey by applying to join EDF's programmes across the UK. They'll benefit from targeted training and development to support their long-term career growth, while contributing to a sustainable energy future. EDF's programmes span key areas, including Science & Engineering, Design Engineering, Supply Chain, Technology and Project Management. Each programme is tailored to align with specific end role positions, providing practical experience across business functions. Placements are complemented by role-specific training to enhance technical, personal and professional skills.

For those earlier in their university journey, EDF offers Industrial Work Placements across a wide range of disciplines - from Science and Engineering to Research and Development and Project Management. A flexible virtual work experience programme is also available in partnership with Springpod, open to anyone aged 14 and over in the UK, offering practical insights into the energy sector. Applications for EDF's graduate programmes open in September 2025. Find out more on the EDF Careers website and join the Graduate Talent Community for the latest updates. Joining EDF means graduates open up their world to opportunities that can support them to shape a career path that reflects their interests and ambitions.

### GRADUATE VACANCIES IN 2026
- ACCOUNTANCY
- ENGINEERING
- FINANCE
- HUMAN RESOURCES
- PURCHASING
- TECHNOLOGY

**NUMBER OF VACANCIES**
50+ graduate jobs

**LOCATIONS OF VACANCIES**

**STARTING SALARY FOR 2026**
£35,000+
*Plus a relocation bonus, performance based bonuses, flexible benefits & excellent pension.*

**UNIVERSITY PROMOTIONS DURING 2025-2026**
BIRMINGHAM, BRISTOL, EDINBURGH, EXETER, IMPERIAL COLLEGE LONDON, LANCASTER, MANCHESTER, NOTTINGHAM, QUEEN MARY LONDON, READING, SHEFFIELD, SOUTHAMPTON
*Please check with your university careers service for full details of EDF's local promotions and events.*

**MINIMUM ENTRY REQUIREMENTS**
2.2 Degree
*Relevant degree required for some roles.*

**APPLICATION DEADLINE**
5th October 2025

**FURTHER INFORMATION**
www.Top100GraduateEmployers.com
*Register now for the latest news, local promotions, work experience and graduate vacancies at EDF.*

# eDF

## SUCCESS IS PERSONAL

"I'm ambitious because I know my **value**."

Find your success at EDF.

# Enterprise Mobility™

enterprisemobility.co.uk/careers

@enterprisemobility.careers.uk
sayhello@em.com
youtube.com/@enterprisemobilitycareersemea
enterprisemobilitycareerseurope
linkedin.com/company/enterprise-mobility-

Enterprise Mobility™ is an organisation that's grown from a pioneering idea and seven cars to a global mobility leader. Staying true to the people-first philosophy that's guided them from day one, their 90,000+ team members are now focused on shaping the mobility experiences of the future.

Enterprise Mobility believes great leaders are made, and as a Graduate Management Trainee, individuals will have the freedom to explore their potential. From their first day, the organisation invests in them within a supportive environment where they will take on real responsibilities, gaining invaluable hands-on experience across all facets of the organisation, including sales, marketing, customer service, finance and operations.

Offering 12-month placements and summer internships, Enterprise Mobility believes that tomorrow's leaders learn by doing. From day one, participants join an environment where they can thrive, gain new experiences, and develop leadership skills to map out their future. While they are busy learning, Enterprise Mobility ensures their efforts are recognised and rewarded.

Whether helping build on existing skills or learning new ones, career development is a top priority for Enterprise Mobility. From classroom settings to on-the-job training and mentorship, there are plenty of opportunities for graduates to refine their skills and prepare for the next step in their career.

Team members and their managers will work closely to create a development plan that matches the specific needs and interests of each trainee. Each day, they will work alongside some of the best in the industry, constantly learning from colleagues who are equally invested in their success. Plus, with their unique promote-from-within culture, graduates will always be making progress in their career – and flourishing in ways they never thought possible.

## GRADUATE VACANCIES IN 2026
GENERAL MANAGEMENT
RETAIL
SALES

### NUMBER OF VACANCIES
**1,100 graduate jobs**

### LOCATIONS OF VACANCIES

### STARTING SALARY FOR 2026
**£30,000**
Plus performance-based bonuses following completion of graduate programme, and relocation allowance if applicable.

### WORK EXPERIENCE
DEGREE PLACEMENTS | SUMMER INTERNSHIPS

### UNIVERSITY PROMOTIONS DURING 2025-2026
ABERDEEN, ABERYSTWYTH, ASTON, BANGOR, BATH, BIRMINGHAM, BOURNEMOUTH, BRADFORD, BRIGHTON, BRISTOL, BRUNEL, CARDIFF, CARDIFF METROPOLITAN, CHICHESTER, CITY, COVENTRY, DERBY, DUNDEE, DURHAM, EDINBURGH, EDINBURGH NAPIER, ESSEX, EXETER, FALMOUTH, GLASGOW, GLASGOW CALEDONIAN, HERIOT-WATT, HUDDERSFIELD, HULL, KEELE, KENT, LANCASTER, LEEDS, LEICESTER, LINCOLN, LIVERPOOL, LIVERPOOL JOHN MOORES, LOUGHBOROUGH, MANCHESTER, NEWCASTLE, NORTHUMBRIA, NOTTINGHAM, NOTTINGHAM TRENT, OXFORD BROOKES, PLYMOUTH, PORTSMOUTH, QUEEN MARY LONDON, QUEEN'S UNIVERSITY BELFAST, READING, ROBERT GORDON, ROYAL HOLLOWAY LONDON, SALFORD, SHEFFIELD, SHEFFIELD HALLAM, SOUTHAMPTON, STIRLING, STRATHCLYDE, SUNDERLAND, SURREY, SUSSEX, SWANSEA, EAST ANGLIA, ULSTER, WARWICK, WEST OF ENGLAND, WINCHESTER, YORK

### APPLICATION DEADLINE
**Year-round recruitment**

### FURTHER INFORMATION
www.Top100GraduateEmployers.com
Register now for the latest news, local promotions, work experience and graduate vacancies at Enterprise Mobility.

# Enterprise Mobility™

# JOIN TO START YOUR JOURNEY.

## STAY FOR A THOUSAND MORE.

Opportunities at Enterprise Mobility™ let you discover your potential, become a leader and find all the support you need to create a meaningful career.

**Learn more**

MAKE YOUR MOVE.
**Become a Management Trainee at**
enterprisemobility.co.uk/careers

# Environment Agency

environmentagencycareers.co.uk

eatalent@environment-agency.gov.uk
@envagency
linkedin.com/company/environment-agency
environmentagency
youtube.com/EnvironmentAgencyTV

The Environment Agency works to create better places for people and wildlife. They employ over 13,000 people with offices across England. Their goals are to protect and enhance air, land and water supporting nature's recovery; build a nation resilient to climate change; and support sustainable growth.

The Environment Agency offers two graduate training schemes: Environment and Science and Engineering. With opportunities across England, both schemes provide structured training, mentorship, and support towards achieving professional chartership. The Environment and Science programme includes roles in biodiversity, water resources, flood modelling, and many more, with opportunities for job shadowing, project work, and professional membership. The Engineering scheme prepares graduates for Chartered Engineer status with experience in sustainability, innovation, design, construction, and project management. Participants benefit from expert guidance, tailored placements, and both national and international development opportunities.

12-week summer internships and 12-month industry placements are available to undergraduates and recent graduates. These are paid opportunities in various environmental disciplines, providing insight into specific areas across the organisation and its core mission to protect and improve the environment.

Career entry programmes provide a pathway into the environmental sector, and serve as a stepping stone to explore different roles or specialise in niche technical areas. There is continued support to learn and develop and shape meaningful careers as the technical and people leaders needed for the future.

The Environment Agency is committed to building an inclusive culture, where employees feel valued and supported. They offer flexible working patterns, options to work from an office or at home, and employee support networks.

## GRADUATE VACANCIES IN 2026
- ENGINEERING
- GENERAL MANAGEMENT
- HUMAN RESOURCES
- LAW
- RESEARCH & DEVELOPMENT

### NUMBER OF VACANCIES
**30-40 graduate jobs**

### LOCATIONS OF VACANCIES

### STARTING SALARY FOR 2026
**£24,000-£30,000**

### WORK EXPERIENCE
DEGREE PLACEMENTS | SUMMER INTERNSHIPS

### UNIVERSITY PROMOTIONS DURING 2025-2026
*Please check with your university careers service for full details of Environment Agency's local promotions and events.*

### APPLICATION DEADLINE
**October 2025 - January 2026**

### FURTHER INFORMATION
www.Top100GraduateEmployers.com
*Register now for the latest news, local promotions, work experience and graduate vacancies at Environment Agency.*

# Bring influence that lasts

**Environment Agency**

Environment Agency employees do vital, purposeful work that influences and protects lives, places and communities now and in the future. This includes managing flood risks, restoring damaged habitats, or finding ways to reduce the effects of climate change. These are complex challenges, but with teamwork, creativity, and determination, the organisation is helping communities adapt and thrive.

The Environment Agency fosters a people-led culture where personal and professional growth is championed at every stage. Known for being trusted, empowering, and committed to development, it offers a dynamic environment where individuals are encouraged to broaden their skills, explore new opportunities, and build a career that truly matters.

**Now's the time to shape your future:** explore career opportunities with the Environment Agency and have influence that lasts.

**environmentagencycareers.co.uk**

# EY
## Shape the future with confidence

ey.com/uk/earlycareers
@eyukcareers
linkedin.com/company/ernstandyoung
EYCareersUK
youtube.com/EYUKCareers

EY is a professional services organisation that helps global companies make better decisions about business, finance, sustainability and technology. They have over 400,000 talented people in more than 150 countries. Their services transform how businesses work through innovative solutions and ideas.

Their purpose is building a better working world, with the help of their people. At EY, people are empowered with the right mindsets and skills to navigate what's next, become the transformative leaders the world needs, pursue careers as unique as they are and help shape the future with confidence.

EY offers graduate programmes within their four key business areas – Assurance, Consulting, EY-Parthenon and Tax – alongside opportunities for work experience, summer internships, and industrial placements. As motivated and passionate members of the organisation, interns and graduates will have a personal impact – no matter which area they join. EY provides the tools, networks, experiences and opportunities needed for graduates to shape their future with confidence. Successful applicants will receive dedicated, structured training, a careers counsellor, a buddy, as well as access to innovative technology.

Whether working from the office, a client site, or home, EY colleagues are encouraged to find their own ways to achieve the balance and flexibility they deserve, adapting to the future working world. EY believe that the ability to invite, leverage and learn from different perspectives is key to delivering for their clients.

Embark on a career adventure at EY – whether that's for two days, four weeks or three years – on one of their early career programmes. Discover the possibilities that await and join EY to shape a career with confidence.

### GRADUATE VACANCIES IN 2026
- ACCOUNTANCY
- CONSULTING
- FINANCE
- LAW
- TECHNOLOGY

### NUMBER OF VACANCIES
**1,000+ graduate jobs**

### LOCATIONS OF VACANCIES

### STARTING SALARY FOR 2026
**£Competitive**

### WORK EXPERIENCE
- INSIGHT COURSES
- DEGREE PLACEMENTS
- SUMMER INTERNSHIPS

### UNIVERSITY PROMOTIONS DURING 2025-2026
ABERDEEN, ASTON, BATH, BIRMINGHAM, BRISTOL, CAMBRIDGE, CARDIFF, DURHAM, EDINBURGH, EDINBURGH NAPIER, EXETER, GLASGOW, HERIOT-WATT, IMPERIAL COLLEGE LONDON, KING'S COLLEGE LONDON, LANCASTER, LEEDS, LEICESTER, LIVERPOOL, LOUGHBOROUGH, LONDON SCHOOL OF ECONOMICS, MANCHESTER, NEWCASTLE, NOTTINGHAM, OXFORD, QUEEN'S BELFAST, READING, ROBERT GORDON, SHEFFIELD, SOUTHAMPTON, ST ANDREWS, STRATHCLYDE, ULSTER, UNIVERSITY COLLEGE LONDON, WARWICK, YORK

*Please check with your university careers service for full details of EY's local promotions and events.*

### MINIMUM ENTRY REQUIREMENTS
*Relevant degree required for some roles.*

### APPLICATION DEADLINE
**September 2025 - June 2026**

### FURTHER INFORMATION
**www.Top100GraduateEmployers.com**
*Register now for the latest news, local promotions, work experience and graduate vacancies at EY.*

# Together, how can we shape the future with confidence?

Start your career adventure at EY and explore our range of undergraduate and graduate programmes.

When you join us, you'll make an impact from the get-go. You'll have the opportunity to make your mark on how we do business and help our clients evolve while being supported every step of the way.

We'll equip you with the skills, tools, networks and experiences you'll need to build a career you can truly be proud of.

**Discover the possibilities and your own potential at EY.**

ey.com/uk/earlycareers

Adeola
Audit Graduate, London

The better the question.
The better the answer.
The better the world works.

©2025 Ernst & Young LLP. All rights reserved. ED None.

# EY

Shape the future with confidence

# forvis mazars

**careers-uk.forvismazars.com/jobs/early-careers**

Forvis Mazars in the UK [f]  mcareers@mazars.co.uk [✉]
linkedin.com/company/forvis-mazars-in-the-uk [in]
@lifeatforvismazarsuk [○]  @lifeatforvismazarsuk [♪]

Forvis Mazars is a leading global professional services network, operating in over 100 countries and territories with over 40,000 professionals and are committed to providing an unmatched client experience across audit & assurance, tax, advisory and consulting services.

Forvis Mazars has opportunities available in audit, tax and consulting for students and recent graduates. These roles are located across 13 of their UK offices, meaning there is an opportunity to suit every individual career pathway. Forvis Mazars offers undergraduates a 12-month placement, based in the UK. Both graduate and placement students are given a high level of responsibility, supporting on projects with prestigious clients. Placement students are also given the opportunity to start their professional qualifications, with the intention to return to Forvis Mazars on a graduate programme after university.

There are a range of internship opportunities available throughout the summer across various service lines in Forvis Mazars' UK offices. Interns receive professional skills training as well as working on real-life innovative and creative projects. Interns can also convert their internship to a graduate role. There are also in-person insight days for first year students to take part in.

Forvis Mazars offer excellent professional skills development and real responsibility from the start, with exposure to a variety of clients and dynamic projects across a range of industry sectors. Graduates at Forvis Mazars are provided with the opportunity to gain a professional qualification whilst earning a competitive salary and gaining invaluable industry experience. Forvis Mazars are known as an engine for rapid and consistent career progression, giving ambitious people the opportunity for early responsibility and exposure to an interesting and rewarding portfolio of work.

## GRADUATE VACANCIES IN 2026
- ACCOUNTANCY
- CONSULTING
- FINANCE
- TECHNOLOGY

### NUMBER OF VACANCIES
**250 graduate jobs**

### LOCATIONS OF VACANCIES

### STARTING SALARY FOR 2026
**£Competitive**

### WORK EXPERIENCE
INSIGHT COURSES | DEGREE PLACEMENTS | SUMMER INTERNSHIPS

### UNIVERSITY PROMOTIONS DURING 2025-2026
BATH, BIRMINGHAM, BOURNEMOUTH, BRISTOL, COVENTRY, DURHAM, EDINBURGH, EXETER, GLASGOW, LANCASTER, LEEDS, LEICESTER, LOUGHBOROUGH, LONDON SCHOOL OF ECONOMICS, MANCHESTER, NEWCASTLE, NOTTINGHAM, QUEEN MARY LONDON, ROYAL HOLLOWAY LONDON, SHEFFIELD, STRATHCLYDE, UNIVERSITY COLLEGE LONDON, WARWICK, YORK

*Please check with your university careers service for full details of Forvis Mazars' local promotions and events.*

### APPLICATION DEADLINE
**Year-round recruitment**

### FURTHER INFORMATION
www.Top100GraduateEmployers.com
*Register now for the latest news, local promotions, work experience and graduate vacancies at Forvis Mazars.*

**Laura**
Manager in Technology & Digital advisory

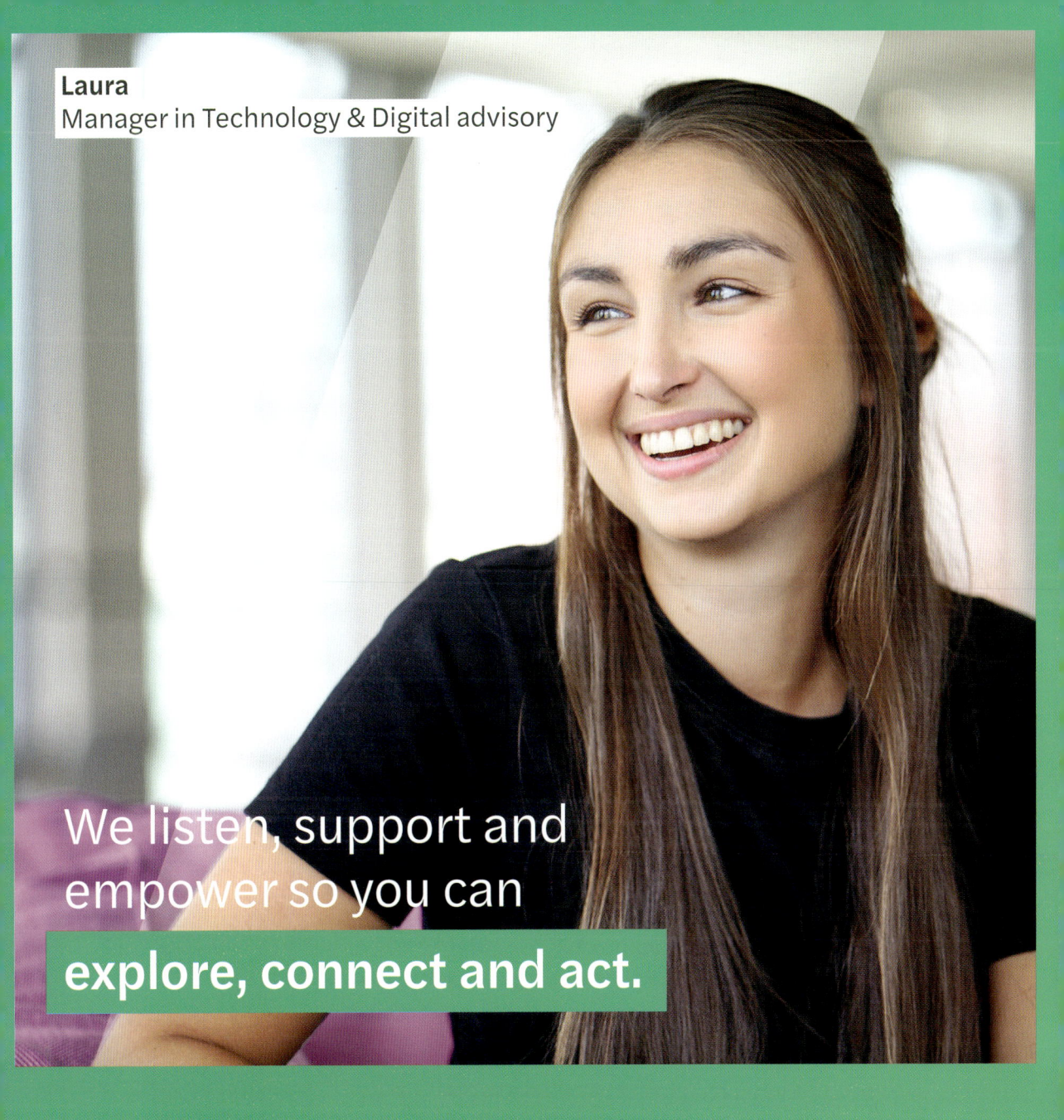

We listen, support and empower so you can **explore, connect and act.**

We are Forvis Mazars.

Grow.
　　**Belong.**
　　　　Impact.

forvismazars.com/uk

**forvis mazars**

# FRESHFIELDS

**freshfields.com/earlycareers**

ukearlycareers@freshfields.com

@freshfieldscareersuk

linkedin.com/company/freshfields

Freshfields is a leading law firm with a long-standing track record of advising the world's largest business and governments on ground-breaking legal issues. With over 2,800 lawyers across 33 offices, their teams bring together individuals with different experiences and skills to turn ambition into meaningful impact.

Freshfields' renowned trainee associate programme helps graduates shape their potential into progress through unrivalled training and experience with global clients.

Graduates rotate seats each three-months, gaining exposure to a range of practice areas including corporate, finance, and dispute resolution, and culminating in a six-month experience in a client or global network office. Collaborating with leading lawyers across Freshfields' global teams on high-profile, precedent-setting matters, trainees gain hands-on responsibility from day one. Working alongside Freshfields' innovation teams, including Freshfields Lab, they can drive legal tech, AI, and data solutions that give clients the edge.

Freshfields offers two schemes for students to explore a career in law: an insight scheme for first-year students and a paid vacation scheme for those further along. Open to all degree subjects, both schemes offer hands-on experience and a focus on growth and development to help clarify whether a legal career is the right path.

A tailored training journey takes students through learning modules aligned to a personal skills framework, plus technical sessions and AI-focused workshops prepare them for the evolving intersection of law and technology.

A strong focus on learning, the support of talented leaders and colleagues, and opportunities for hands-on experiences provide trainees with the knowledge and confidence to shape their ambition into impact.

## GRADUATE VACANCIES IN 2026
### LAW

**NUMBER OF VACANCIES**
Please check website for training contracts starting in 2028.

**LOCATIONS OF VACANCIES**

Vacancies also available in Europe, the USA and Asia.

**STARTING SALARY FOR 2026**
**£56,000**
Raising to £61,000 in 2nd year of Trainee Associate Programme, and a NQ salary of £150,000.

**WORK EXPERIENCE**
INSIGHT COURSES | SUMMER INTERNSHIPS

**UNIVERSITY PROMOTIONS DURING 2025-2026**
BIRMINGHAM, BRISTOL, CAMBRIDGE, DURHAM, EDINBURGH, EXETER, KENT, KING'S COLLEGE LONDON, LEEDS, LEICESTER, LIVERPOOL, LONDON SCHOOL OF ECONOMICS, MANCHESTER, NOTTINGHAM, NOTTINGHAM TRENT, OXFORD, QUEEN MARY LONDON, SOAS, UNIVERSITY COLLEGE LONDON, WARWICK
Please check with your university careers service for full details of Freshfields' local promotions and events.

**APPLICATION DEADLINE**
**Rolling recruitment**

**MINIMUM ENTRY REQUIREMENTS**
**2.1 Degree**

**FURTHER INFORMATION**
**www.Top100GraduateEmployers.com**
Register now for the latest news, local promotions, work experience and graduate vacancies at *Freshfields*.

# FRESHFIELDS

## Shape your ambition

A career at Freshfields isn't just a path
- it's a launchpad.

Here, you'll find opportunities, support and challenges that push you to new heights. You'll have the chance to do meaningful work that drives lasting impact, advising clients and shaping the future through innovation and collaboration.

**Explore opportunities:**

📷 @FreshfieldsCareersUK

in #ShapeYourAmbition

freshfields.com/earlycareers

# Google

**careers.google.com**

GoogleStudents
@GoogleStudents   linkedin.com/company/google
@GoogleStudents   youtube.com/GoogleStudents

Larry Page and Sergey Brin founded Google in September 1998 with a mission to organise the world's information and make it universally accessible and useful. Since then, Google has grown, and its parent company, Alphabet, has over 182,000 employees worldwide, with a wide range of popular products and platforms.

Google aims to solve problems for everyone, with everyone, and its employees (or "Googlers") build products that help create opportunities for people globally. They bring insight, imagination, and a passion for tackling challenges. It's the people who make Google the unique company it is.

Google hires individuals who are intelligent, driven, and determined, valuing ability over experience. They recruit graduates from diverse disciplines, from humanities and business to engineering and computer science. Ideal candidates demonstrate a passion for the online industry and have actively engaged in their university experience through clubs, societies, or relevant internships. Technical roles within engineering teams may require specific skills. Google have a dedicated page on their website to help applicants prepare for the hiring process, offering tips and key focus areas.

Whether it's providing online marketing consultancy, selling advertising solutions, recruiting new talent, or building products, Google offers full-time roles and internships across various teams, including global customer solutions, sales, people operations, legal, finance, operations, cloud, and engineering. Opportunities include their Associate Product Manager (APM) programme, Associate Product Marketing Manager programme (APMM), the BOLD internship programme, and Spark at Google. With programmes and internships across the globe, there are many opportunities to grow with Google and help create products and services used by billions.

## GRADUATE VACANCIES IN 2026
- CONSULTING
- ENGINEERING
- HUMAN RESOURCES
- MARKETING
- SALES
- TECHNOLOGY

## NUMBER OF VACANCIES
**No fixed quota**

## LOCATIONS OF VACANCIES
*Vacancies also available in Europe.*

## STARTING SALARY FOR 2026
**£Competitive**

## WORK EXPERIENCE
SUMMER INTERNSHIPS

## UNIVERSITY PROMOTIONS DURING 2025-2026
*Please check with your university careers service for full details of Google's local promotions and events.*

## MINIMUM ENTRY REQUIREMENTS
*Relevant degree required for some roles.*

## APPLICATION DEADLINE
**Year-round recruitment**

## FURTHER INFORMATION
www.Top100GraduateEmployers.com
*Register now for the latest news, local promotions, work experience and graduate vacancies at Google.*

# Google

At Google, we create products that make a meaningful difference for billions of users around the world. Interested in joining? Learn more about our roles, hiring process, application tips, scholarship opportunities, and more!

Careers.Google.com

# Grant Thornton

grantthornton.co.uk/early-careers

traineerecruitment@uk.gt.com
@gt_trainees | linkedin.com/company/grant-thornton-uk
@grantthorntonuk | youtube.com/UKGrantThornton

Grant Thornton UK is part of a global network of professional services firms, spanning 140+ countries. In the UK, 5,000+ people work across 23 offices, collaborating with dynamic businesses, communities and individuals to help them make a real impact.

The three-year graduate programme is more than a route to qualification – it's a launchpad for a fulfilling career in audit, tax or advisory. With guidance and insight from subject-matter experts and a career coach, trainees get real-world experience, innovative skills, and exposure to exciting projects and clients.

For students in their penultimate or sandwich-year, their summer internships and 12-month placements give a hands-on introduction to professional services and life at the firm – an introduction that can offer a fast-track to a graduate programme. Returning placement students are also eligible for an accelerated training agreement, where they can qualify up to six months earlier than their standard graduate programmes.

Grant Thornton looks beyond grades and assesses potential not only through exam performance, but also by considering curiosity, motivation, and alignment with the firm's values. With new technology, evolving markets and shifting client needs in accounting, the firm is looking for bright minds to challenge the status quo, contribute to change, and shape what comes next.

From early client exposure, real responsibility and access to senior business leaders, trainees are given the tools and opportunities to thrive. Once qualified, trainees can explore new business areas, progress within their teams, or even work abroad at one of the firm's global member firms.

With a culture grounded in their values of being purposefully driven, actively curious and candid but kind, their future is bright – and so are their graduates'.

## GRADUATE VACANCIES IN 2026
- ACCOUNTANCY
- FINANCE
- TECHNOLOGY

## NUMBER OF VACANCIES
**200 graduate jobs**

## LOCATIONS OF VACANCIES

## STARTING SALARY FOR 2026
**£Competitive**

## WORK EXPERIENCE
- INSIGHT COURSES
- DEGREE PLACEMENTS
- SUMMER INTERNSHIPS

## UNIVERSITY PROMOTIONS DURING 2025-2026
ASTON, BATH, BIRMINGHAM, BOURNEMOUTH, BRIGHTON, BRISTOL, CAMBRIDGE, CARDIFF, COVENTRY, DERBY, DURHAM, EDINBURGH, ESSEX, EXETER, HULL, KENT, KING'S COLLEGE LONDON, LEEDS, LEICESTER, LIVERPOOL, LONDON SCHOOL OF ECONOMICS, MANCHESTER, NOTTINGHAM, NOTTINGHAM TRENT, OXFORD, READING, ROYAL HOLLOWAY LONDON, SOUTHAMPTON, SURREY, SWANSEA, WARWICK, WEST OF ENGLAND, WINCHESTER

*Please check with your university careers service for full details of Grant Thornton's local promotions and events.*

## APPLICATION DEADLINE
**Year-round recruitment**

## FURTHER INFORMATION
www.Top100GraduateEmployers.com
*Register now for the latest news, local promotions, work experience and graduate vacancies at Grant Thornton.*

# Grant Thornton

# Our future's bright.
# Yours should be, too.

**We're shaping the future of accountancy – and we want you to join us.**

Accountancy is evolving – and so are we. We need curious, digital-first thinkers ready to challenge convention and spark real change.

Our trainees get support from expert mentors, a people manager and a career coach, enabling them to do challenging and meaningful work from day one.

And we know everyone deserves to thrive. We're a firm built on inclusion and purpose, where you'll be empowered to make a real impact.

*23 OFFICES*

## Programmes

Graduate programmes    Internships

12-month placements

## Careers in

Audit    Advisory    Tax

**Discover more**

*5,000+ PEOPLE*

© 2025 Grant Thornton UK LLP and Grant Thornton UK Advisory & Tax LLP. All rights reserved.

Grant Thornton UK LLP and Grant Thornton UK Advisory & Tax LLP are member firms of Grant Thornton International Ltd (GTIL). GTIL and the member firms are not a worldwide partnership. Services are delivered by the member firms. GTIL does not provide services to clients. GTIL and its member firms are not agents of, and do not obligate, one another and are not liable for one another's acts or omissions. Please see grantthornton.co.uk for further details. DTSK-10841

# HM Revenue & Customs

**civil-service-careers.gov.uk/hmrc-tax-specialist-programme**

tsprecruitmentteam@hmrc.gov.uk
@hmrcgovuk  linkedin.com/company/hmrc
@HMRCcareers  HMRCcareers

**GRADUATE VACANCIES IN 2026**
- ACCOUNTANCY
- FINANCE
- LAW

**NUMBER OF VACANCIES**
500 graduate jobs

**LOCATIONS OF VACANCIES**

**STARTING SALARY FOR 2026**
£36,000

**UNIVERSITY PROMOTIONS DURING 2025-2026**
*Please check with your university careers service for full details of HMRC's local promotions and events.*

**MINIMUM ENTRY REQUIREMENTS**
2.2 Degree

**APPLICATION DEADLINE**
20th October 2025

**FURTHER INFORMATION**
www.Top100GraduateEmployers.com
*Register now for the latest news, local promotions, work experience and graduate vacancies at **HMRC**.*

HMRC is one of the UK's largest organisations with over 66,000 employees, collecting the money that powers public services. Their flagship graduate Tax Specialist Programme delivers industry-recognised training from a world-leading tax authority, with an above-market starting salary and guaranteed career progression.

The Tax Specialist Programme is a standout career opportunity for ambitious graduates ready to shape the nation's future while building their own. This comprehensive 3-4 year graduate programme offers high quality training and on-the-job learning, enabling trainees to build practical skills to resolve high-stakes tax disputes, lead teams, and interact with senior business figures. With opportunities nationwide across fourteen regional centres, the programme welcomes graduates from all degree disciplines, with or without prior tax knowledge. HMRC are looking for analytical thinkers and problem solvers committed to becoming the future leaders in ensuring money is collected fairly and effectively, supporting the services that millions rely on every day.

All Tax Specialist Programme trainees complete an immersive learning journey led by HMRC's in-house expert trainers. The programme provides structured learning that builds technical expertise, leadership capabilities, and professional skills combining theoretical knowledge with practical application through hands-on casework.

Graduates work directly on cases that shape the nation's financial landscapes making an impact every day. They contribute to high-stakes tax disputes, conduct compliance checks, and work across different areas of tax. HMRC's inclusive environment empowers people of all ages, cultures, and backgrounds to develop their skills, knowledge, and experience.

# HM Revenue & Customs

# Start with us, grow with us.

Secure your future with HMRC's **Tax Specialist Programme.**

Join us to shape the nation's future while building your own. Gain financial security, expert training from a world leading tax authority, and the pride of funding vital public services.

With HMRC's Tax Specialist Programme, your growth isn't just a possibility, but a guarantee, mapped out from day one!

**Starting salary of at least £36,000.** — 1

2 — A 3 to 4 year programme to become an expert in tax.

3 — **Completion salary of at least £56,000.**

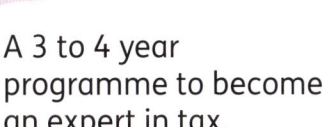

## Scan the QR to learn more

## Follow us

- HMRCcareers
- HMRCcareers
- company/hmrc
- hmrcgovuk

> **The community at HMRC is fantastic.**
> You're never alone, there's always someone to turn to for advice or expertise. Our managers are there to provide the support you need to ensure you're on the right track.
>
> Kyra, Tax Specialist Programme trainee

# Hogan Lovells

ukearlycareers.hoganlovells.com
ukearlycareers@hoganlovells.com
@hoganlovellsearlycareers
linkedin.com/company/hoganlovells
@hoganlovellsearlycareers.uk
youtube.com/@HoganLovells

With the combined talent of 2,800+ lawyers spanning six continents and 35 offices, Hogan Lovells bring a world of relevant experience to every matter. They empower people to make innovative choices that drive progress, and make meaningful contributions to clients and society.

Hogan Lovells understand that finding the right firm is one of the most important decisions graduates make at the start of their legal careers. This is why they continue to offer opportunities to students looking to get to know the firm. From vacation schemes to insight events, law fairs, webinars, workshops, and more, all their opportunities are packed with insight and practical experience. Students will meet Hogan Lovells lawyers, delve into broad practice groups and high-profile projects, develop their own commercial awareness, and learn more about the role of a trainee solicitor.

The firm's two-year training contract focuses on practical hands-on learning guided by experienced colleagues. Trainees develop a deep understanding of Hogan Lovells' bold and distinctive approach to collaborating to create valuable global solutions, as they learn from a diverse network of industry leading lawyers. Trainees do four six-month seats across different practice groups – corporate and finance, global regulatory and intellectual property, media and technology, litigation arbitration, and employment. Plus, for one of those seats, they will have the chance to apply for an international or client secondment.

Regardless of background or chosen path, Hogan Lovells provide graduates with opportunities to grow their legal acumen, sharpen their commercial edge, and tackle real challenges presented by major global clients. With support, mentoring and encouragement at every stage, Hogan Lovells provide an exceptional platform for graduates to build skills for now and their future.

## GRADUATE VACANCIES IN 2026
LAW

**NUMBER OF VACANCIES**
**50 graduate jobs**
For training contracts starting in 2028.

**LOCATIONS OF VACANCIES**

**STARTING SALARY FOR 2026**
**£56,000**

**WORK EXPERIENCE**
INSIGHT COURSES | SUMMER INTERNSHIPS

**UNIVERSITY PROMOTIONS DURING 2025-2026**
BIRMINGHAM, BRISTOL, CAMBRIDGE, DURHAM, EXETER, KENT, KING'S COLLEGE LONDON, LEEDS, LEICESTER, LONDON SCHOOL OF ECONOMICS, NOTTINGHAM, OXFORD, QUEEN MARY LONDON, UNIVERSITY COLLEGE LONDON, WARWICK
*Please check with your university careers service for full details of Hogan Lovells' local promotions and events.*

**MINIMUM ENTRY REQUIREMENTS**
**2.1 Degree**

**APPLICATION DEADLINE**
**Year-round recruitment**

**FURTHER INFORMATION**
www.Top100GraduateEmployers.com
*Register now for the latest news, local promotions, work experience and graduate vacancies at Hogan Lovells.*

# Define your Future.

## The power to shape your future, and ours.

**Hogan Lovells**

- £56k trainee starting salary
- 2,800+ colleagues worldwide
- 63 FTSE 100 clients
- 35+ offices across 18 countries
- 54% of our work involves 3+ countries
- 150,000+ pro bono hours per year
- +50% of UK Partners trained at the firm
- 70 vacation scheme places and 50 training contracts a year

Meet us at ukearlycareers.hoganlovells.com

www.hoganlovells.com
© Hogan Lovells 2024. All rights reserved. BT-REQ-3864

# HSBC

hsbc.com/careers/students-and-graduates

uk.graduaterecruitment@hsbc.com
@lifeathsbc
linkedin.com/company/hsbc
hsbccareers
youtube.com/lifeatHSBC

**HSBC is one of the world's largest financial organisations. Worldwide, they have over 200,000 employees serving around 41 million customers across 58 countries, who range from individuals to some of the world's largest organisations, financial and government institutions.**

HSBC are interested in skills, not subject studied. They look at who the applicant is to make sure the programme they're applying for matches their unique qualities. HSBC teach them all the technical skills to succeed and give them the tools to build a long, exciting career. Whether they're suited for a role in relationship management, trading, investment banking, software engineering, cyber or data analytics, HSBC's structured support and development programmes will ensure they don't just reach their goals, they go beyond them.

Opportunities are open to applicants from all degree disciplines, and HSBC have programmes based across the UK. Use their online skills matcher tool on their graduate careers website to discover where a career at HSBC could lead. They offer insight programmes, internships, and industrial placement opportunities, which are the perfect way to prepare to join them on a graduate programme. Participants will begin to develop skills that will open doors to a long and varied career and build relationships with a network of colleagues.

Participants will develop technical and behavioural skills needed to succeed as a graduate and beyond, learn from world-class professionals and work on live, business-critical projects. Their impact will be felt from day one. HSBC's mentor and buddy schemes, networking and wellbeing initiatives provide support. With opportunities to work on cross-bank initiatives and projects outside of day-to-day responsibilities, participants continue to grow – broadening their horizons and developing future-ready skills that will take them in multiple directions.

## GRADUATE VACANCIES IN 2026
FINANCE
GENERAL MANAGEMENT
INVESTMENT BANKING
TECHNOLOGY

**NUMBER OF VACANCIES**
600+ graduate jobs

**LOCATIONS OF VACANCIES**

*Vacancies also available in Asia and elsewhere in the world.*

**STARTING SALARY FOR 2026**
£Competitive
*Plus bonuses.*

**WORK EXPERIENCE**
INSIGHT COURSES | DEGREE PLACEMENTS | SUMMER INTERNSHIPS

**UNIVERSITY PROMOTIONS DURING 2025-2026**
ASTON, BATH, BIRMINGHAM, BRISTOL, CAMBRIDGE, CARDIFF, EDINBURGH, EXETER, GLASGOW, IMPERIAL COLLEGE LONDON, KING'S COLLEGE LONDON, LEEDS, LEICESTER, LOUGHBOROUGH, LONDON SCHOOL OF ECONOMICS, MANCHESTER, OXFORD, SHEFFIELD, SHEFFIELD HALLAM, SUSSEX, SWANSEA, UNIVERSITY COLLEGE LONDON, WARWICK, YORK
*Please check with your university careers service for full details of HSBC's local promotions and events.*

**MINIMUM ENTRY REQUIREMENTS**
2.1 Degree

**APPLICATION DEADLINE**
September 2025 - December 2025

**FURTHER INFORMATION**
www.Top100GraduateEmployers.com
*Register now for the latest news, local promotions, work experience and graduate vacancies at HSBC.*

# It's where you want to be, not have to be

At HSBC we give you the support
you need step by step, to grow and grow.
**Apply now at hsbc.com/careers**

**HSBC** | Opening up a world of opportunity

# IBM

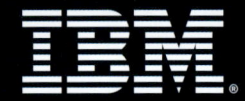

**ibm.com/uk-en/careers/search**

linkedin.com/company/ibm
@lifeatibm
youtube.com/ibm

With operations in over 170 countries, IBM is a different kind of technology company. Restlessly reinventing since 1911, they're not only one of the largest corporate organisations in the world, but also one of the biggest technology and consulting employers, with many Fortune 50 companies relying on IBM Cloud.

Successful candidates join IBM as full-time sales professionals through the Sales Accelerator Program. The first 12 months will be a learning journey. After a 12-month strategic career launch, there is a transition to the next step. IBM's career paths match candidates' passions. The Digital Sales roles start in cities like Valencia, Spain or Dublin.

In Client Engineering, graduates work side by side with clients to co-create tech prototypes and build Minimum Viable Products. This path is for problem solvers who want to be close to tech without needing to code. The Customer Success Manager guides clients through their digital transformation.

IBM are looking for recent graduates, ready to launch a long-term career in tech sales. Ideal candidates will be curious and driven learners, who thrive with structure, mentorship, and hands-on experience. Suited to the roles are tech-interested communicators, who can translate innovation into client value. IBM UK offers university undergraduates in their penultimate year a 12-month Industrial Placement or 12-Week Summer Placement in London. Students engage in technical sales roles across Data, AI & Automation.

The programme includes structured learning pathways, blending online and in-person sessions with expert-led workshops and seminars. Supported by a dual management structure, interns acquire the latest industry knowledge and practical skills. They emerge with enhanced technical and sales acumen, soft skills, a robust network, and a strong foundation for their future careers.

---

**GRADUATE VACANCIES IN 2026**
- SALES
- TECHNOLOGY

**NUMBER OF VACANCIES**
30+ graduate jobs

**LOCATIONS OF VACANCIES**

**STARTING SALARY FOR 2026**
£34,000 or €34,000
*Once completing initial sales training, applicants will then move on to a sales incentive plan with commission.*

**WORK EXPERIENCE**
- DEGREE PLACEMENTS
- SUMMER INTERNSHIPS

**UNIVERSITY PROMOTIONS DURING 2025-2026**
*Please check with your university careers service for full details of IBM's local promotions and events.*

**MINIMUM ENTRY REQUIREMENTS**
2.1 Degree

**APPLICATION DEADLINE**
Year-round recruitment

**FURTHER INFORMATION**
www.Top100GraduateEmployers.com
*Register now for the latest news, local promotions, work experience and graduate vacancies at IBM.*

# Take your career to the *next level.*

Find a career that makes a difference, where your skills could define a better world.

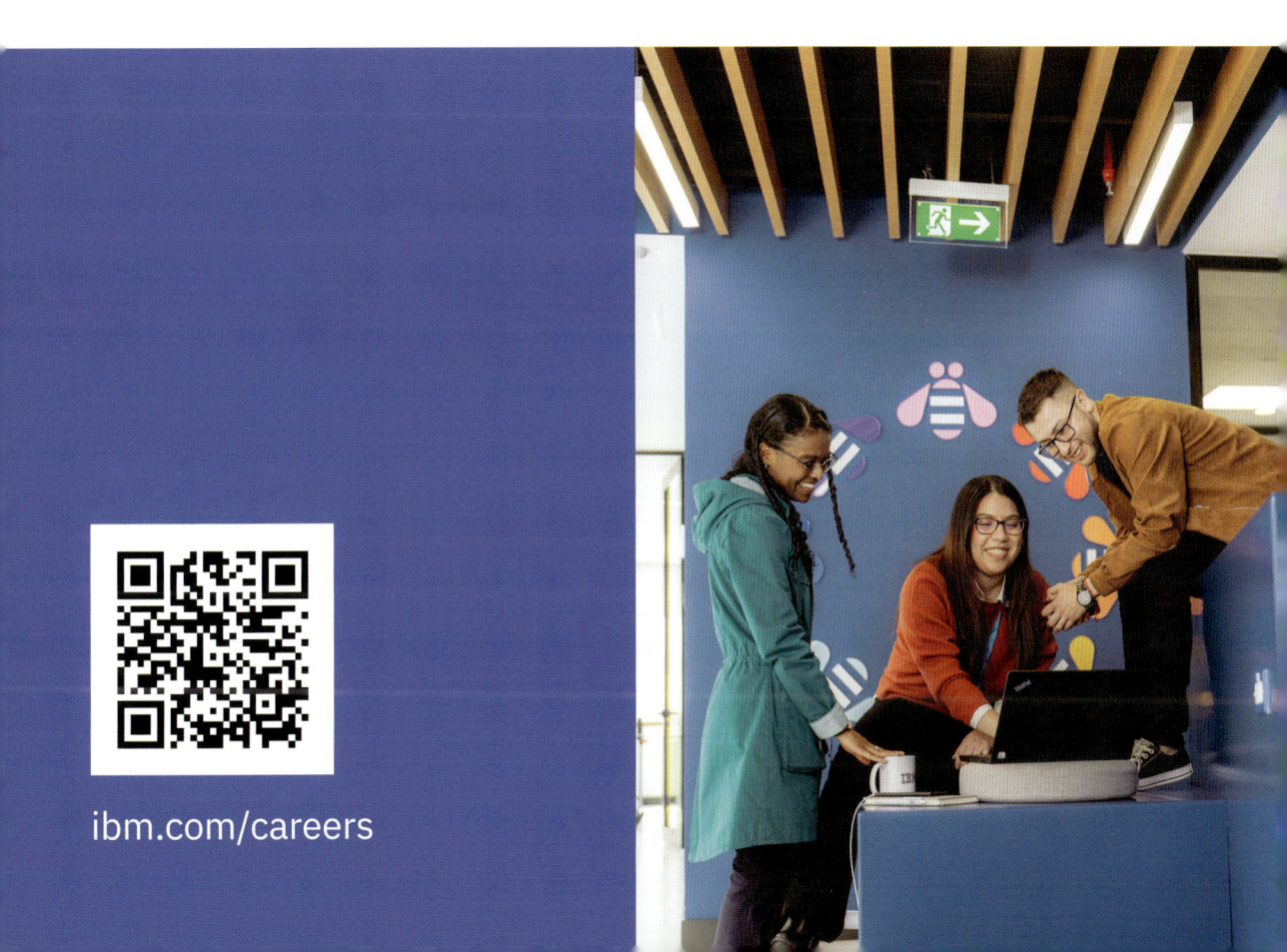

ibm.com/careers

# itv

**careers.itv.com/teams/early-careers**

@ITVCareers  ITVCareers
@CareersAtITV  linkedin.com/company/itv

ITV is a vertically integrated producer, broadcaster and streamer, consisting of ITV Studios and Media & Entertainment. ITV Studios is a scaled and global creator, owner and distributor of high-quality TV content. It operates in 13 countries, across 60+ labels and has a global distribution network.

ITV's strategic vision is to be a digitally led media and entertainment company that creates and brings its content to audiences wherever, whenever, and however they choose; this is aligned to its purpose to be More than TV.

ITV is the largest free-to-air commercial television network in the UK and is a leading creative force in global content production and distribution, with exciting opportunities for early careers talent.

The Technology Graduate Scheme is a two-year rotational programme working across areas such as software development, data, cyber security and video engineering. In the first year, participants will work within each of the business areas, attend structured training in a development language (Scala, Java or front-end) and do an extended placement with one of the software engineering teams.

A tailored blend of placements, projects and learning opportunities will provide a rounded foundation for a career in media technology and set participants up for a long-lasting career at ITV. They are looking for dynamic and driven people with an appetite for learning. Applicants may have, or be working towards, a science, maths or engineering degree, or have relevant suitable experience.

The ITV Academy offers a range of apprenticeships, traineeship schemes and programmes across the business and in different ITV locations over the country. These serve as entry-level pathways or are open to their own staff, ensuring further development and training is always available. There are also corporate roles in HR, finance, legal, marketing, comms and more.

## GRADUATE VACANCIES IN 2026
- ACCOUNTANCY
- FINANCE
- GENERAL MANAGEMENT
- HUMAN RESOURCES
- LAW
- MARKETING
- MEDIA
- RESEARCH & DEVELOPMENT
- SALES
- TECHNOLOGY

**NUMBER OF VACANCIES**
No fixed quota

**LOCATIONS OF VACANCIES**

**STARTING SALARY FOR 2026**
£Competitive
*Plus an annual bonus.*

**WORK EXPERIENCE**
INSIGHT COURSES | DEGREE PLACEMENTS | SUMMER INTERNSHIPS

**UNIVERSITY PROMOTIONS DURING 2025-2026**
*Please check with your university careers service for full details of ITV's local promotions and events.*

**MINIMUM ENTRY REQUIREMENTS**
2.2 Degree
*Relevant degree required for some roles.*

**FURTHER INFORMATION**
www.Top100GraduateEmployers.com
*Register now for the latest news, local promotions, work experience and graduate vacancies at ITV.*

# Build an incredible career – the ITV Way.

In their offices and studios, they love celebrating individuality and they're committed to creating an organisation where everyone feels included. This means building a diverse and creative team that represents everyone, that gives people the opportunity to thrive, and where everyone can feel valued.

**Find out why we are More than TV at itvjobs.com**

# JPMorganChase

jpmorganchase.com/careers#students

**GRADUATE VACANCIES IN 2026**
- ACCOUNTANCY
- FINANCE
- GENERAL MANAGEMENT
- HUMAN RESOURCES
- INVESTMENT BANKING
- TECHNOLOGY

**NUMBER OF VACANCIES**
450 graduate jobs

**LOCATIONS OF VACANCIES**

JPMorganChase is a global leader in financial services, providing strategic advice and products to the world's most prominent corporations, governments, wealthy individuals and institutional investors. Their first-class business in a first-class way approach to serving clients drives everything they do.

JPMorganChase's full-time programmes are available to undergraduate, postgraduate and PhD-level candidates and run from 24 to 36 months, depending on the role. They offer a wide range of programmes across their entire business in areas such as: Markets, Investment Banking, Software Engineering, Corporate Functions. Successful candidates will join global teams committed to their success and be part of a fast-paced work environment that's constantly challenging them to learn and develop.

JPMorganChase offer a range of programmes including work experience, apprenticeships, pre-internships and internships. Their internship programmes are designed to help interns explore the firm and gain hands-on work experience before applying for one of their full-time roles. Their apprenticeships allow apprentices to experience the best of both worlds by having the opportunity to work on projects that impact the firm, with time set aside to complete their course. The work experience programmes offer insights into career possibilities and inspire students to see what role might be right for them.

Graduates and interns can set their career in motion through mentorship programmes, networking opportunities and chances to connect with colleagues dedicated to their success. The internships and early career programmes are designed with professional growth in mind. They offer the opportunity to contribute to meaningful projects and gain significant experiences while working towards helping businesses, people and communities grow.

**UNIVERSITY PROMOTIONS DURING 2025-2026**
*Please check with your university careers service for full details of JPMorganChase's local promotions and events.*

**STARTING SALARY FOR 2026**
£Competitive

**APPLICATION DEADLINE**
2nd November 2025

**FURTHER INFORMATION**
www.Top100GraduateEmployers.com
*Register now for the latest news, local promotions, work experience and graduate vacancies at JPMorganChase.*

# Find a career that fits you.

We're looking for students from all backgrounds to help us create innovative solutions for clients, customers and communities.

**We can't wait to watch you grow in your career.**

©2025 JPMorgan Chase & Co. All rights reserved. JPMorgan Chase & Co. is an Equal Opportunity Employer, including Disability/Veterans.

JPMorganChase

# KPMG

**kpmgcareers.co.uk**

KPMGRecruitment (f)  graduate@kpmg.co.uk
@kpmgukcareers (Instagram)  linkedin.com/company/kpmg-uk/
@kpmgukcareers (TikTok)  youtube.com/@KPMGUKCareers

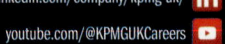

KPMG work across advisory, audit, consulting, technology, tax and law. Their clients span a range of industries, and their work covers everything from environment and social governance, to innovating with AI and improving healthcare. KPMG provide opportunities for growth and building skills for life.

KPMG's graduate programmes are designed to build solid foundations in a supportive, collaborative environment, while gaining a professional qualification. Programmes span audit, consulting, tax and technology. Audit is KPMG's biggest practice, helping to build trust in businesses and the economy. All graduates will work with clients from day one to transform businesses, find innovative solutions, and understand the commercial world.

For undergraduates, KPMG offers insight programmes, available for students from lower socioeconomic backgrounds, Black Heritage, or disabilities. These paid opportunities include a final assessment, guaranteeing participants a place on their chosen programme for the following year.

Careers at KPMG encourage growth, learning and development as graduates become experienced professionals in their field. Over three to four years, graduates are exposed to various clients, projects and opportunities. Working with senior leaders and owning their work, graduates are supported across their work life, and encouraged to forge their own path at the firm.

There are lots of opportunities to get involved with KPMG employee networks and volunteering initiatives, from office netball, to celebrating Pride Month, to volunteering in the community.

KPMG looks for graduates from all degree backgrounds. Those who are resilient, curious, and have an eye for detail will get the opportunity to thrive in a successful career and really make the difference.

## GRADUATE VACANCIES IN 2026
- ACCOUNTANCY
- CONSULTING
- TECHNOLOGY

**NUMBER OF VACANCIES**
1,000 graduate jobs

**LOCATIONS OF VACANCIES**

**STARTING SALARY FOR 2026**
£Competitive

**WORK EXPERIENCE**
- DEGREE PLACEMENTS
- SUMMER INTERNSHIPS

**UNIVERSITY PROMOTIONS DURING 2025-2026**
ABERDEEN, ASTON, BIRMINGHAM, BRIGHTON, BRISTOL, BRUNEL, CARDIFF, CITY, COVENTRY, EAST ANGLIA, ESSEX, GLASGOW, GLASGOW CALEDONIAN, HERIOT-WATT, KING'S COLLEGE LONDON, LEEDS, LIVERPOOL, LIVERPOOL JOHN MOORES, MANCHESTER, NEWCASTLE, NORTHUMBRIA, NOTTINGHAM, NOTTINGHAM TRENT, PLYMOUTH, READING, ROBERT GORDON, ROYAL HOLLOWAY LONDON, SHEFFIELD HALLAM, SOUTHAMPTON, STIRLING, STRATHCLYDE, SURREY, SWANSEA

*Please check with your university careers service for full details of KPMG's local promotions and events.*

**MINIMUM ENTRY REQUIREMENTS**
2.1 Degree

**APPLICATION DEADLINE**
Year-round recruitment

**FURTHER INFORMATION**
www.Top100GraduateEmployers.com
*Register now for the latest news, local promotions, work experience and graduate vacancies at KPMG.*

# Deepak, Ali & Elena

## got the 26 bus moving on time.

Come and make a real-world difference, like Deepak, Ali & Elena, on a KPMG graduate programme.

**Apply to 2026 graduate roles at**
**kpmgcareers.co.uk/graduate**

# L'ORÉAL
## UK & IRELAND

careers.loreal.com/en_US/content/UK

@lorealgroupe · linkedin.com/company/loréal

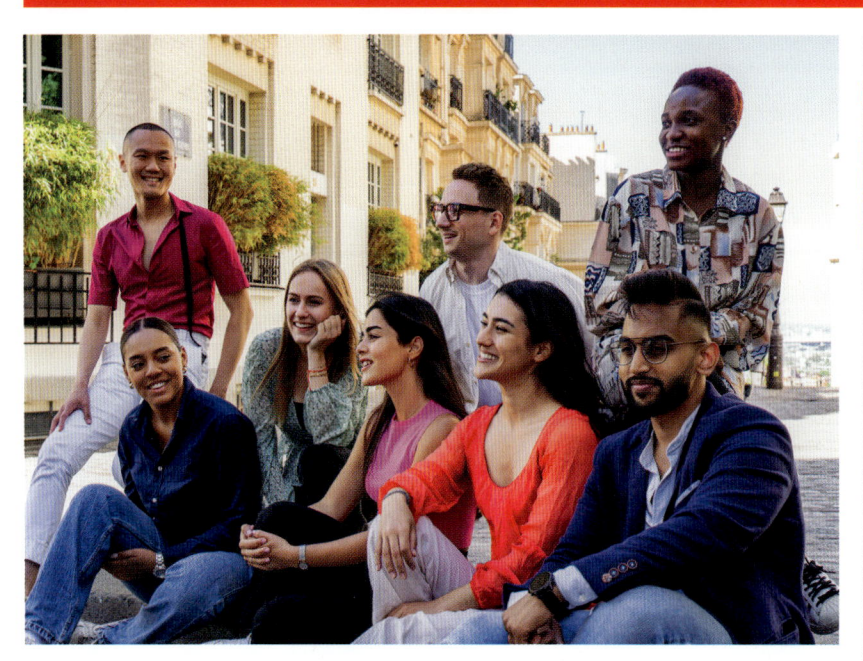

L'Oréal Groupe is the world's number one beauty company, with a portfolio of 40 international brands. Their goal is to offer each and every person around the world the best of beauty in terms of quality, efficacy, safety, sincerity, and responsibility, to satisfy all beauty needs and desires in their infinite diversity.

L'Oréal UK & Ireland, the leading player in the multi-billion pound beauty industry in the UK, look for an entrepreneurial mindset in their graduates. They believe in developing their people from the ground up, providing their employees with the opportunity to grow within the company, develop a broad future focused skill set and build a dynamic career. As a result, a portion of graduate roles are filled by talents from their Internship and Spring Insights Programs, creating a future focused early careers journey at L'Oréal. The remainder of the graduate roles are sourced from the external market, to ensure an equal opportunity for all candidates to join this exciting business.

On the Management Trainee Program, they will work in different functions and brands across the business, gaining multiple perspectives of life at L'Oréal. With three different rotations in their chosen stream, graduates are free to develop their strengths and discover new possibilities, shaping their future career as they go. With development programmes and their own mentor, graduates will progress into operational roles in as little as 18 months.

L'Oréal is committed to being one of the top employers in the UK, fostering a workplace where everyone feels welcomed and valued. Promoting gender equality, driving diversity and inclusion, addressing mental health, and establishing evolving workplace practices are a key focus. Through 'L'Oréal for the Future', their global sustainability programme, the business is driving change across all areas including product design, supply chain and consumer behaviour.

**GRADUATE VACANCIES IN 2026**
- FINANCE
- GENERAL MANAGEMENT
- HUMAN RESOURCES
- MARKETING
- PURCHASING
- SALES

**NUMBER OF VACANCIES**
40+ graduate jobs

**LOCATIONS OF VACANCIES**

**STARTING SALARY FOR 2026**
£35,000

**WORK EXPERIENCE**
- INSIGHT COURSES
- DEGREE PLACEMENTS
- SUMMER INTERNSHIPS

**UNIVERSITY PROMOTIONS DURING 2025-2026**
Please check with your university careers service for full details of L'Oréal's local promotions and events.

**APPLICATION DEADLINE**
15th September - 15th November 2025

**FURTHER INFORMATION**
www.Top100GraduateEmployers.com
Register now for the latest news, local promotions, work experience and graduate vacancies at *L'Oréal*.

# FREEDOM TO GO BEYOND, THAT'S THE BEAUTY OF L'ORÉAL.

L'ORÉAL

Our brands, dynamic culture, and a mindset of always being our own challenger, mean that we offer autonomy and opportunities you won't get anywhere else.

**At L'Oréal UK and Ireland you are trusted to succeed.**

Graduate and Internship opportunities at:
CAREERS.LOREAL.COM

# LATHAM & WATKINS

lw.com

@lathamwatkins
youtube.com/@lathamwatkinsglobal
AssociateRecruiting.Graduate.LO@lw.com
linkedin.com/company/latham-&-watkins

Latham & Watkins is one of the leading global law firms, advising businesses and institutions that drive the global economy. They lead the market in major financial centres and offer unmatched expertise and resources to help graduates grow from intellectually curious self-starters into exceptional lawyers.

The two-year training contract combines real responsibility on global matters with supervision from world-class lawyers who foster professional development. Trainees rotate through four practice areas, gaining experience in commercial law, including both corporate and finance. In their second year, trainees can apply for secondments, with both client and international options on offer.

Latham & Watkins runs two vacation schemes over the academic year for applicants to get to know the firm and life as a trainee lawyer. Throughout the scheme, participants gain insight into two practice areas, participating in client calls, court visits, Q&As and training sessions, group work and social events. These schemes equip participants with a sense of the kind of lawyer they want to become, and afterwards participants can interview for a training contract.

Latham & Watkins invest in growing their people and preparing them for the next stage of their careers. All trainees are supported through the Solicitors Qualifying Exam (SQE), which involves a one-year preparatory course that the firm sponsors. Trainees are provided with a £20,000 maintenance to cover the SQE. Non-law students are sponsored to complete the Postgraduate Diploma in Law (PGDL), and given a further £20,000 to cover the PGDL if required.

Upon joining, trainees benefit from a two-week induction to bridge the gap between law school and practice, and department specific training with every new seat. The training and career enhancement combines personal mentoring, career coaching, and hands-on learning with rigorous education.

## GRADUATE VACANCIES IN 2026
LAW

### NUMBER OF VACANCIES
**32 graduate jobs**
*For training contracts starting in 2028.*

### LOCATIONS OF VACANCIES

### STARTING SALARY FOR 2026
**£60,000**

### WORK EXPERIENCE
INSIGHT COURSES | DEGREE PLACEMENTS | SUMMER INTERNSHIPS

### APPLICATION DEADLINE
*Please see website for full details.*

### UNIVERSITY PROMOTIONS DURING 2025-2026
BIRMINGHAM, BRISTOL, BATH, CAMBRIDGE, CARDIFF, DURHAM, EXETER, KING'S COLLEGE LONDON, LEEDS, LIVERPOOL, LONDON SCHOOL OF ECONOMICS, MANCHESTER, NOTTINGHAM, OXFORD, QUEEN MARY, UNIVERSITY COLLEGE LONDON, WARWICK, YORK
*Please check with your university careers service for full details of Latham & Watkins' local promotions and events.*

### MINIMUM ENTRY REQUIREMENTS
**2.1 Degree**

### FURTHER INFORMATION
**www.Top100GraduateEmployers.com**
*Register now for the latest news, local promotions, work experience and graduate vacancies at **Latham & Watkins**.*

# Access a limitless network of expertise

Latham & Watkins is one of the world's leading global law firms advising the businesses and institutions that drive the global economy. We are the market leaders in major financial and business centers globally and offer unmatched expertise and resources to help you grow from an intellectually curious self-starter into an exceptional lawyer. If you aspire to be the best, this is where you belong. Explore more at lwcareers.com.

## WHERE AMBITION MEETS EXCELLENCE

### LATHAM&WATKINS

# Lidl

lidlearlycareers.co.uk

Lidl is a global supermarket leader, known for their quality products and low prices. With a fresh approach to food retail and commitment to customers, Lidl also offer the best graduate programmes in the business – giving ambitious grads the chance to make their mark.

Lidl grads get stuck in from day one, learning the ropes across the business. They'll take on real responsibility, learn fast, and build the kind of experience that sets them up for a big future.

Whether it's working in Lidl's stores, warehouses, or offices, every grad gets a proper look at how Lidl runs – and how they can make an impact. They pick up the skills, knowledge, and confidence to lead teams in a fast-paced, hands-on environment – helping them become an expert on all things Lidl.

There's also plenty of structure and support along the way. Lidl grads learn from people who know the business inside out, gaining insight from the experienced leaders who have been there and done it. They're trusted to make decisions, solve problems, and drive things forward – all while building a career to be proud of.

With over 980 stores and 14 warehouses across the UK, grad opportunities are truly nationwide – including head office roles in Tolworth, Southwest London. Lidl are looking for sharp thinkers and future leaders from all walks of life, because it's what makes their teams unique.

For grads who are ready to work hard, learn loads, and make things happen, Lidl is the perfect place to kickstart careers. Plus, graduates get all the perks they deserve - including a £40,000 salary, 30 days holiday per year, a 10% in-store discount, and much more.

There has never been a better time to become a Lidl grad.

**GRADUATE VACANCIES IN 2026**
GENERAL MANAGEMENT
LOGISTICS
PROPERTY
PURCHASING
RETAIL

**NUMBER OF VACANCIES**
30-50 graduate jobs

**LOCATIONS OF VACANCIES**

**STARTING SALARY FOR 2026**
£40,000

**UNIVERSITY PROMOTIONS DURING 2025-2026**
LOUGHBOROUGH, SURREY
*Please check with your university careers service for full details of Lidl's local promotions and events.*

**MINIMUM ENTRY REQUIREMENTS**
2.2 Degree

**APPLICATION DEADLINE**
October - November 2025

**FURTHER INFORMATION**
www.Top100GraduateEmployers.com
*Register now for the latest news, local promotions, work experience and graduate vacancies at Lidl.*

# Step into our world

**LIDL**

Our graduate programmes do more than teach the basics - they set you up for success. Whether you see a future in our stores, warehouses, or offices, we'll give you the tools to thrive at Lidl.

**Find your place at lidlearlycareers.co.uk**

# Linklaters

careers.linklaters.com

trainee.recruitment@linklaters.com
@linklaterscareersuk
@linklaterscareersuk
linkedin.com/company/linklaters
youtube.com/linklaterscareers

Unlike many law firms, Linklaters has consistent, market-leading global teams across the full range of practice areas within corporate law. Wherever their lawyers focus, they are involved in the most interesting and dynamic work. Linklaters provides its people with the opportunity to shape their careers from day one.

With 30 offices across 20 countries, Linklaters lawyers act for the world's leading corporates, banks, funds, governments and non-profit organisations on their most complex and challenging assignments. As a truly global business, they solve unique problems and provide exceptional development opportunities.

When people join Linklaters, they find colleagues they want to work with in a truly high performance culture. Linklaters has inspiring and personable professionals who are generous with their time and always happy to help. Their success is built on working together and they look for individuals who will collaborate and innovate to deliver the smartest solutions for clients.

Linklaters recruits candidates from a range of different backgrounds and disciplines, not just law, because those candidates bring with them a set of unique skills and perspectives that can help to challenge conventional thinking and inspire different approaches to client problems.

Over two years, trainees rotate through four seats (placements) in different practice areas, with most trainees going on international or client secondments. Linklaters are committed to providing world-class training and practical experience, alongside support, mentorship and coaching. They offer a fully rounded programme to rapidly develop understanding of commercial law.

Attend an insight event, join a diversity and access programme, participate in a vacation scheme or start as a trainee solicitor, and graduates will find Linklaters offers outstanding, career-long opportunities.

## GRADUATE VACANCIES IN 2026
LAW

### NUMBER OF VACANCIES
**100 graduate jobs**
For training contracts starting in 2028.

### LOCATIONS OF VACANCIES

### STARTING SALARY FOR 2026
**£56,000**

### WORK EXPERIENCE
INSIGHT COURSES | DEGREE PLACEMENTS

### UNIVERSITY PROMOTIONS DURING 2025-2026
BIRMINGHAM, BRISTOL, CAMBRIDGE, CARDIFF, DURHAM, EDINBURGH, GLASGOW, IMPERIAL COLLEGE LONDON, KENT, KING'S COLLEGE LONDON, LANCASTER, LEEDS, LEICESTER, LIVERPOOL, LOUGHBOROUGH, LONDON SCHOOL OF ECONOMICS, MANCHESTER, NEWCASTLE, NOTTINGHAM, OXFORD, QUEEN MARY LONDON, QUEEN'S BELFAST, SHEFFIELD, SOAS, SOUTHAMPTON, SURREY, UNIVERSITY COLLEGE LONDON, WARWICK, YORK

*Please check with your university careers service for full details of Linklaters' local promotions and events.*

### MINIMUM ENTRY REQUIREMENTS
**2.1 Degree**

### APPLICATION DEADLINE
**3rd December 2025**

### FURTHER INFORMATION
**www.Top100GraduateEmployers.com**
*Register now for the latest news, local promotions, work experience and graduate vacancies at Linklaters.*

# Linklaters

## WHERE TALENT

## MEETS OPPORTUNITY

This is the place where talent meets opportunity, where ambition meets impact and where you start your future. Start your legal career with Linklaters.

**Find out more at careers.linklaters.com**

- LinkedIn – Linklaters
- Instagram – Linklaterscareersuk
- TikTok – Linklaterscareersuk
- Youtube – Linklaterscareers

# lloydsbankinggrouptalent.com

**LLOYDS BANKING GROUP**

@lbgearlytalent (Instagram)
linkedin.com/company/lloydsbankinggroup
lbgearlytalent (Facebook)
youtube.com/lloydsbankinggroupcareers

---

Lloyds Banking Group is the UK's largest digital bank - serving 28 million customers through household names like Lloyds Bank, Halifax, Bank of Scotland and Scottish Widows. With major hubs across the UK, the Group offers careers in tech, data, finance and more. Big brands. Big impact. No dull days.

Lloyds Banking Group offers graduate programmes built for people who want to get stuck in, think big and shape the future. Be at the heart of the bank's digital transformation. Programmes run across key regional hubs - including Leeds, Edinburgh, Bristol, Manchester and Birmingham - where grads work on real-world challenges from day one. That could mean innovating smarter tech, cracking complex datasets, protecting against evolving threats or rethinking how financial services supports lives. Open to all degree backgrounds, these opportunities are for ambitious minds, not perfect CVs. The pace is real. The work matters. And the opportunity? Bigger than most expect.

Summer internships and industrial placements are available across technology, engineering, data, finance, risk and more. Open to penultimate-year students, these placements go beyond the basics. They contribute to real projects with real responsibility - supported by expert mentors and colleagues. It's a high-energy, high-impact glimpse into a fast-moving organisation that's reshaping how millions bank, save and plan.

Structured development, professional qualifications, technical training and the opportunity to grow across specialisms over time come as standard at Lloyds Banking Group. This is a business that backs initiative, rewards progress and runs on ideas. Whether building a technical path or exploring new territory, grads are trusted to lead, learn and push things forward. All while shaping a career - and future - that actually means something.

---

### GRADUATE VACANCIES IN 2026
- ACCOUNTANCY
- FINANCE
- HUMAN RESOURCES
- INVESTMENT BANKING
- MARKETING
- TECHNOLOGY

### NUMBER OF VACANCIES
**250+ graduate jobs**

### LOCATIONS OF VACANCIES

### STARTING SALARY FOR 2026
**£42,000**

### WORK EXPERIENCE
- INSIGHT COURSES
- DEGREE PLACEMENTS
- SUMMER INTERNSHIPS

### UNIVERSITY PROMOTIONS DURING 2025-2026
ASTON, BATH, BIRMINGHAM, BRISTOL, CARDIFF, COVENTRY, DURHAM, EDINBURGH, EXETER, GLASGOW, GLASGOW CALEDONIAN, IMPERIAL COLLEGE LONDON, LEEDS, LIVERPOOL, MANCHESTER, NOTTINGHAM, OXFORD, SHEFFIELD HALLAM, ST ANDREWS, UNIVERSITY COLLEGE LONDON, WARWICK, YORK

*Please check with your university careers service for full details of Lloyds Banking Group's local promotions and events.*

### MINIMUM ENTRY REQUIREMENTS
**2.2 Degree**

### APPLICATION DEADLINE
**October - December 2025**

### FURTHER INFORMATION
**www.Top100GraduateEmployers.com**
*Register now for the latest news, local promotions, work experience and graduate vacancies at Lloyds Banking Group.*

# Bring your authentic self. Even your TikTok drafts

28 million people trust us to plan, protect and manage their finances, through brands including Lloyds Bank, Halifax, Bank of Scotland and Scottish Widows. Big names, big responsibilities.

And big opportunities for you. We're putting £3 billion into sharper systems, smarter services and people who bring all of themselves to the table. Creativity, curiosity, TikTok drafts and all.

Finance, Data Science, HR, Risk, Technology Engineering and so much more – whatever your interest and wherever you jump in, this is work that grows with you. Bring your energy and fresh thinking. You'll build skills that stick and see your ideas make an impact all across the UK.

An open culture, different perspectives, people who back you - that's how we roll. Great pay. Benefits that lift you up, and space to shape your future.

Bring your authentic self. And start something big.

**Move us. Make you**

Explore opportunities at
lloydsbankinggrouptalent.com

**Explore more**

LLOYDS BANKING GROUP

Move us. Make you

# LOCKHEED MARTIN

lockheedmartin.com/en-gb/careers.html

@lockheedmartin (Instagram)
earlycareers.fc-lmuk@global.lmco.com
lockheedmartin (Facebook)
linkedin.com/company/lockheed-martin
@LMUKNews (X)
youtube.com/@LockheedMartin

---

Lockheed Martin is a global defence and aerospace company with a strong UK presence, supporting national security through advanced technologies like the F-35 and missile defence. With 1,700 employees across multiple sites, it partners with government, industry, and academia to drive innovation.

Lockheed Martin offers graduate programmes across engineering, cyber, operations, business, and manufacturing, with roles based throughout the UK. From day one, graduates get involved in meaningful work, contributing to real projects and gaining exposure to the future of defence and advanced technology. Each graduate follows a structured two-year development programme designed to sharpen both technical skills and professional instincts. The experience includes mentoring, formal training, and opportunities to learn how Lockheed Martin operates across its UK business.

For students still at university, Lockheed Martin offers 12-month internships beginning each June. These are not work experience in name only. Interns take on real responsibilities, join project teams, and learn by doing. Many go on to receive return offers to join the graduate programme, making this a strong first step toward a full-time role. More than half of interns come back.

Training and development continue beyond the initial programme. Whether through rotational assignments, stretch projects, or leadership development, early-career professionals are given room to grow. Career progression is supported by internal mobility and a culture that values initiative and follow-through.

For those ready to contribute, explore, and build something that matters, Lockheed Martin offers more than a job, it's a proving ground. It's a place where ideas are heard, careers are built, and impact is real.

---

**GRADUATE VACANCIES IN 2026**
ENGINEERING
FINANCE
TECHNOLOGY

**NUMBER OF VACANCIES**
15+ graduate jobs

**LOCATIONS OF VACANCIES**

**STARTING SALARY FOR 2026**
£34,000
Plus a £2,000 sign on bonus and 6-monthly pay increases throughout duration of 2-year graduate programme.

**WORK EXPERIENCE**
DEGREE PLACEMENTS

**UNIVERSITY PROMOTIONS DURING 2025-2026**
Please check with your university careers service for full details of Lockheed Martin's local promotions and events.

**MINIMUM ENTRY REQUIREMENTS**
2.1 Degree
Relevant degree required for some roles.

**APPLICATION DEADLINE**
30th September 2025 - 1st March 2026

**FURTHER INFORMATION**
www.Top100GraduateEmployers.com
Register now for the latest news, local promotions, work experience and graduate vacancies at Lockheed Martin.

**LOCKHEED MARTIN**

# Where the *best* are *built*

Learn More

# M&S

jobs.marksandspencer.com/early-careers

@lifeatmands | LifeatMandS
linkedin.com/company/marks-and-spencer

**GRADUATE VACANCIES IN 2026**
GENERAL MANAGEMENT
PURCHASING
RETAIL

**NUMBER OF VACANCIES**
40+ graduate jobs

**LOCATIONS OF VACANCIES**

**STARTING SALARY FOR 2026**
£32,000

**UNIVERSITY PROMOTIONS DURING 2025-2026**
*Please check with your university careers service for full details of Marks & Spencer's local promotions and events.*

**APPLICATION DEADLINE**
*Please see website for full details.*

**FURTHER INFORMATION**
www.Top100GraduateEmployers.com
*Register now for the latest news, local promotions, work experience and graduate vacancies at **Marks & Spencer**.*

---

**M&S has been setting the standard in retail for over 100 years - built on trust, quality, and innovation. From fashion, home & beauty to iconic food, they do it all. With 65,000+ colleagues and 32 million customers, they continue to reinvent retail with the biggest transformation in history.**

M&S offers two early careers programmes for graduates: the Retail Leaders Programme and the Food Business Programme. Open to applicants from all degree disciplines, these programmes are designed to develop future leaders who are passionate about retail, providing exceptional customer service, and making a real impact from day one.

The Retail Leaders Programme gives graduates the opportunity to step into a leadership role early. Through hands-on store experience, people management, and commercial decision-making, graduates build the skills and confidence to run their own M&S store within 12 months.

The Food Business Programme provides exposure to one of the UK's most iconic food retailers. Starting with a store placement, graduates work shoulder-to-shoulder with teams who bring the M&S brand to life every day, shaping experiences for the 32 million customers who shop with them worldwide.

All graduates join M&S on a permanent contract and benefit from structured development from day one. This includes mentoring, tailored learning modules, business masterclasses, and support from experienced leaders.

Whether in food or retail leadership, graduates take on real responsibility early and are supported to grow into future leaders. Many go on to secure roles as Store Managers, Category Specialists or Commercial Leads across the UK.

M&S is committed to nurturing long-term careers, backed by a strong culture of inclusion, progression and continuous development.

# GEN: IMPACT.

## THIS IS THE FUTURE OF M&S.

We're transforming how we deliver quality, value, and innovation and it's your chance to be part of it.

Join us on our Early Careers programmes and help shape the next chapter of M&S.

Scan the QR code below to find out more.

GEN: M&S

# Microsoft

careers.microsoft.com/students

MicrosoftLife
@MicrosoftLife   linkedin.com/company/microsoft
@MicrosoftLife   youtube.com/WorkingAtMicrosoft

## GRADUATE VACANCIES IN 2026
- CONSULTING
- MARKETING
- SALES
- TECHNOLOGY

**NUMBER OF VACANCIES**
No fixed quota

**LOCATIONS OF VACANCIES**

**STARTING SALARY FOR 2026**
£Competitive
Plus benefits.

**WORK EXPERIENCE**
DEGREE PLACEMENTS

**UNIVERSITY PROMOTIONS DURING 2025-2026**
Please check with your university careers service for full details of Microsoft's local promotions and events.

**MINIMUM ENTRY REQUIREMENTS**
Varies by function
Relevant degree required for some roles.

**APPLICATION DEADLINE**
February 2026

**FURTHER INFORMATION**
www.Top100GraduateEmployers.com
Register now for the latest news, local promotions, work experience and graduate vacancies at **Microsoft**.

---

Over the last four decades, Microsoft has helped people and organisations use technology to transform how they work, live, and play. Microsoft enables digital transformation for the era of an intelligent cloud and an intelligent edge, empowering every person and every organisation to achieve more.

Alongside traditional engineering opportunities, Microsoft has a range of internships and graduate jobs in project management, sales, marketing, consulting and technology. Regardless of role or title, all graduate hires are enrolled on a customised on-boarding process: the Microsoft Aspire Experience.

During a 2-year period, Aspire graduates are given additional training, tools and connections to help them thrive at Microsoft and maximise their performance and learning. Internships and graduate positions are designed for those who thrive in dynamic environments and enjoy a challenge; who believe that technology has the power to transform the world for better. Whatever skill set a new hire has, Microsoft has positions available that will challenge and develop their existing capabilities to help achieve their full potential.

Successful candidates will gain valuable experience by working on real projects that drive real impact, while being exposed to some of the brightest minds in the industry. Over the course of the programme, they will work alongside other Aspire graduates to build a rich network of connections in over 60 countries.

Microsoft does not just value difference, they seek it out and invite it in. They bring together people from across the globe and support them with employee networks and resource groups to accelerate their professional development and help build a long-term career. Play a vital part in the success of a high-tech global leader. Start a Microsoft journey now.

# MAKE IT.
# BREAK IT.
# MAKE IT BETTER.

When smart, creative, passionate people get together, the result can be astounding and the opportunities limitless. Microsoft are looking ahead and empowering their customers to do more and achieve more. They are obsessing about building products to solve hard challenges. They are reinventing productivity. As a graduate you will help build the future in a cloud-first, mobile-first world.

www.microsoft.co.uk/students

**Microsoft**

# MOTT MACDONALD

mottmac.com/en/careers/early-careers

linkedin.com/company/mott-macdonald

Mott MacDonald is a global engineering, development and management consultancy, who design, deliver and maintain integral transport, energy, water, buildings and infrastructure. They use expertise to overcome complex challenges to deliver benefits for their clients and communities they serve.

Students and recent graduates can apply to one of Mott MacDonald's graduate career paths, across various business sectors they operate in and to one of the 35 offices in the UK or in mainland Europe.

Mott MacDonald's early careers paths equip graduates to build the foundation for a successful and impactful career. They will learn from industry experts, receive structured training, and gain experience on community-enhancing projects that make a difference.

All graduates join 'Accelerating Your Future', a three-year development programme that introduces the key business and commercial competencies needed to succeed at Mott MacDonald. Virtual and face-to-face workshops are used to deliver the programme.

Upon joining, graduates are partnered with a mentor who assists with a personalised development plan, and the company provide professional routes that are accredited by industry recognised professional bodies.

Mott MacDonald also offers summer and year-in-industry placements for students currently pursuing an undergraduate or master's degree. Working on projects with graduates and experienced professionals, participants will focus on one of the many sectors and gain valuable experience on community-enhancing projects, learning about the industry and Mott MacDonald as a company. This is the perfect springboard onto one of their award-winning graduate career paths, as many of the placement students return to Mott MacDonald after graduating.

## GRADUATE VACANCIES IN 2026
CONSULTING
ENGINEERING

### NUMBER OF VACANCIES
**350 graduate jobs**

### LOCATIONS OF VACANCIES
*Vacancies also available in Europe.*

### STARTING SALARY FOR 2026
**£30,000+**
*Plus a personal performance bonus and group performance bonus.*

### WORK EXPERIENCE
DEGREE PLACEMENTS | SUMMER INTERNSHIPS

### UNIVERSITY PROMOTIONS DURING 2025-2026
ASTON, BIRMINGHAM, BRIGHTON, BRISTOL, CAMBRIDGE, CARDIFF, DURHAM, EDINBURGH, EXETER, GLASGOW, HERIOT-WATT, IMPERIAL COLLEGE LONDON, LANCASTER, LEEDS, LIVERPOOL, LOUGHBOROUGH, NEWCASTLE, NOTTINGHAM, QUEEN'S BELFAST, READING, SHEFFIELD, SOUTHAMPTON, ULSTER, UNIVERSITY COLLEGE LONDON, WARWICK, YORK
*Please check with your university careers service for full details of Mott MacDonald's local promotions and events.*

### MINIMUM ENTRY REQUIREMENTS
*Relevant degree required for some roles.*

### APPLICATION DEADLINE
**Year-round recruitment**

### FURTHER INFORMATION
**www.Top100GraduateEmployers.com**
*Register now for the latest news, local promotions, work experience and graduate vacancies at Mott MacDonald.*

# MM
## MOTT MACDONALD

## SHAPE YOUR STORY

A career at Mott MacDonald means an opportunity to deliver value, innovation and excellence in some of the world's most pivotal industries. Apply now to be part of a global team of experts pushing each other to be brilliant every day.

**Apply today:**

search **Mott MacDonald early careers**

# NetworkRail

earlycareers.networkrail.co.uk

linkedin.com/company/network-rail
@networkrail / networkrail
@networkrail / youtube.com/networkrail

Network Rail own, operate, maintain and develop the railway infrastructure in England, Scotland and Wales. That's 20,000 miles of track, 30,000 bridges, tunnels and viaducts and the thousands of signals, level crossings and stations. They manage 20 of the country's largest stations.

Their graduate schemes offer the expert training and professional development needed to build a secure and successful future. Graduates gain hands-on experience across a range of roles and projects, rotating between placements to discover what interests them, where their passions lie and what their future career direction could be.

Network Rail offer two distinct graduate pathways: Engineering and Business. Within the Engineering pathway, they have three specialised schemes available: Mechanical, Electrical, and Civil Engineering. The Business pathway includes a wide range of schemes, such as IT, Finance, and many more. Opportunities are available across the country.

Whether applicants are looking to spend a year with Network Rail or just a summer, they'll give them the chance to experience their culture, discover what a career with them is like and gain exposure to projects and possibilities. Develop personal experience. Enhance skillsets. Build a strong network. Voice opinions. The undergraduate schemes will offer support from experienced managers, past graduates and other professionals to provide the guidance and support needed.

On the graduate programme, enjoy immense variety and gain unrivalled experience, training, development, and qualifications in a range of roles and projects. Be immersed in all aspects of the industry whilst rotating through different placements to further develop in an area of interest.

**GRADUATE VACANCIES IN 2026**
- ACCOUNTANCY
- ENGINEERING
- FINANCE
- GENERAL MANAGEMENT
- PROPERTY
- PURCHASING
- TECHNOLOGY

**NUMBER OF VACANCIES**
120+ graduate jobs

**LOCATIONS OF VACANCIES**

**STARTING SALARY FOR 2026**
£32,000
Plus a £2,000 bonus.

**WORK EXPERIENCE**
DEGREE PLACEMENTS

**UNIVERSITY PROMOTIONS DURING 2025-2026**
ASTON, BIRMINGHAM, CARDIFF, CARDIFF METROPOLITAN, COVENTRY, DERBY, EDINBURGH, GLASGOW, GLASGOW CALEDONIAN, HERIOT-WATT, LEEDS, LEICESTER, LIVERPOOL, LIVERPOOL JOHN MOORES, MANCHESTER, SHEFFIELD, SHEFFIELD HALLAM, STRATHCLYDE, SWANSEA, WEST OF ENGLAND, YORK
Please check with your university careers service for full details of Network Rail's local promotions and events.

**MINIMUM ENTRY REQUIREMENTS**
2.2 Degree
Relevant degree required for some roles.

**APPLICATION DEADLINE**
December 2025

**FURTHER INFORMATION**
www.Top100GraduateEmployers.com
Register now for the latest news, local promotions, work experience and graduate vacancies at **Network Rail**.

# NetworkRail

# We Matter to Millions

If finding a wide range of amazing career opportunities matters to you. **It matters to us.**

**Graduate engineering** and **business opportunities** available.

Choose from a variety of career routes and experience the support you need to create a future to be proud of.

# Newton

newtonimpact.com/careers/earlycareers

graduates@newtonimpact.com
@lifeatnewton
linkedin.com/company/newtonimpact
LifeAtNewton
youtube.com/@newton.impact

Newton is a strategic delivery consultancy that partners with organisations to solve their most complex challenges and deliver real-world change. Working with clients across a range of industries, they need exceptional talent ready to bring bold, fresh thinking into their graduate consultant roles.

Newton's clients face some of the most difficult challenges in their sectors but seemingly impossible is where Newton thrives best. They're so confident in their ability to create change that they put 100% of their implementation fees at risk. From day one graduates work side-by-side, on-site with clients to go as deep as it takes to find answers and forge the client relationships needed to deliver meaningful, measurable impact.

What does meaningful impact look like? It shows up in many ways. For example, when working on a major train upgrade programme, their graduates worked in teams to achieve a 480% increase in throughout. Or, when they helped to save £729 million working with a UK government department. Graduates join a community of exceptional people where they progress at pace and gain responsibility from day one. Results require intensity, and intensity unlocks unique opportunities to develop further. Graduates are expected to challenge and be challenged within a culture that balances high autonomy, hard work and first-hand client experience. They receive tailored support to help them take on diverse and complex work. They regularly travel across the UK to work with a range of clients and collaborate with colleagues on regular whole-company days tackling challenges together.

Roles are open to applicants from all degree disciplines and can be based anywhere in the UK. Newton empowers ambitious and dedicated graduates to push themselves and each other in the pursuit of personal growth.

**GRADUATE VACANCIES IN 2026**
CONSULTING

**NUMBER OF VACANCIES**
130+ graduate jobs

**LOCATIONS OF VACANCIES**

**STARTING SALARY FOR 2026**
£48,000
Plus a £2,500 sign on bonus and biannual profit share.

**WORK EXPERIENCE**
SUMMER INTERNSHIPS

**UNIVERSITY PROMOTIONS DURING 2025-2026**
BATH, BIRMINGHAM, BRISTOL, CAMBRIDGE, DURHAM, EDINBURGH, EXETER, IMPERIAL COLLEGE LONDON, LONDON SCHOOL OF ECONOMICS, MANCHESTER, NOTTINGHAM, OXFORD, SHEFFIELD, ST ANDREWS, UNIVERSITY COLLEGE LONDON, WARWICK
Please check with your university careers service for full details of Newton's local promotions and events.

**MINIMUM ENTRY REQUIREMENTS**
136 UCAS points

**APPLICATION DEADLINE**
End of 2025

**FURTHER INFORMATION**
www.Top100GraduateEmployers.com
Register now for the latest news, local promotions, work experience and graduate vacancies at *Newton*.

# Impossible problem or irresistible challenge?

It's a matter of perspective

Find a career that inspires you as much as you push yourself. Own your work from day one. Collaborate with exceptional people across sectors and industries. Unlock complexity to create meaningful impact.

To find out if a career as a Newton consultant is right for you, search **Newton Graduate Careers**

VISIT WORKATNEWTON.COM

**Newton**

# NHS
## Graduate Management Training Scheme

graduates.nhs.uk
linkedin.com/company/nhs-graduate-management-training-scheme

**GRADUATE VACANCIES IN 2026**
- ACCOUNTANCY
- FINANCE
- GENERAL MANAGEMENT
- HUMAN RESOURCES
- TECHNOLOGY

**NUMBER OF VACANCIES**
**200 graduate jobs**

**LOCATIONS OF VACANCIES**

**STARTING SALARY FOR 2026**
**£30,277**

**UNIVERSITY PROMOTIONS DURING 2025-2026**
ASTON, BATH, BIRMINGHAM, BRISTOL, COVENTRY, EAST ANGLIA, ESSEX, EXETER, IMPERIAL COLLEGE LONDON, LEEDS, LIVERPOOL, MANCHESTER, NOTTINGHAM, PLYMOUTH, READING, SHEFFIELD, SURREY, SUSSEX, WEST OF ENGLAND
*Please check with your university careers service for full details of the NHS's local promotions and events.*

**MINIMUM ENTRY REQUIREMENTS**
**2.2 Degree**

**APPLICATION DEADLINE**
**29th October 2025**

**FURTHER INFORMATION**
www.Top100GraduateEmployers.com
*Register now for the latest news, local promotions, work experience and graduate vacancies at the NHS.*

---

The National Health Service (NHS) is Europe's largest employer, employing over 1.3 million people. It provides universal, high-quality healthcare to over 57 million people across England. The Graduate Management Training Scheme (GMTS) offers graduates the opportunity to become future healthcare leaders.

GMTS trainees specialise in one of four areas: General Management, Human Resources, Finance, and Health Informatics (Data Analytics). Their work is often in hospital or office settings and can range from A&E data analysis to service improvement to financial planning and much more. Trainees get access to a comprehensive development package, including on-the-job training within placements where they gain specialist skills and postgraduate qualifications from leading universities. There is a wealth of on-scheme support available including placement managers and individual trainee support managers. With GMTS alumni across the NHS, there are many opportunities to build far-reaching networks and learn from others going through the same experience.

The Scheme has won awards, offering almost endless opportunities to grow personally and professionally while taking on early leadership responsibility. Graduates are selected based on their leadership potential, values and ambition to make a difference through a management career in health and care.

The NHS offers great responsibility and development potential. On this fast track to senior leadership, graduates face the exhilarating challenge of handling complex problems and high-profile situations. Facing these challenges, future NHS leaders need the resilience, tenacity and focus to achieve the best results in a compassionate way. It's an incredibly rewarding path where hard work and commitment can affect the lives of millions – and be completely life-changing for graduates themselves – in an organisation like no other in the world.

# NHS Graduate Management Training Scheme

# Life-changing.
# For you.
# And potentially millions.

**When you work for the NHS, it's about making a difference. Not just for you and your journey, but for millions of patients and their families and communities.**

The NHS Graduate Management Training Scheme offers you a fast track to a senior non-clinical role. It's your opportunity to get post-graduate qualifications from leading universities, on-the-job training and experience, early leadership responsibility and dedicated trainee support. Not to mention building a supportive peer network with 250 other graduate trainees.

With placements across England in a variety of hospital and office settings, you could be improving patient care, developing better ways to use data, creating new strategies and much more.

**Your days will be challenging but exceptionally rewarding, and every day you'll move towards becoming a healthcare leader of the future.**

THE TIMES GRADUATE RECRUITMENT AWARDS 2025 — Graduate Employer of Choice — GENERAL MANAGEMENT

THE TIMES GRADUATE RECRUITMENT AWARDS 2025 — Graduate Employer of Choice — HUMAN RESOURCES

**Start your journey here**

www.graduates.nhs.uk

# P&G

**pgcareers.com**
linkedin.com/showcase/procter-gamble-uk-ireland
@proctergamble
youtube.com/ProcterGamble

### GRADUATE VACANCIES IN 2026
- ACCOUNTANCY
- ENGINEERING
- FINANCE
- HUMAN RESOURCES
- LOGISTICS
- MARKETING
- RESEARCH & DEVELOPMENT
- SALES
- TECHNOLOGY

**NUMBER OF VACANCIES**
100 graduate jobs

**LOCATIONS OF VACANCIES**

*Vacancies also available in Europe.*

**STARTING SALARY FOR 2026**
£45,000
*For management graduate roles.*

**WORK EXPERIENCE**
DEGREE PLACEMENTS | SUMMER INTERNSHIPS

**UNIVERSITY PROMOTIONS DURING 2025-2026**
CAMBRIDGE, DURHAM, EDINBURGH, IMPERIAL COLLEGE LONDON, LEEDS, LIVERPOOL, MANCHESTER, NEWCASTLE, NORTHUMBRIA, OXFORD, UNIVERSITY COLLEGE LONDON, WARWICK
*Please check with your university careers service for full details of P&G's local promotions and events.*

**MINIMUM ENTRY REQUIREMENTS**
*Relevant degree required for some roles.*

**APPLICATION DEADLINE**
*Please see website for full details.*

**FURTHER INFORMATION**
www.Top100GraduateEmployers.com
*Register now for the latest news, local promotions, work experience and graduate vacancies at P&G.*

---

Procter & Gamble (P&G) owns iconic global brands like Gillette, Pampers, Head & Shoulders and Oral-B. With employees from over 140 countries, and operations in approximately 70 countries, P&G aspires to build a better world and enhance the lives of the world's consumers.

As a 'build from within' company, P&G expects those who join at entry level to become their next generation of accomplished leaders. There are no rotational programmes or gradual onboarding at P&G. Instead, from day one, employees are entrusted with meaningful work that has a tangible impact on P&G's leading brands and their careers. This build-from-within approach means P&G invests heavily in career development with senior leaders supporting graduates to continuously grow their skills and capabilities.

Whether helping to design the latest front-end innovation, selling to some of the UK's biggest retailers, or designing a full-blown product launch, P&G employees will be empowered to succeed.

P&G is committed to creating an environment where all of its employees can be their full and authentic selves, and to foster a culture that inspires employees to perform at their best, by creating a culture of acceptance and inclusion for everyone, so they can bring their unique voices to work. They believe in equal voice and representation for all and take their responsibility to build a more equitable world seriously.

Joining P&G means being part of an organisation that strives for excellence in consumer products and values making a positive impact on society. With their strong emphasis on leadership development, responsibility from day one, and senior leaders who are invested in supporting the next generation, P&G offers not only a fulfilling career but one where graduates can make an impact right from the start.

# DAY 1

# Make an Impact from Day 1

To learn more about careers at P&G visit **pgcareers.com**

**penguinrandomhousecareers.co.uk**

linkedin.com/company/penguin-random-house-uk
@PenguinUKJobs
youtube.com/penguinrandomhouseuknews

Penguin are the UK's largest publisher and their doors are open to all kinds of talent. They want everyone to feel a deep sense of belonging, supported to do their best work and motivated to play a part in realising their shared purpose: to connect more people with great stories and ideas.

Collaboration, creativity, and entrepreneurship lie at the heart of what Penguin do. In a constantly evolving industry, they work hard to stretch the definition of the word publisher. At Penguin, graduates will work with a breadth of talent from editors, technologists, designers, salespeople, publicists, digital marketers, distributors, and many others, to make each of their books a success. Together, Penguin make books for everyone, because a book can change anyone.

Penguin is one of the most widely recognised book publishers in the world, with more than 2,000 people and publishing over 1,500 books each year. Penguin offer a range of vacancies and all that's needed to start a great career. Successful applicants will be supported to make decisions for themselves, and contribute to Penguin's shared mission. Penguin have amazing opportunities, great benefits, and the stability and support to be expected from a big organisation.

Each year Penguin have hundreds of entry level and early-career roles available across their creative book publishing houses and specialist support function teams. Graduates will develop skills through their variety of learning and development training, mentoring, and career pathways.

Find out 'what's next?'. Penguin's emerging talent programmes for those at the start of their career are a great way for graduates to make their mark on a paid traineeship in one of Penguin's welcoming, collaborative and supportive teams.

### GRADUATE VACANCIES IN 2026
- ACCOUNTANCY
- FINANCE
- HUMAN RESOURCES
- MARKETING
- MEDIA
- RESEARCH & DEVELOPMENT
- RETAIL
- SALES
- TECHNOLOGY

**NUMBER OF VACANCIES**
250 graduate jobs

**LOCATIONS OF VACANCIES**

**STARTING SALARY FOR 2026**
£27,500-£30,000

**WORK EXPERIENCE**
INSIGHT COURSES | SUMMER INTERNSHIPS

**UNIVERSITY PROMOTIONS DURING 2025-2026**
Please check with your university careers service for full details of Penguin's local promotions and events.

**APPLICATION DEADLINE**
Year-round recruitment

**FURTHER INFORMATION**
www.Top100GraduateEmployers.com
Register now for the latest news, local promotions, work experience and graduate vacancies at Penguin.

# Start your story with a globally recognised brand

## Made up of small, friendly teams.

bit.ly/PenguinUKCareers

# Pfizer

pfizer.co.uk/careers

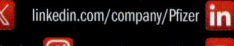

Pfizer – facebook  
studentprogrammesuk@pfizer.com  
@Pfizer_News – X  
linkedin.com/company/Pfizer  
@PfizerInc – Instagram  
youtube.com/Pfizer

For more than 170 years, Pfizer has worked to make a difference for all. It applies science and global resources to bring therapies to people that extend and significantly improve their lives. Every day, Pfizer colleagues work to advance wellness, prevention, treatments, and cures.

Each year, Pfizer offers up to 100 university undergraduates a 12-month industrial placement, based at one of the company's four UK sites. Whether they join in research & development, commercial, or global operations, placement students will be part of one global team, working to bring vital breakthroughs to patients. They are given a high level of responsibility as they support, manage, and deliver projects in one of the world's most innovative biopharmaceutical companies. During the programme, students will be part of a team that lets them ask questions, share ideas, make discoveries and retain a healthy work-life balance.

Staying true to its values, Pfizer supports its new joiners to gain the courage to run with new ideas and to contribute fully to the success of the team in which they work. It provides undergraduates with a unique set of experiences that will broaden and develop the critical skill sets and competencies they will need to be successful in the business environment and to excel in their degree. Placements are listed on Pfizer's Undergraduate Vacancies webpage from September each year, with new positions added through to December.

Undergraduates who complete a successful 12-month industrial placement can apply for Pfizer UK's Future Leader Graduate Programme; but this isn't the only route available for graduates looking for a career within Pfizer. A number of entry-level roles are available across its UK sites and these opportunities are advertised throughout the year on the Pfizer Careers website.

### GRADUATE VACANCIES IN 2026
- FINANCE
- GENERAL MANAGEMENT
- MARKETING
- SALES
- TECHNOLOGY

### NUMBER OF VACANCIES
**15-20 graduate jobs**

### LOCATIONS OF VACANCIES

### STARTING SALARY FOR 2026
**£27,000+**

### WORK EXPERIENCE
- DEGREE PLACEMENTS
- SUMMER INTERNSHIPS

### UNIVERSITY PROMOTIONS DURING 2025-2026
*Please check with your university careers service for full details of Pfizer's local promotions and events.*

### MINIMUM ENTRY REQUIREMENTS
*Relevant degree required for some roles.*

### APPLICATION DEADLINE
**Year-round recruitment**

### FURTHER INFORMATION
www.Top100GraduateEmployers.com  
*Register now for the latest news, local promotions, work experience and graduate vacancies at Pfizer.*

# Pfizer

# Are you ready to make breakthroughs that change patients' lives?

**pfizer.co.uk/undergraduate-placements**

#FindItAtPfizer

# POLICE:NOW
### INFLUENCE FOR GENERATIONS

**policenow.org.uk**

graduates@policenow.org.uk
PoliceNow  linkedin.com/school/police-now
@policenowgraduates  youtube.com/PoliceNowChangeTheStory

---

The challenges facing policing have never been greater and public trust has declined to devastating lows. It is time for change. Police Now is a charity with a mission to build a more representative police service by recruiting outstanding, diverse graduates to be leaders in society and on the policing frontline.

Police Now offers the only National Graduate Programme into policing, working with police forces across England and Wales. Graduates work on big societal issues; help create safer communities; support victims and drive a positive and fair internal culture in policing. Graduates get paid a salary from day one while they train to become neighbourhood police officers or detectives.

The training empowers graduates to make an immediate and real impact and gain the confidence needed to drive transformative change and rebuild trust.

Over two years, graduates develop their problem-solving and leadership skills, beginning with an award-winning training academy, while receiving support from a dedicated performance and development coach to aid their growth and help them to navigate a new career.

Those training to be neighbourhood police officers can apply for a four-week secondment. This is a unique opportunity to develop skills and gain valuable experience working with external partners like the Home Office. After successfully completing the two-year programme, graduates become fully warranted officers.

Graduates from all degree disciplines can bring skills to policing and contribute to Police Now's mission. Ongoing career and promotion support is provided by Police Now beyond the programme. Few careers offer the combination to make a meaningful difference where it matters most, and a breadth of opportunities for progression.

---

**GRADUATE VACANCIES IN 2026**
POLICING

**NUMBER OF VACANCIES**
**400 graduate jobs**

**LOCATIONS OF VACANCIES**

**STARTING SALARY FOR 2026**
**£29,907-£40,776**
*Dependent on location.*

**UNIVERSITY PROMOTIONS DURING 2025-2026**
*Please check with your university careers service for full details of Police Now's local promotions and events.*

**MINIMUM ENTRY REQUIREMENTS**
**2.2 Degree**

**APPLICATION DEADLINE**
*Please see website for full details.*

**FURTHER INFORMATION**
www.Top100GraduateEmployers.com
*Register now for the latest news, local promotions, work experience and graduate vacancies at Police Now.*

# FOR EVERY LIFE YOU'LL CHANGE

For the fight to stop violence against women and girls. For the battle to end knife crime's grip. For a police force as diverse as our streets.

Become a neighbourhood police officer or detective through our National Graduate Programme.

**Our two-year programme gives you:**

- ✓ Starting salary of £29,907 - £40,776 depending on location.
- ✓ A dedicated Performance and Development Coach to support you.
- ✓ A peer network of over 3,500 Police Now officers.

Join the only National Graduate Programme into policing.

Visit policenow.org.uk

**POLICE:NOW**
INFLUENCE FOR GENERATIONS

**Caroline Anderson** Police Now graduate
**Shielding vulnerable children from harm.**

**Anokhi Chouhan** Police Now graduate
**Protecting victims of domestic abuse.**

**Upile Mtitimila** Police Now graduate
**Bringing criminals to justice.**

# pwc

**pwc.co.uk/careers**

PwCCareersUK  linkedin.com/company/pwc-uk
@pwc_uk_careers  youtube.com/careerspwc

---

PwC is a hugely diverse business, bound by their global purpose - to build trust in society and solve important problems. The greatest opportunity to deliver their purpose is through meaningful work that makes a difference to their clients and society.

With c.23,000 people across the UK, PwC's strength comes from their people. They're the driving force behind the PwC brand, the ones who define them in the market. PwC is a collective of curious minds, embracing change and seizing opportunities. They don't just adapt to what's next, they shape it. Working with emerging technologies and leading organisations, PwC challenges assumptions and empowers their people to deliver groundbreaking work. They believe in shared success, which is why the growth of their people is their priority.

With pathways for students in all year groups and degree disciplines and many routes offering the chance to work towards a professional qualification, PwC offers the chance to explore opportunities based on personal interests, location and degree. They provide clear guidance throughout their recruitment process to support applicants in making the decision that's right for them.

It's an exciting time to join PwC. They're on a journey to become a skills-enabled organisation, allowing them to identify, develop and future-proof the skills their people need today and for tomorrow. By focusing on human and technical skills, they promote cross-functional teamwork, driving inclusive growth, and maximising value for their clients. And by doing this, they do more than develop skills – they cultivate potential. Enabling graduates to develop the skills they need, for the career they want, so they can go further.

At PwC, graduates can uncover hidden talents, build lifelong relationships rooted in trust and empathy, and turn challenges into opportunities.

---

**GRADUATE VACANCIES IN 2026**
- ACCOUNTANCY
- CONSULTING
- FINANCE
- LAW
- TECHNOLOGY

**NUMBER OF VACANCIES**
c.1,000 graduate jobs

**LOCATIONS OF VACANCIES**

**STARTING SALARY FOR 2026**
£Competitive

**WORK EXPERIENCE**
| INSIGHT COURSES | DEGREE PLACEMENTS | SUMMER INTERNSHIPS |

**UNIVERSITY PROMOTIONS DURING 2025-2026**
ABERDEEN, ABERYSTWYTH, ASTON, BANGOR, BATH, BIRMINGHAM, BIRMINGHAM CITY, BOURNEMOUTH, BRADFORD, BRIGHTON, BRISTOL, BRUNEL, CAMBRIDGE, CARDIFF, CARDIFF METROPOLITAN, CHICHESTER, CITY, COVENTRY, DERBY, DUNDEE, DURHAM, EAST ANGLIA, EDINBURGH, EDINBURGH NAPIER, ESSEX, EXETER, FALMOUTH, GLASGOW, GLASGOW CALEDONIAN, GREENWICH, HERIOT-WATT, HUDDERSFIELD, HULL, IMPERIAL COLLEGE LONDON, KEELE, KENT, KING'S COLLEGE LONDON, LANCASTER, LEEDS, LEICESTER, LINCOLN, LIVERPOOL, LIVERPOOL JOHN MOORES, LOUGHBOROUGH, LONDON SCHOOL OF ECONOMICS, MANCHESTER, MANCHESTER METROPOLITAN, NEWCASTLE, NORTHUMBRIA, NOTTINGHAM, NOTTINGHAM TRENT, OXFORD, OXFORD BROOKES, PLYMOUTH, PORTSMOUTH, QUEEN MARGARET EDINBURGH, QUEEN MARY LONDON, QUEEN'S BELFAST, READING, ROBERT GORDON, ROYAL HOLLOWAY LONDON, SALFORD, SHEFFIELD, SHEFFIELD HALLAM, SOAS, SOUTHAMPTON, ST ANDREWS, STIRLING, STRATHCLYDE, SUNDERLAND, SURREY, SUSSEX, SWANSEA, ULSTER, UNIVERSITY COLLEGE LONDON, WARWICK, WEST OF ENGLAND, WESTMINSTER, WINCHESTER, YORK

**APPLICATION DEADLINE**
Year-round recruitment

**FURTHER INFORMATION**
www.Top100GraduateEmployers.com
*Register now for the latest news, local promotions, work experience and graduate vacancies at PwC.*

# pwc

## We'll help you grow your skills
# so you can
## go further

Fuel your development. At PwC, we provide opportunities, mentorship and learning that accelerate your career from day one. From working at the cutting-edge of tech to collaborating with industry experts, we empower you to shape tomorrow.

# ROYAL AIR FORCE
**REGULAR & RESERVE**

recruitment.raf.mod.uk

@rafrecruitment | linkedin.com/company/royal-air-force

RAFRecruitment | youtube.com/royalairforce

---

The Royal Air Force (RAF) plays a vital role in defending the UK and its allies. They offer an exceptional opportunity for graduates to launch dynamic, purposeful careers as commissioned Officers - combining leadership, technical excellence, and the chance to make a global impact.

Graduates joining the RAF step into a force that is forward-thinking, inclusive, and committed to operating at the forefront of technology and defence. Success in today's RAF requires more than just academic qualifications - Officers are trusted from the outset to lead teams, make critical decisions, and manage resources in a wide range of specialist roles, from air operations and engineering to intelligence, logistics, cyberspace, and healthcare.

New Officers begin their journey with world-class leadership training at RAF College Cranwell, where they develop the mindset, confidence, and skills needed to command. From there, they move on to specialist training in their chosen career specialisation, preparing them to take on meaningful responsibilities from the start. The RAF offers more than just a job - it's a lifestyle built around service, adventure, and development. Officers benefit from a highly competitive salary with structured annual pay increases, subsidised accommodation and food, excellent medical and dental care, and access to a range of sports, travel, and adventurous training opportunities.

They receive support to pursue further qualifications, including fully funded degrees and professional accreditation, while gaining unmatched career experience. For personnel who are ambitious, resilient, and eager to make a difference, the RAF is a place to lead, grow, and be part of something bigger. It's more than a career - it's a way to shape the future, contribute to national security, and represent values of integrity, service, respect, and excellence.

---

### GRADUATE VACANCIES IN 2026
- ENGINEERING
- GENERAL MANAGEMENT
- HUMAN RESOURCES
- LAW
- LOGISTICS
- TECHNOLOGY

### NUMBER OF VACANCIES
**No fixed quota**

### LOCATIONS OF VACANCIES

*Vacancies also available elsewhere in the world.*

### STARTING SALARY FOR 2026
**£41,456**
*after initial training. Plus subsidised living and food charges, free gym, paid holiday and a non-contributory pension.*

### MINIMUM ENTRY REQUIREMENTS
*Relevant degree required for some roles.*

### APPLICATION DEADLINE
**Year-round recruitment**

### FURTHER INFORMATION
www.Top100GraduateEmployers.com
*Register now for the latest news, local promotions, work experience and graduate vacancies at RAF.*

# ROYAL AIR FORCE
**REGULAR & RESERVE**

**FIND YOUR FORCE**

# GRADUATE OPPORTUNITIES

**AIRCREW**
Pilot
Weapon Systems Officer

**AIR & SPACE OPERATIONS**
Control Officer
Operations Officer

**CYBERSPACE**
Engineer Officer •
(Communications Electronics)

**MEDICAL SERVICES**
Medical Officer •
Nursing Officer •
Medical Support Officer (MSO)
MSO Environmental Health
MSO Physiotherapist •
Dental Officer •

**LOGISTICS**
Logistics Officer

• Degree required

**PEOPLE OPERATIONS**
People Operations Officer

**LEGAL**
Legal Officer •

**ENGINEERING**
Engineer Officer • (Aerosystems)

**GROUND COMBAT & SECURITY**
RAF Police Officer
RAF Regiment Officer

**CHAPLAINCY**
Chaplain •

**INTELLIGENCE**
Intelligence Officer

## SEARCH RAF RECRUITMENT

All information correct at time of publication.

06/25 CRN 31_1903 GRADUATE OPPORTUNITIES ADVERT

# Revolut

revolut.com/talent-programmes

linkedin.com/company/revolut
@revolutinsider
revolutapp
@RevolutApp
youtube.com/@RevolutApp

---

Revolut is a global fintech powering all things money – from spending and saving to investing and trading. Since 2015, they've grown to 60+ million customers, 10,000+ employees, and offices worldwide. Revolut's programmes enable graduates to launch meaningful, high-impact careers in tech and finance.

The Rev-celerator Graduate Programme is a 12-month experience for high-potential grads to launch bold careers in fintech. Roles span engineering (Python, Java, iOS, Android), product, design, data, operations, and information security. Graduates join fast-moving teams, solving complex, global problems, drive real impact from day one, and help shape the future of finance.

Revolut welcomes top graduates (2024–2026), and for those based outside its hiring locations, they offer international relocation to their hubs in the UK, Spain, Portugal, Poland, or UAE – including visa support, relocation costs, and initial accommodation. The programme runs in a hybrid format across Revolut's global hubs. Wherever graduates start, their growth won't stop.

The Rev-celerator Internship Programme is a 10-week summer experience for students in their penultimate year (graduating in 2027). They can join teams across engineering, product, design, data, or operations, working on real projects with clear goals, strong mentorship, and global exposure. Interns are treated as Revoluters from day one – with the same expectations, ownership, and impact. Top performers may be offered a place on the graduate programme. Internships run in a hybrid format across Revolut's global hubs, with full relocation support where needed.

Revolut provides mentorship, learning pathways, and early ownership. They prioritise continuous growth, with live project experience, cross-functional exposure, regular feedback, and a personal development plan.

---

### GRADUATE VACANCIES IN 2026
- CONSULTING
- ENGINEERING
- GENERAL MANAGEMENT
- RESEARCH & DEVELOPMENT
- TECHNOLOGY

### NUMBER OF VACANCIES
**150 graduate jobs**

### LOCATIONS OF VACANCIES

*Vacancies also available in Europe, the USA, Asia and elsewhere in the world.*

### STARTING SALARY FOR 2026
**£Competitive**
*Top-performing graduates may be eligible for a performance bonus. Revolut also offers an ergonomic budget to help you set up a home workspace and deliver wow.*

### WORK EXPERIENCE
SUMMER INTERNSHIPS

### UNIVERSITY PROMOTIONS DURING 2025-2026
*Please check with your university careers service for full details of Revolut's local promotions and events.*

### MINIMUM ENTRY REQUIREMENTS
**2.1 Degree**
*Relevant degree required for some roles.*

### APPLICATION DEADLINE
**14th December 2025**

### FURTHER INFORMATION
**www.Top100GraduateEmployers.com**
*Register now for the latest news, local promotions, work experience and graduate vacancies at Revolut.*

# THIS WAY, INNOVATORS

We're not just reimagining finance, we're revolutionising careers.

Whether you're starting anew or aiming high, we've got the programme for you.

# Revolut

Rev-celerator Internship and Graduate Programmes.
**Your future in fintech starts here.**

**SCAN THE QR CODE TO LEARN MORE**

revolut.com/talent-programmes

# ROLLS ROYCE

**careers.rolls-royce.com**

@RollsRoyce_Careers   linkedin.com/company/rolls-royce

Rolls-Royce has been at the forefront of innovation for over a hundred years, helping to power, protect and connect people. Through complex power and propulsion solutions, this business plays an important role in supporting the energy transition. They are proud to call themselves a force for progress.

When graduates kickstart their career with Rolls-Royce, they're defining the future on their own terms. Each journey with the company starts with a strong but simple belief – everyone is unique and every Rolls-Royce journey is different. Along with the freedom to choose opportunities that will help them develop in the way they want, successful applicants will get the space, skills and support to discover who they can be.

Whether they choose engineering or technology, the programmes extend across the whole company, offering different experiences to graduates. Learning-focused, programmes concentrate on providing real-world experiences and work on live projects across the different divisions and functions.

Rolls-Royce are focused on shaping the future of cleaner, safer and more sustainable power, and are looking for people who share this vision. They are seeking candidates with a diverse range of talents and different ways of thinking, who will challenge perceptions. That's why the Engineering & Technology programme is open to all STEM degree subjects, and their Enterprise Skills Accelerator and Business Capabilities programmes are open to all subjects.

Their 12-month internships and 10-week summer internships provide a fantastic insight into life and work at Rolls-Royce. They also offer 6-month internships if needed, as well as direct entry-level positions, so candidates don't have to wait to get started in the career they want. Learn, grow, and thrive in an inclusive environment that values each employee as an individual.

**GRADUATE VACANCIES IN 2026**
ENGINEERING
GENERAL MANAGEMENT
TECHNOLOGY

**NUMBER OF VACANCIES**
No fixed quota

**LOCATIONS OF VACANCIES**

**STARTING SALARY FOR 2026**
£31,000
*Plus a £2,000 joining bonus.*

**WORK EXPERIENCE**
DEGREE PLACEMENTS | SUMMER INTERNSHIPS

**UNIVERSITY PROMOTIONS DURING 2025-2026**
*Please check with your university careers service for full details of Rolls-Royce's local promotions and events.*

**MINIMUM ENTRY REQUIREMENTS**
*Relevant degree required for some roles.*

**APPLICATION DEADLINE**
November 2025

**FURTHER INFORMATION**
www.Top100GraduateEmployers.com
*Register now for the latest news, local promotions, work experience and graduate vacancies at Rolls-Royce.*

# Be You.
# Be Rolls-Royce.

**At Rolls-Royce, we have a long history of setting out to achieve extraordinary goals. Join us and you can help transform the way we power, protect, and connect people across the globe, secure our world, and explore the universe.**

We develop and deliver complex power and propulsion solutions for safety-critical applications in the air, at sea and on land. Whether you're supporting the UK Royal Navy's nuclear submarines, enabling the transition to net zero carbon air travel, or learning what it takes to operate a leading global company, you can't innovate if you can't be yourself.

That's why we look for people with diverse talents and different ways of thinking, and give them the space, skills and support to discover their passions. All in an environment where you can be your best.

Graduate, internship and graduate direct opportunities at **careers.rolls-royce.com**

# ROYAL NAVY

**royalnavy.mod.uk/careers**

@RoyalNavy  RoyalNavyRecruitment

The Royal Navy is, first and foremost, a fighting force. Serving alongside Britain's allies in conflicts around the world, the Royal Navy also vitally protects UK ports, fishing grounds, and merchant ships, helping to combat international smuggling, terrorism, and piracy.

Throughout the course of history, a life at sea has always attracted those with a taste for travel and adventure; but there are plenty of other reasons for graduates and final-year students to consider a challenging and wide-ranging career with the Royal Navy. Graduates will receive a structured route through the ranks, with fast-track, on-the-job training as a constant feature.

Graduates can join the Royal Navy as Officers – the senior leadership and management team in the various professions, which range from engineering, sub-surface, and warfare to medical, the Fleet Air Arm, and logistics. Starting salaries of £34,000, rising to £41,400 in the second year, compare well with those in industry. Those wanting to join the Royal Navy as an Engineer – with Marine, Weapon, or Air Engineer Officer, above or below the water – could work on anything from sensitive electronics to massive gas-turbine engines and nuclear weapons. Increasingly, its 30,000 personnel are involved in humanitarian and relief missions; situations where their skills, discipline, and resourcefulness make a real difference to people's lives. What's more, the Royal Navy can offer a secure, flexible career, with the potential to extend to age 50.

The Royal Navy offers opportunities for early responsibility, career development, sport, recreation, and travel which exceed any in civilian life. With its global reach and responsibilities, the Royal Navy offers plenty of adventure and the chance to see the world, while pursuing one of the most challenging, varied, and fulfilling careers available.

---

**GRADUATE VACANCIES IN 2026**
- ENGINEERING
- FINANCE
- GENERAL MANAGEMENT
- HUMAN RESOURCES
- LAW
- LOGISTICS
- MEDIA
- RESEARCH & DEVELOPMENT
- TECHNOLOGY

**NUMBER OF VACANCIES**
No fixed quota

**LOCATIONS OF VACANCIES**

*Vacancies also available elsewhere in the world.*

**STARTING SALARY FOR 2026**
£34,000
*Raising to £41,400 in the second year.*

**WORK EXPERIENCE**
INSIGHT COURSES | DEGREE PLACEMENTS | SUMMER INTERNSHIPS

**UNIVERSITY PROMOTIONS DURING 2025-2026**
*Please check with your university careers service for full details of the Royal Navy's local promotions and events.*

**MINIMUM ENTRY REQUIREMENTS**
*Relevant degree required for some roles.*

**APPLICATION DEADLINE**
Year-round recruitment

**FURTHER INFORMATION**
www.Top100GraduateEmployers.com
*Register now for the latest news, local promotions, work experience and graduate vacancies at the Royal Navy.*

## A CAREER THAT MAKES
# A WORLD OF DIFFERENCE

A career in the Royal Navy is like no other. A job where no two days are the same, where you can challenge yourself and solve problems on the go. Plus, you get to travel the world, all while helping those that are in need.

**For more information call 0345 607 5555**
**Visit royalnavy.mod.uk/careers**

# savills

**savills.co.uk/graduates/current-graduate-vacancies.aspx**

@SavillsInstagrad  gradrecruitment@savills.com

Savills is a world leading property agent, employing over 40,000 people across 700 offices. Savills take pride in providing the best-in-class advice as they help individuals, businesses and institutions make better property decisions. The goal is simple: to help people thrive through places and spaces.

Savills' graduate programme offers the chance to gain internationally recognised professional qualifications. The company offers roles within surveying, planning, sustainability, energy, engineering, rural, food & farming and forestry, with half of these vacancies in regional locations. The company has offices in exciting locations around the UK, where fee earners work with varied and prestigious clients. The diversity of Savills' services means there is the flexibility to carve out a fulfilling, self-tailored career path in many locations.

Savills offers around 120 placement opportunities, each year, including a one week insight programme for first year students, a one month summer scheme for second year property students, or final year non-property students, and a 12 month year in industry, called the Sandwich Placement, for relevant 3rd year students. Savills passionately believe that their graduates are future leaders, and as such make a huge investment in them.

Savills graduates are given responsibility from day one, in teams who highly value their contribution, and are involved in some of the world's most high-profile property deals and developments. They are surrounded by expert professionals and experienced team members from whom they learn and seek advice. Individual achievement is rewarded, and Savills look for graduates with entrepreneurial flair. Work-life balance, structured training and a dynamic working environment are amongst the factors which see Savills as The Times Graduate Recruitment Award's winning employer for Property year-on-year.

## GRADUATE VACANCIES IN 2026
ENGINEERING
PROPERTY

**NUMBER OF VACANCIES**
120+ graduate jobs

**LOCATIONS OF VACANCIES**

**STARTING SALARY FOR 2026**
£27,000-£30,000
*Plus a sign-on bonus of up to £1,500.*

**WORK EXPERIENCE**
DEGREE PLACEMENTS | SUMMER INTERNSHIPS

**UNIVERSITY PROMOTIONS DURING 2025-2026**
ABERDEEN, BATH, BIRMINGHAM, BRIGHTON, BRISTOL, CAMBRIDGE, CARDIFF, DURHAM, EDINBURGH, EDINBURGH NAPIER, EXETER, GLASGOW, HERIOT-WATT, KING'S COLLEGE LONDON, LEEDS, LIVERPOOL, LIVERPOOL JOHN MOORES, LOUGHBOROUGH, LONDON SCHOOL OF ECONOMICS, MANCHESTER, NEWCASTLE, NORTHUMBRIA, NOTTINGHAM, NOTTINGHAM TRENT, OXFORD BROOKES, QUEEN MARY LONDON, QUEEN'S UNIVERSITY BELFAST, READING, ROYAL HOLLOWAY LONDON, SALFORD, SHEFFIELD, SHEFFIELD HALLAM, SOUTHAMPTON, ST ANDREWS, STRATHCLYDE, SUSSEX, UNIVERSITY COLLEGE LONDON, WARWICK, WEST OF ENGLAND, YORK
*Please check with your university careers service for full details of Savills's local promotions and events.*

**APPLICATION DEADLINE**
28th November 2025

**FURTHER INFORMATION**
www.Top100GraduateEmployers.com
*Register now for the latest news, local promotions, work experience and graduate vacancies at **Savills**.*

# Shape **your** future

"I have helped progress over 300 Megawatts of energy for the UK power grid through renewable developments - enough to power over 200,000 homes".

**18**
POSSIBLE CAREER PATHS

**2-3**
YEAR TRAINING PROGRAMME WITH PERMANENT EMPLOYMENT CONTRACT

**19**
YEARS AS THE TIMES GRADUATE EMPLOYER OF CHOICE FOR PROPERTY

**40%**
OF OUR MAIN BOARD JOINED AS GRADUATE TRAINEES

**40,000+**
GLOBAL EMPLOYEES

**700+**
OFFICES IN OVER 70 COUNTRIES

A career in real estate offers an exciting and dynamic career path with the opportunity to specialise in several different areas thet help shape the future of our built environment.

## Become **the future of Savills**

Awards
2nd PLACE
2025 - 2026

@savillsinstagrad    #careersinproperty

**savills**

# SCOTTISHPOWER

scottishpower.com/pages/careers.aspx
earlycareers@scottishpower.com
linkedin.com/company/scottish-power
@scottishpowerhq
youtube.com/ScottishPowerUK

ScottishPower is the first integrated energy company in the UK to generate 100% green electricity. Their focus is on wind energy, smart grids and driving the change to a cleaner, electric future and they are investing over £18m every working day to make this happen.

ScottishPower offers a diverse range of graduate opportunities designed to launch careers in the energy sector while supporting the UK's transition to net zero. Their graduate programmes span engineering, cyber security, land management, cyber security and data & technology, with roles available across SP Energy Networks, ScottishPower Renewables, and other business areas. Roles are open to applicants from all degree disciplines and opportunities are available across the UK.

Graduates can expect hands-on learning, technical training, and cohort-based development activities that build real-world experience. The programmes are tailored for aspiring engineers, technical specialists, and future business leaders, with a strong support network.

ScottishPower offer year in industry placements in partnership with the EDT. These span across various functions including; Engineering, HR, procurement, finance, project management, marketing and more.

Graduates embark on a two-year journey that includes structured placements across different areas of the business, allowing them to explore their interests and strengths while gaining a holistic understanding of the energy industry. These placements span functions such as asset management, customer service, financial planning, and network planning and regulation.

Training is delivered through a mix of technical and behavioural modules, ensuring graduates develop the skills needed to thrive in a fast-evolving sector.

## GRADUATE VACANCIES IN 2026
- ENGINEERING
- FINANCE
- GENERAL MANAGEMENT
- MARKETING
- PROPERTY
- PURCHASING
- TECHNOLOGY

**NUMBER OF VACANCIES**
160 graduate jobs

**LOCATIONS OF VACANCIES**

**STARTING SALARY FOR 2026**
£34,000
Plus a £3,000.

**WORK EXPERIENCE**
DEGREE PLACEMENTS | SUMMER INTERNSHIPS

**UNIVERSITY PROMOTIONS DURING 2025-2026**
BANGOR, CARDIFF, CARDIFF METROPOLITAN, DUNDEE, EDINBURGH, EDINBURGH NAPIER, GLASGOW, GLASGOW CALEDONIAN, HERIOT-WATT, IMPERIAL COLLEGE LONDON, LANCASTER, LIVERPOOL, LIVERPOOL JOHN MOORES, MANCHESTER, NORTHUMBRIA, QUEEN MARGARET EDINBURGH, ST ANDREWS, STIRLING, STRATHCLYDE, SWANSEA

*Please check with your university careers service for full details of Scottish Power's local promotions and events.*

**MINIMUM ENTRY REQUIREMENTS**
2.2 Degree

**APPLICATION DEADLINE**
4th January 2026

**FURTHER INFORMATION**
www.Top100GraduateEmployers.com
*Register now for the latest news, local promotions, work experience and graduate vacancies at Scottish Power.*

# Solve problems, shape our industry and make your mark.

At ScottishPower, accelerating net zero is at the heart of everything we do - imagine being part of that.

Our graduate programmes offer exciting opportunities for aspiring engineers, technical experts, and future business leaders.

We're invested in your development, providing hands-on learning, technical training, and cohort events to help you build real-world experience and achieve your career goals. Every day brings fresh challenges, with a strong support network to guide your journey.

Start your career in clean energy with us and see where it takes you!

£34,000 plus £3,000 sign on bonus

Honours degree at a minimum of 2:2

Roles across Scotland, England & Wales

ScottishPower

shell.co.uk/about-us/careers.html

linkedin.com/company/shell
@shell   @shell_uk
Shell   youtube.com/Shell

Shell is an international energy company and one of the largest in the UK's energy sector. It has been present in the UK since 1897. Today, around 6,000 people work at Shell UK across a range of energy-related activities, playing a major role in powering and fueling the UK's industry, transport, and homes.

   The Shell Graduate Programme is a three-year programme, enabling graduates to grow their careers and contribute to the energy sector. Shell match graduates into one of four pathways based on skills and preference, including Trading & Supply, Commercial, Finance and IDT. Graduates have the opportunity to work on innovative solutions to help provide communities with secure and affordable energy and enable Shell to become a net-zero emissions business. They will explore new technologies and trends while working with experts from various fields. New graduates are based in Shell's London office.

   The Assessed Internship Programme is a 10-12 week placement for penultimate year students from all degree disciplines. It gives students a real role, along with the mentoring and support they need to succeed while working on a major project with clear deliverables and outcomes. Assessed interns will undergo formal mid-term and end-of-internship reviews, and if successful, might be offered a position in the Graduate Programme.

   The Graduate Programme provides development and career opportunities with a global leader in energy. Graduates are placed in roles that offer stimulating challenges and the chance to learn from professionals, with access to further training and coaching. They are supported in creating a personalized development plan that aligns with their strengths and interests, to cultivate the skills to become future leaders. Upon completion of the programme, graduates embark on the next chapter of their career within a selected business area.

**GRADUATE VACANCIES IN 2026**
ENGINEERING
FINANCE
GENERAL MANAGEMENT
LOGISTICS
MARKETING
RETAIL
SALES
TECHNOLOGY

**NUMBER OF VACANCIES**
30+ graduate jobs

**LOCATIONS OF VACANCIES**

**STARTING SALARY FOR 2026**
£Competitive

**WORK EXPERIENCE**
SUMMER INTERNSHIPS

**UNIVERSITY PROMOTIONS DURING 2025-2026**
Please check with your university careers service for full details of Shell's local promotions and events.

**MINIMUM ENTRY REQUIREMENTS**
2.1 Degree
Relevant degree required for some roles.

**APPLICATION DEADLINE**
10th December 2025

**FURTHER INFORMATION**
www.Top100GraduateEmployers.com
Register now for the latest news, local promotions, work experience and graduate vacancies at Shell.

# Do you want to be a future leader?
## Power Your Progress through the Shell Graduate Programme

The Shell Graduate Programme is a leadership development program that develops future leaders of Shell. Our Graduates, while diverse in background and skillsets, come together with key traits and behaviours that aid their success in the programme. These include qualities such as their capacity to analyse situations and propose purposeful solutions that align with our strategic goals, adaptability towards learning and growing from feedback in order to deliver results, and how they nurture relationships and work effectively with a diverse team.

Shell Graduate Programme lasts three years on average and you are invited to explore multiple career opportunities in Trading & Supply, Commercial, Finance, IDT and Global Functions. Programme is devised to bring you the necessary tools and realise your full potential through on-the-job trainings, formal training and coaching.

Join us as a Graduate at Shell where you can grow and thrive as we power progress together.

**National Graduate Recruitment Awards 2024 — WINNER** — The most popular graduate recruiter in energy and utilities award

**RATEMYPLACEMENT 2024 - 2025 Best 100 Student Employers**

Scan this QR code to apply now!

**Power Your Progress**

# SLAUGHTER AND MAY/

slaughterandmay.com
earlycareers@slaughterandmay.com
@SlaughterandMayCareers

Slaughter and May is one of the most prestigious law firms in the world. The strength of their global practice is reflected both in the multi-jurisdictional nature of their work and their international client base. The firm is a trusted adviser to some of the largest global companies in the world.

There are distinct differences that set Slaughter and May apart from other global law firms. These differences are in relation to their international approach, multi-specialist training, and lack of billable targets.

Slaughter and May work with the very best law firms across the globe to support their clients, handpicked to meet the needs of each matter, to deliver integrated legal advice. Fundamental to their business model is the ability to work in partnership with other law firms – this is how they have built their successful global practice.

Slaughter and May lawyers are all trained to be multi-specialists across a broad range of legal matters. This is hard work, but their lawyers say it makes for a far more fulfilling career. It provides challenge and interest, and also allows their lawyers to develop deeper relationships with clients as they have a better understanding of their businesses. Their lawyers are not set billing targets, and are therefore free to work collaboratively. They share expertise and knowledge in order to concentrate on what matters most – the quality of their work and client service.

Slaughter and May takes great pride in drawing strength from diversity and believes that an inclusive workplace drives collaboration and enhances business performance. They are looking to employ the brightest minds regardless of what or where they studied. They offer open days and work experience schemes to enable applicants to gain an insight into life as a commercial lawyer.

---

**GRADUATE VACANCIES IN 2026**
LAW

**NUMBER OF VACANCIES**
**90 graduate jobs**
*For training contracts starting in 2028.*

**LOCATIONS OF VACANCIES**

**STARTING SALARY FOR 2026**
**£56,000**

**WORK EXPERIENCE**
INSIGHT COURSES | SUMMER INTERNSHIPS

**UNIVERSITY PROMOTIONS DURING 2025-2026**
*Please check with your university careers service for full details of Slaughter and May's local promotions and events.*

**MINIMUM ENTRY REQUIREMENTS**
**2.1 Degree**

**APPLICATION DEADLINE**
*Please see website for full details.*

**FURTHER INFORMATION**
www.Top100GraduateEmployers.com
*Register now for the latest news, local promotions, work experience and graduate vacancies at Slaughter and May.*

# SLAUGHTER AND MAY/

# A WORLD OF DIFFERENCE

Laws, international markets, global institutions... all changing every day. So how do we, as an international law firm, create the agility of mind that enables us to guide some of the world's most influential organisations into the future?

By allowing bright people the freedom to grow. By training lawyers in a way that develops a closer understanding of clients through working on a wider range of transactions. By fostering an ethos of knowledge sharing, support and mutual development by promoting from within and leaving the clocks outside when it comes to billing. To learn more about how our key differences not only make a world of difference to our clients, but also to our lawyers and their careers, visit:

## slaughterandmay.com/careers

**90**
Training Contracts

Lawyers from
**50+**
universities

**300+**
places on
open days and schemes

# Teach First

teachfirst.org.uk/training-programme

linkedin.com/company/teach-first
@teachfirstuk (TikTok)    @teachfirstuk (Instagram)
teachfirst (Facebook)    youtube.com/TeachFirstUK

At Teach First, they believe that where people start in life shouldn't determine where they finish. That's why, since 2003, they've been training talented graduates to become inspiring teachers and influential leaders in schools serving disadvantaged communities.

Right now, too many children in the UK are denied the life chances they deserve. It's not right. It's not fair. And it won't change - unless people step up. Graduates have options. But, few programmes offer the impact, challenge and opportunity for growth that Teach First's does.

The two-year Training Programme is the UK's largest and most ambitious teaching and leadership development scheme. From day one, trainees will be in the classroom, leading lessons and making a real difference, all while earning a competitive salary and working towards a fully funded qualification.

But, this is about more than teaching. It's about leading change. Trainees receive over £10,000 of world-class coaching and development, building skills that open doors across sectors, from education to business, public service, policy and beyond. Become a qualified teacher by the end of the first year, and a proven leader by the end of the second. In fact, trainees are seven times more likely to progress into leadership roles early in their careers.

And the support doesn't stop when the programme ends, with the chance to join the network of over 20,000 leaders making a difference for the pupils who need it the most, both in and out of the classroom. With access to exclusive development opportunities across the UK.

This is not the easy route. It's the ambitious one. It demands drive, resilience, and a deep belief in the potential of every child. But for those ready to lead the fight for a fairer future - it's a career-defining opportunity.

---

**GRADUATE VACANCIES IN 2026**
TEACHING

**NUMBER OF VACANCIES**
1,300 graduate jobs

**LOCATIONS OF VACANCIES**

**STARTING SALARY FOR 2026**
£Competitive

**WORK EXPERIENCE**
INSIGHT COURSES

**UNIVERSITY PROMOTIONS DURING 2025-2026**
ASTON, BATH, BIRMINGHAM, BRISTOL, CAMBRIDGE, CARDIFF, CITY, DURHAM, EAST ANGLIA, EDINBURGH, ESSEX, EXETER, HERIOT-WATT, HULL, IMPERIAL COLLEGE LONDON, KENT, KING'S COLLEGE LONDON, LANCASTER, LEEDS, LEICESTER, LIVERPOOL, LOUGHBOROUGH, LONDON SCHOOL OF ECONOMICS, MANCHESTER, NEWCASTLE, NORTHUMBRIA, NOTTINGHAM, NOTTINGHAM TRENT, OXFORD, OXFORD BROOKES, QUEEN MARY LONDON, READING, ROYAL HOLLOWAY LONDON, SHEFFIELD, SOAS, SOUTHAMPTON, ST ANDREWS, SURREY, SUSSEX, SWANSEA, UNIVERSITY COLLEGE LONDON, WARWICK, YORK

*Please check with your university careers service for full details of Teach First's local promotions and events.*

**MINIMUM ENTRY REQUIREMENTS**
2.1 Degree

**APPLICATION DEADLINE**
Year-round recruitment

**FURTHER INFORMATION**
www.Top100GraduateEmployers.com
*Register now for the latest news, local promotions, work experience and graduate vacancies at **Teach First**.*

# Lead. Advance.
# Inspire.

You've got it in you to make the world a better place. To open doors for the children who need it most.

Join our Training Programme and discover your potential. As a teacher. And as a leader.

Registered charity, no. 1098294

**Teach First**

# TESCO

tesco.com/early-careers

linkedin.com/company/-tesco
tesco | @tesco | @Tesco
youtube.com/Tescomedia

From food to fashion, Tesco is one of the world's largest retailers of consumer goods that serves customers, communities and the planet a little better every day. Over 330,000 colleagues work across the UK, Europe and Asia. For graduates and interns, there are opportunities in every corner of Tesco.

With ten graduate programmes across tech, finance, marketing, online and more, there's plenty of choice – and plenty to look forward to – as a graduate. Each programme is designed to help people grow and get to know Tesco inside and out, starting with in-store experience and quickly picking up new skills in a supportive and inclusive environment.

Tesco is a place where everyone's welcome, valued and encouraged to be themselves. It's a community where colleagues empower each other to flourish in their own way, with a strong focus on wellbeing, flexibility, and work-life balance from day one, which people will feel and benefit from on the 2 or 3-year graduate programmes.

Those studying at university and working towards a 2:2 or above could also join a 10-week paid internship – with the chance to land a place on a graduate programme after. No matter what degree applicants are studying, they can apply to any programme.

From early responsibility to personalised support, learning resources, workshops, on-site training, and a buddy system, Tesco helps careers take off. Whether it's learning how to make the most of professional networks, developing personal resilience, or nurturing people's unique skills – there's a lot in store. The end goal: to become their future leaders, and take Tesco's business from strength to strength.

Explore Tesco's early careers opportunities on their website.

### GRADUATE VACANCIES IN 2026
ENGINEERING
FINANCE
LOGISTICS
MARKETING
PURCHASING
TECHNOLOGY
OTHER

### NUMBER OF VACANCIES
50+ graduate jobs

### LOCATIONS OF VACANCIES

### STARTING SALARY FOR 2026
£32,000-£40,000

### WORK EXPERIENCE
DEGREE PLACEMENTS | SUMMER INTERNSHIPS

### UNIVERSITY PROMOTIONS DURING 2025-2026
ANGLIA RUSKIN, BIRMINGHAM, COVENTRY, IMPERIAL COLLEGE LONDON, KING'S COLLEGE LONDON, KINGSTON, LEICESTER, LONDON METROPOLITAN, LOUGHBOROUGH, MANCHESTER, NOTTINGHAM, QUEEN MARY LONDON, STRATHCLYDE, UNIVERSITY COLLEGE LONDON, UNIVERSITY OF HERTFORDSHIRE

*Please check with your university careers service for full details of Tesco's local promotions and events.*

### MINIMUM ENTRY REQUIREMENTS
2.2 Degree

### APPLICATION DEADLINE
1st October - 31st October 2025

### FURTHER INFORMATION
www.Top100GraduateEmployers.com
*Register now for the latest news, local promotions, work experience and graduate vacancies at Tesco.*

# Inclusive culture, included.

And we don't just stop there for our graduate programmes. Fantastic benefits? Included. Affinity networks? Included. Top-notch wellbeing support? You guessed it – included. In fact, we include so much, we can't include it all here.

To find out more search **Tesco early careers**

# Early Careers at TESCO

# Transport for London

**tfl.gov.uk/corporate/careers/graduates**

transportforlondon • earlycareerscampaigns@tfl.gov.uk
@tfl • linkedin.com/company/transport-for-london
@transportforlondon • youtube.com/transportforlondon

## Our city. Made better by you.

Transport for London (TfL) are responsible for the day-to-day operation of London's public transport network and manage London's main roads. They are committed to achieving the Mayor's goal of making London carbon neutral by 2030 and supporting a green recovery to become a world-leading smart city.

TfL offers a diverse range of opportunities including graduate schemes, summer placements and industry internships. Opportunities vary from engineering, project management, real estate, operations, technology, finance and many other areas. Each programme provides comprehensive training and development opportunities to help build a successful career. Individuals will gain hands-on experience, work on impactful projects, and contribute to the smooth functioning of London's transport network. Roles are based across London with hybrid working depending on the placement.

The graduate development programme consists of up to 6 structured placement rotations which vary from 3 to 6 months, giving graduates the opportunity to work on several projects. Technical and professional development is supported through a wide range of on-the-job practical experiences including a combination of classroom-led and online training courses, mentoring and structured networking opportunities with scheme alumni. Some programmes will result in industry recognised qualifications such as Institution of Engineering and Technology (IET), Institution of Civil Engineers (ICE) and others.

One-to-one support is provided through a placement manager, responsible for day-to-day management and support; a scheme sponsor, a senior manager who acts as a technical and professional adviser; and a development adviser, who will support professional development through career coaching and career progression at TfL.

---

### GRADUATE VACANCIES IN 2026
- ENGINEERING
- FINANCE
- GENERAL MANAGEMENT
- HUMAN RESOURCES
- MEDIA
- PROPERTY
- PURCHASING
- TECHNOLOGY

### NUMBER OF VACANCIES
**50+ graduate jobs**

### LOCATIONS OF VACANCIES

### STARTING SALARY FOR 2026
**£31,000**
*2026 salary to be confirmed.*

### WORK EXPERIENCE
INSIGHT COURSES | SUMMER INTERNSHIPS

### UNIVERSITY PROMOTIONS DURING 2025-2026
BRUNEL, CITY, EAST ANGLIA, ESSEX, IMPERIAL COLLEGE LONDON, LONDON SCHOOL OF ECONOMICS, QUEEN MARY LONDON, UNIVERSITY COLLEGE LONDON
*Please check with your university careers service for full details of TfL's local promotions and events.*

### MINIMUM ENTRY REQUIREMENTS
**2.2 Degree**
*Relevant degree required for some roles.*

### APPLICATION DEADLINE
**October - December 2025**

### FURTHER INFORMATION
www.Top100GraduateEmployers.com
*Register now for the latest news, local promotions, work experience and graduate vacancies at TfL.*

# Our city.
# Made better by you.

At TfL, we invest a lot in our apprentices and graduates because we want you to be the future of our business.

tfl.gov.uk/corporate/careers/graduates

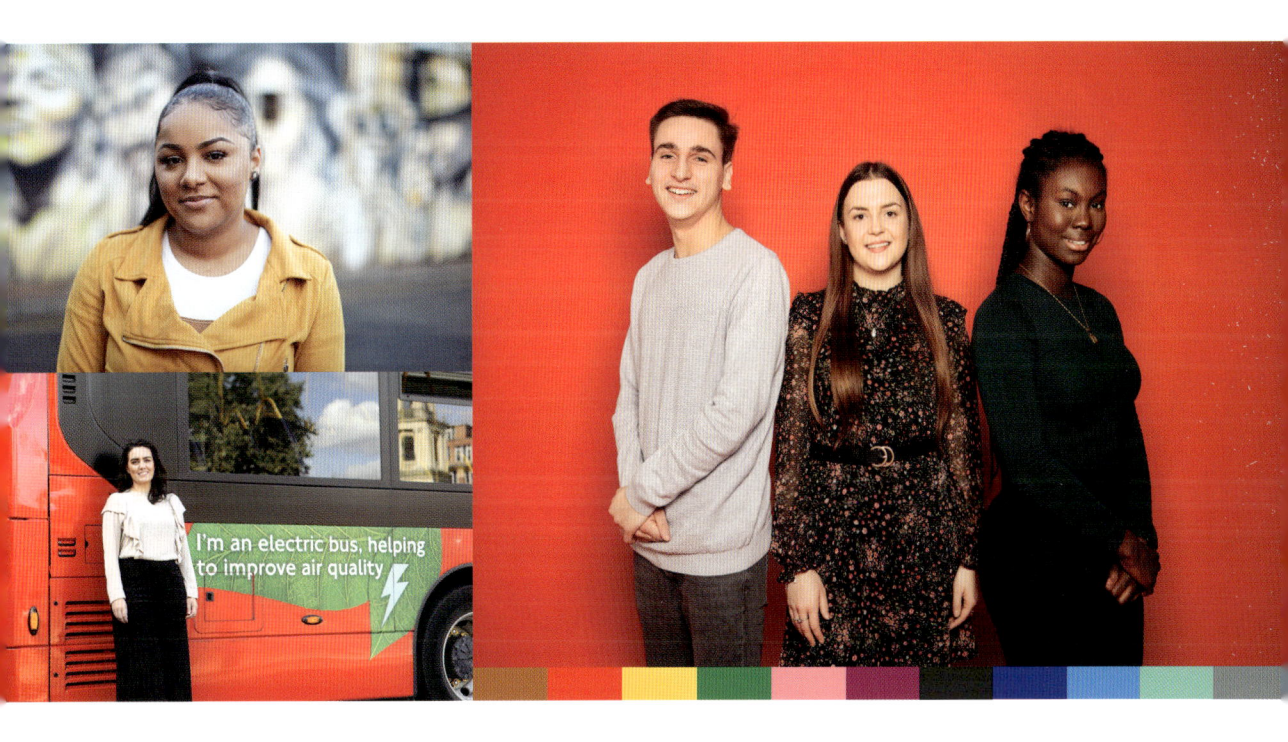

"TfL offers a diverse range of opportunities which has enabled me to complete multiple different placements across the business. For instance, Piccadilly Line Upgrade, Business and Digital Engineering, Trains Systems Performance Modelling and Data & Analysis in Safety, Health and Environment.

Outside of the Engineering & Technology graduate scheme, I was also the Vice Chair of the Graduates, Apprentices and Interns Committee, which aims to build an inclusive and visible community of graduates, apprentices and interns within TfL. It is these great opportunities that make the TfL graduate schemes exciting and engaging."

Bianca Agapito
Engineering & Techology
Graduate Alumni

Transport for London

# careers.unilever.com/uk-futurecareers

UFLP.recruitmentUK@unilever (graduates)
futurecareers.recruitment@unilever.com (placements/apprenticeships)
@UnileverCareersUK
linkedin.com/company/unilever

## GRADUATE VACANCIES IN 2026
- ENGINEERING
- FINANCE
- GENERAL MANAGEMENT
- HUMAN RESOURCES
- MARKETING
- MEDIA
- RESEARCH & DEVELOPMENT
- SALES
- TECHNOLOGY

### NUMBER OF VACANCIES
**40+ graduate jobs**

### LOCATIONS OF VACANCIES

### STARTING SALARY FOR 2026
**£35,000**
Plus a £5,000 interest-free loan.

### WORK EXPERIENCE
DEGREE PLACEMENTS

### UNIVERSITY PROMOTIONS DURING 2025-2026
BATH, BIRMINGHAM, EDINBURGH, IMPERIAL COLLEGE LONDON, KING'S COLLEGE LONDON, LEEDS, LEICESTER, LIVERPOOL, LOUGHBOROUGH, MANCHESTER, NOTTINGHAM, NOTTINGHAM TRENT, SURREY

*Please check with your university careers service for full details of Unilever's local promotions and events.*

### MINIMUM ENTRY REQUIREMENTS
*Relevant degree required for some roles.*

### APPLICATION DEADLINE
**September - November 2025**

### FURTHER INFORMATION
**www.Top100GraduateEmployers.com**
*Register now for the latest news, local promotions, work experience and graduate vacancies at Unilever.*

---

Unilever are one of the world's largest consumer goods companies who make over 400 of the best loved brands, such as Dove, TRESemmé, Lynx, Hellman's, Persil, Marmite, Vaseline, Colman's and Pot Noodle. Over 3.4 billion consumers use their products daily. Their purpose is 'to brighten everyday life'.

The Unilever Future Leaders Programme is a three-year scheme designed to prepare graduates for business leadership roles. The programme consists of placements within and across functions, formal training, and business mentorship. All degree levels and disciplines are accepted, except for the Research and Development stream which requires a STEM degree background.

Unilever offer industrial placements, for students who are completing a year in industry as part of their degree and apprenticeship programmes which are inclusive to anyone who meets the requirements. High performers across these two programmes may also have the opportunity to be fast-tracked to the final stage of the UFLP selection process! No matter what stage applicants are at, there are a variety of opportunities within Unilever's multiple functions: HR, Finance, Supply Chain, R&D, Sales, Marketing, Technology, Legal (placement only), Communications (placement only) and, Sustainability (placement only).

At Unilever, diversity is about championing inclusion, embracing differences, and growing together for business performance. Every Unilever employee should bring their authentic self to work irrespective of ethnicity, ability, sexual orientation, or gender. They have a variety of programmes for passionate talent with fresh ideas who want exposure to real world challenges.

All new joiners have a significant impact on the business and are given real responsibility. They are also provided with one-to-one mentoring and support to assist their development and achievement of future goals.

## BRIGHTENING EVERYDAY LIFE FOR ALL

Sold in 190 countries!

€60.8 billion turnover in 2024 with 58% in emerging markets!

Over 400 Brands!

€987 million spend on Research and Development!

3.4 billion people use our products daily!

Scan the QR code to visit our website and learn more!

# WHITE & CASE

whitecasetrainee.com

WhiteCase — londontrainee@whitecase.com
@WhiteCase — linkedin.com/company/white-&-case
@WhiteCase — youtube.com/WhiteCaseGlobal

White & Case is a global law firm of more than 2,500 lawyers worldwide. They've built an unrivalled network of 43 offices in 29 countries. That investment is the foundation for their client work in over 200 countries today. White & Case work with clients that are multinational organisations with complex needs.

White & Case trainees will work on fast-paced, cutting-edge cross-border projects from the outset of their career. As such, White & Case is looking to recruit ambitious trainees who have a desire to gain hands-on practical experience from day one and a willingness to take charge of their own career. They value globally minded citizens of the world who are eager to work across borders and cultures, and who are intrigued by solving problems within multiple legal systems. The White & Case training contract consists of four six-month seats, one in finance, one in a contentious practice area, and one of which is guaranteed to be spent in one of their overseas offices.

They offer vacation scheme placements over the winter, spring, and summer, open days, and two-day insight schemes. These provide a great way to experience first-hand what life is like as a White & Case trainee as well as gain useful insight into the firm and the training they offer.

The firm's virtual learning programme offers the opportunity to gain insight into life as a White & Case trainee and experience the realities of cross-border law. There is no cost to access the platform, it is self-paced to fit around users' schedules, and no application form or legal knowledge is required. Students will gain insight into the fast-paced, cutting-edge projects their lawyers and trainees work on, and gain valuable skills by undertaking true-to-life legal tasks. Participation in the learning platform will be recognised on their application forms.

## GRADUATE VACANCIES IN 2026
LAW

### NUMBER OF VACANCIES
**50 graduate jobs**
For training contracts starting in 2028.

### LOCATIONS OF VACANCIES

### STARTING SALARY FOR 2026
**£62,000**

### WORK EXPERIENCE
INSIGHT COURSES | SUMMER INTERNSHIPS

### UNIVERSITY PROMOTIONS DURING 2025-2026
Please check with your university careers service for full details of White & Case's local promotions and events.

### MINIMUM ENTRY REQUIREMENTS
**2.1 Degree**

### APPLICATION DEADLINE
Please see website for full details.

### FURTHER INFORMATION
**www.Top100GraduateEmployers.com**
Register now for the latest news, local promotions, work experience and graduate vacancies at *White & Case*.

# Together we make a mark

## Graduate careers in law

As a trainee in our London office, you will have the opportunity to work on challenging cross-border client matters providing you with international experience and exposure from day one. Join us and make your mark.

whitecasetrainee.com

**1**
of the only law firms to offer a guaranteed overseas seat

**75**
vacation scheme places per year in London

**£62k**
year-one starting salary

**43**
offices across 29 countries

**50**
trainees recruited per year in London

**£175k**
salary on qualification

Learn more about the career opportunities in our London office, the work our trainees do and stories from our people in our graduate careers brochure at whcs.law/UKStudentsandGraduates.

**WHITE & CASE**

# Useful Information

| EMPLOYER | GRADUATE RECRUITMENT WEBSITE | EMPLOYER | GRADUATE RECRUITMENT WEBSITE |
|---|---|---|---|
| A&O SHEARMAN | earlycareersuk.aoshearman.com | HSBC | hsbc.com/careers/students-and-graduates |
| AECOM | aecom.com/graduates-and-early-careers/uk-ireland | IBM | ibm.com/uk-en/careers/search |
| ALDI | aldirecruitment.co.uk | ITV | careers.itv.com/teams/early-careers |
| AMAZON | amazon.jobs/content/en/career-programs | JPMORGANCHASE | jpmorganchase.com/careers#students |
| AON | aon.com/careers/uk | KPMG | kpmgcareers.co.uk |
| ARMY | jobs.army.mod.uk | L'ORÉAL | careers.loreal.com/en_US/content/UK |
| ARUP | careers.arup.com/earlycareers | LATHAM & WATKINS | lw.com |
| ASTRAZENECA | careers.astrazeneca.com/early-talent | LIDL | lidlearlycareers.co.uk |
| ATKINSRÉALIS | careers.atkinsrealis.com/uk-early-careers | LINKLATERS | careers.linklaters.com |
| BABCOCK | earlycareers.babcockinternational.com/graduates | LLOYDS BANKING GROUP | lloydsbankinggrouptalent.com |
| BAE SYSTEMS | careers.baesystems.com | LOCKHEED MARTIN | lockheedmartin.com/en-gb/careers.html |
| BANK OF AMERICA | campus.bankofamerica.com | M&S | jobs.marksandspencer.com/early-careers |
| BARCLAYS | search.jobs.barclays/grads-interns | MICROSOFT | careers.microsoft.com/students |
| BBC | bbc.co.uk/earlycareers | MOTT MACDONALD | mottmac.com/en/careers/early-careers |
| BCG | careers.bcg.com | NETWORK RAIL | earlycareers.networkrail.co.uk |
| BLACKROCK | careers.blackrock.com/students-and-graduates | NEWTON | newtonimpact.com/careers/earlycareers |
| BLOOMBERG | bloomberg.com/company/early-careers/full-time | NHS | graduates.nhs.uk |
| BNY | bny.com/corporate/global/en/careers | P&G | pgcareers.com |
| BRITISH AIRWAYS | careers.ba.com/graduates-bps-and-interns | PENGUIN | penguinrandomhousecareers.co.uk |
| CAPGEMINI | capgemini.com/gb-en/careers/career-paths | PFIZER | pfizer.co.uk/careers |
| CIVIL SERVICE | faststream.gov.uk | POLICE NOW | policenow.org.uk |
| CLYDE & CO | careers.clydeco.com | PWC | pwc.co.uk/careers |
| DELOITTE | deloitte.com/uk/en/careers/early-careers | RAF | recruitment.raf.mod.uk |
| DEUTSCHE BANK | careers.db.com/students-graduates | REVOLUT | revolut.com/talent-programmes |
| DIAGEO | diageo.com | ROLLS-ROYCE | careers.rolls-royce.com |
| DLA PIPER | careers.dlapiper.com/early-careers | ROYAL NAVY | royalnavy.mod.uk/careers |
| EDF | careers.edfenergy.com/early-careers | SAVILLS | savills.co.uk/graduates/current-graduate-vacancies.aspx |
| ENTERPRISE MOBILITY | enterprisemobility.co.uk/careers | SCOTTISH POWER | scottishpower.com/pages/careers.aspx |
| ENVIRONMENT AGENCY | environmentagencycareers.co.uk | SHELL | shell.co.uk/about-us/careers.html |
| EY | ey.com/uk/earlycareers | SLAUGHTER AND MAY | slaughterandmay.com |
| FORVIS MAZARS | careers-uk.forvismazars.com/jobs/early-careers | TEACH FIRST | teachfirst.org.uk/training-programme |
| FRESHFIELDS | freshfields.com/earlycareers | TESCO | tesco.com/early-careers |
| GOOGLE | careers.google.com | TRANSPORT FOR LONDON | tfl.gov.uk/corporate/careers/graduates |
| GRANT THORNTON | grantthornton.co.uk/early-careers | UNILEVER | careers.unilever.com/uk-futurecareers |
| HMRC | civil-service-careers.gov.uk/hmrc-tax-specialist-programme | WHITE & CASE | whitecasetrainee.com |
| HOGAN LOVELLS | ukearlycareers.hoganlovells.com | | |